D1548466

"Nature, by an absolute and uncontrollable necessity, has determined us to judge as well as to breathe and feel."

—DAVID HUME (1738)

"Questions such as these—responding to persistent human wonderings—lie behind the wide and demanding lay interest in psychology. Academic and research psychologists sometimes forget, or do not recognize, that these lay questions are fair questions ultimately, even if sometimes ingenuously framed. They deserve far more serious scientific attention than yet has been granted them by the busily preoccupied field of scientific psychology."

—JACK BLOCK (1991)

"A specter is haunting U.S. intellectual life [that includes] claims for a certain kind of empiricism, for common sense, for linguistic transparency... that is founded on notions of the real."

—FROM A FLIER PROMOTING A CONFERENCE ON POSTMODERNISM AT UC SANTA CRUZ (HELD JANUARY 31, 1998)

"Consider this rule of thumb: to the extent that philosophical positions both confuse us and close doors to further inquiry, they are likely to be wrong."

—E. O. WILSON

"It is only shallow people who do not judge by appearances. The mystery of the world is in the visible, not the invisible."

—OSCAR WILDE

Personality

JUDGMENT A Realistic

Approach

to Person

Perception

Personality
JUDGMENT
A Realistic

Approach

to Person

Perception

David C. Funder
University of California, Riverside

Academic Press

San Diego   London   Boston   New York   Sydney   Tokyo   Toronto

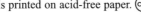
Academic Press
a division of Harcourt Brace & Company
525 B Street, Suite 1900, San Diego, California 92101-4495, USA
http://www.apnet.com

Academic Press
24-28 Oval Road, London NW1 7DX, UK
http://www.hbuk.co.uk/ap/

Library of Congress Catalog Card Number: 99-61411

International Standard Book Number: 0-12-269930-0

PRINTED IN THE UNITED STATES OF AMERICA
99 00 01 02 03 04 MM 9 8 7 6 5 4 3 2 1

For Patti

Contents

3   *Error and Accuracy in the Study of Personality Judgment*

4   *Methodological and Philosophical Considerations*

Preface

It is difficult for me to believe that I have been doing research on accuracy in personality judgment for 20 years. This work has taken various forms, including investigations of the relations between personality judgments and behavior and the conditions under which personality judgments are made with more and lesser accuracy. Most recently, I attempted to develop a theoretical approach, called the Realistic Accuracy Model, that might be sufficient to account for some of what is now known about accuracy and to suggest directions for further research (Funder, 1995a).

Over the years my colleagues and I have managed to publish a fair number of journal articles and chapters that present data relevant to accuracy, survey bits of the literature on behavioral consistency and on judgmental error, and attempt to justify our theoretical approach. However, this varied material has never been brought together into one place. Of course, it might be possible for a dedicated reader to go to the library and find for himself or herself nearly everything—both theoretical and empirical—that is presented on the following pages. But it has lately dawned on me that few readers are sufficiently motivated to do a PsychLit search under my name and to study everything that pops up. Thus, if I hope for anyone to be able to understand the entire range of interpretations of the literature, theoretical development, and empirical findings that underlie the Realistic Accuracy Model, the job of pulling this material together is one that I must do myself.

That is the purpose of this book. It draws on nearly all of the research that has come out of my lab so far (actually three labs, at Harvard, Illinois, and Riverside), and most of the major publications of my graduate students, collaborators, and myself. Indeed, parts of this book were, for the first draft, taken verbatim out of prior publications, although over the course of revision most of these passages have been substantially changed. Of some relevance to the reader is that—in case you have read some of this prior work—passages in this book here and there may sound familiar. This is not merely déjà vu.

As might be expected, I found myself saying both more and different things on a large number of subjects than before. I also managed to bring in a fair amount of work from other investigators in laboratories—not enough to do them justice, probably, but enough to illustrate that accuracy in personality judgment is a reborn topic of research with many different approaches and participants around the world.

Acknowledgments

I am grateful to Academic Press, the American Psychological Association, and the American Psychological Society (via Blackwell Publishers) for permission to reuse some material previously published under their copyright.

I have been fortunate in the students and colleagues with whom I have collaborated over the years and, of course, the most fun occurs when a student, over time, turns into a full collaborator and finally becomes someone on whom you rely for ideas and wisdom. Dr. C. Randall Colvin of Northeastern University did this, and I thank him for all his help, which over the years has ranged from collating Q-sort decks to sharply criticizing some of my conceptual blunders. Research on the "accuracy project," as we call it, has also been greatly assisted by Melinda Blackman, Alex Creed, Kate Dobroth, Leslie Eaton, Robert Fuhrman, R. Michael Furr, David Kolar, Carl Sneed, and Jana Spain, all of whom have developed or are developing into significant psychological researchers in their own right. Our lab has also been assisted by an army of undergraduate research assistants, too numerous to list, at Harvey Mudd College, Harvard University, the University of Illinois, and the University of California, Riverside. I do have to give special mention to Doretta Massaro and Robert Eblin, my first two undergraduate assistants at Harvard. Bob was the first to say to a subject, "You can talk about anything you like and I'll be back in about 5 minutes." Doretta was the first to explain to an undergraduate how to do a Q-sort. Both were important in getting this project off the ground and both went off to great careers outside of psychology. I also need to acknowledge Mary Verdier, who organized the first army of videotape coders at the University of Illinois, and Rayanne Notareschi, who did the same thing at Riverside.

The bulk of the writing of this book was completed while I was on a sabbatical visit holding an Erskine Fellowship at the University of Canterbury in Christchurch, New Zealand. Canterbury provided a stimulating and supportive academic atmosphere and a truly superb, computer-based library of the psychological literature. New Zealand is a wonderful country and Christchurch is a lovely city. Garth Fletcher both made my Erskine fellowship possible and was a most hospitable as well as intellectually stimulating host, ably assisted by his then-student, Dr. Geoff Thomas. I also enjoyed and learned from long conversations about philosophy of science with Dr. Brian Haig.

At Academic Press, Nikki Levy was a consistently supportive and encouraging editor. Rebecca Orbegoso patiently shepherded the final draft through production.

My wife, Patti, was supportive and helpful during the whole process of writing this book. This project is just one of the many things I could not have done without her. To Patti, I dedicate this book.

CHAPTER 1

Approaching Accuracy

This is a book about accuracy in personality judgment. It presents theory and research concerning the circumstances under which and processes by which one person might make an accurate appraisal of the psychological characteristics of another person, or even of oneself.

Accuracy is a practical topic. Its improvement would have clear advantages for organizations, for clinical psychology, and for the lives of individuals. With accurate personality judgment, organizations would become more likely to hire the right people and place them in appropriate positions. Clinical psychologists would make more accurate judgments of their clients and so serve them better. Moreover, a tendency to misinterpret the interpersonal world is an important part of some psychological disorders. If we knew more about accurate interpersonal judgment, this knowledge might help people to correct the kinds of misjudgments that can cause problems. Most important of all, if individuals made more accurate judgments of personality they might do better at choosing friends, avoiding people who cannot be trusted, and understanding their interpersonal worlds (Nowicki & Mitchell, 1998). This last-named advantage—improving interpersonal understanding—is the worthiest justification for doing research on accuracy and the most powerful reason why people find the topic interesting.

CURIOSITY AND ITS FULFILLMENT

When George Miller (1969) urged researchers to "give psychology away" to the wider public, the gifts he described were the ways in which psychological knowledge might be used to create more useful instruments for aircraft cockpits, allow more accurate selection of qualified employees, and ensure racial harmony, world peace, and increased sales of soap. Psychology can—to a greater or lesser degree—do all of these things, and these accomplishments help to justify its existence. Moreover, it certainly can be useful to predict what another person will do, or even to know what another person is thinking, and our interest in these matters is heightened when we feel a need to control what is going on (Swann, Stephenson, & Pittman, 1981).

But its practical accomplishments are not the primary reason that psychology exists, and our everyday interest about other people goes beyond pragmatic considerations. People are *intrinsically* interested in each other. How else can we explain the vast amount of otherwise pointless gossip that occupies so much of our time, gossip that consists largely of highly speculative judgments about why some other person is doing what he or she is doing, what he or she is thinking, and what he or she is likely to do next. How else can we explain the frequency of sidewalk cafes, confessional television programs, and telescopes in the windows of high-rise apartment complexes, all of which provide the opportunity to watch other people who, with any luck, you need never encounter nor be directly affected by in any other way. And how else, indeed, can we explain the existence of the highly paid occupation of "celebrity," the function of which seems to be to give everybody on earth a few individuals in common that they can all gossip about?

Psychology arose to institutionalize, formalize, and satisfy the intrinsic curiosity people have about each other and about themselves. To paraphrase a comment by Sal Maddi (1996), if all of psychology were abolished tomorrow and all memory of its existence erased, before very long it would have to be reinvented, because some questions simply will not go away. If the reader of this book is a psychologist or graduate student in psychology, chances are that a burning interest in one or more of these questions is the reason the reader got into the field in the first place (Funder, 1998).

The fundamental questions people have about each other have two foci. The job of a local television news reporter is to satisfy the curiosity, sometimes morbid, of his or her viewers. When interviewing the person who just survived a plane crash or whose house has burned to the ground, the reporter invariably asks, "How did it *feel?* What were you *thinking?*" And when interviewing the surviving postal workers after one of their coworkers has gone on yet another murderous rampage, the reporter inevitably asks, "What *kind* of person was he? What was he *like?*"

In other words, included among the fundamental questions that underlie psychological curiosity are the ones that ask what people are thinking and feeling, and what they are like. The first concerns what Ickes (1993) has called "empathic accuracy," defined as the ability to describe another person's thoughts and feelings (see also Ickes, 1997). The second question concerns judgments of personality, of traits such as extraversion, honesty, sociability, and happiness. The two topics are relevant to each other. What one is thinking and feeling surely offers a clue as to the kind of person that he or she is. And different kinds of people no doubt think and feel differently, even in the same situation. The two topics are therefore not completely separable, and it will become apparent as we go along that the research findings concerning one of these topics is highly relevant to (and generally consistent with) the findings from the other (Colvin, Vogt, & Ickes, 1997). But this book is primarily about the latter topic. This is a book about how people make judgments of what each other is like, the degree to which these judgments achieve accuracy, and the factors that make accuracy in personality judgment more and less likely.

WHAT IS ACCURACY?

Accuracy is a topic that has only recently come back into acceptance, if not fashion, in research psychology (Funder & West, 1993). For the better part of four decades (1950–1990) psychologists were prone either to ignore accuracy or to redefine it out of existence. The reasons for this state of affairs range from the daunting methodological issues that confront the study of accuracy to the infiltration of deconstructionist philosophies into social psychology. The infiltration of these philosophies has had the subtle but unmistakable effect of causing many psychologists to be uncomfortable with the idea of assuming, defining, or even discussing the nature of social reality.

So at the outset it should be said that when this book talks about *accuracy,* the term is used advisedly yet in the most disingenuous possible way. Herein, accuracy refers not to any sophisticated reconstructionist, deconstructionist, or convenient operational definition of this very loaded word. Rather, it refers to the relation between what is perceived and what is.

This definition raises a large number of issues. The most central as well as the most daunting is the criterion issue, which concerns how reality—especially, psychological reality—can ever be known so that judgments can be compared with it to assess their accuracy. Other issues, only slightly less central and slightly less daunting, include the nature of personality, the quality of human judgment, and a host of methodological complications that arise in the study of personality and person perception.

These are all worthy issues. They deserve to be addressed directly. The topic of accuracy is too important to be ignored, sidestepped, or operationally redefined out of existence. The goal of this book, therefore, is to confront this topic, and these issues, as directly as possible.

CHAPTER ORGANIZATION

The remainder of this introductory chapter is in four parts. The first discusses in detail the reasons why the topic of accuracy in personality judgment is so important. These reasons are practical, theoretical, and even philosophical. The second part introduces the basic orienting assumptions of the particular approach to accuracy that will be taken in this book. Three seemingly simple but sometimes controversial assumptions entail an approach to accuracy that trespasses across the otherwise well-defended, traditional border between social and personality psychology. The third part of this chapter outlines some of the differences (and sometimes antagonisms) between social and personality psychology, and proposes a rapprochement. The need for the reintegration of personality and social psychology is a direct implication of the present approach to accuracy research, and is a persistent theme throughout this book. The fourth part of this chapter describes the historical roots of the Realistic Accuracy Model and outlines its research agenda and the overall plan of the remainder of the book.

THE IMPORTANCE OF ACCURACY

The accuracy of personality judgment touches on many areas of life. It is important for reasons that are practical, theoretical, and intrinsic.

Practical Considerations

Accuracy in personality judgment has important practical implications for people living their daily lives as well as for psychologists attempting to do work that has a positive effect on individuals and society.

Daily Life

A moment's reflection will confirm that personality judgment is an important part of daily existence. Conversations about what other people are like fill our waking hours, and our impressions of others' personality attributes drive decisions about who to trust, befriend, hire, fire, date, and marry. This process is formalized in the "letter of recommendation," a common vehicle for one person to describe his or her impressions of another. "The candidate is cheerful, hard-working, resourceful, energetic, cooperative . . ." Trait terms like these abound in such letters and presumably are intended to mean something to, and to influence decisions made by, those who read them.

The sum total of the judgments made about you by everybody who knows you is your reputation. And as Robert Hogan has noted, your reputation may be your most important possession (Hogan, 1982; Hogan & Hogan, 1991). The care and maintenance of one's reputation is the business of much if not all of social life, and how this endeavor turns out has large implications. People will kill to maintain their reputations and will sometimes kill themselves if their reputations are sufficiently and irreparably damaged. As Shakespeare's Casio lamented,

> Reputation, reputation, reputation! O, I have lost my reputation! I have lost the immortal part of myself, and what remains is bestial. My reputation, Iago, my reputation![1]

Why is reputation seen as so important? There are at least three reasons. First, many doors in life are opened or closed to you as a function of how your personality is perceived. Someone who thinks you are cold will not date you, someone who thinks you are uncooperative will not hire you, and someone who thinks you are dishonest will not lend you money. This will be the case regardless of how warm, cooperative, or honest you might *really* be. Second, a long tradition of research on expectancy effects shows that to a small but important degree, people have a way of living up, or down, to the impressions others have of them. Children expected to improve their academic performance to some degree will do just that (Rosenthal, 1994), and young women expected to be warm and friendly tend to become so (Snyder, Tanke, & Berscheid, 1977).[2]

There is another important reason to care about what others think of us: They might be right. To learn the state of one's health, one consults a medical expert. To learn whether one's car is safe, one consults a mechanical expert. And if you want to learn what your personality is like, just look around. Experts surround you. The people in your social world have observed your behavior and drawn conclusions about your personality and behavior, and they can therefore be an important source of feedback about the nature of your own personality and abilities. This observation is not quite equivalent to the symbolic interactionist "looking glass self-hypothesis" that claims we cannot help but think about ourselves as others do (e.g., Mead, 1934; Shrauger & Schoeneman, 1979). Rather, the idea is that looking to the natural experts in our social world is a rational way to learn more about what we are really like.

In an important sense, a reputation has a life of its own and operates and can be studied separately from the person who happens to own it. But that is not what will be done here. The present concern with the *accuracy* of personality judgment leads

---

[1]Perhaps Casio was overreacting. To this speech, Iago replied, in part, "Reputation is an idle and most false imposition, oft got without merit, and lost without deserving" (*Othello,* Act 2, Scene 3).

[2]Lee Jussim (1991, 1993) has persuasively argued that these impressions in most real-life cases are accurate to begin with, and so "expectancy effects" include both accurate prediction and behavioral influence. Moreover, expectancy effects tend to work only about aspects of a person about which he or she is unsure. When people are certain about their self-conceptions to begin with, they tend to maintain them while perceivers eventually abandon discrepant expectancies (Swann & Ely, 1984). But the behavioral influence component, while perhaps smaller than once thought, is real (see also Madon, Jussim & Eccles, 1997; Rosenthal, 1994).

to a focus on the degree to which one's reputation might be among the indicators of what a person is *really* like.

Applied Psychology

Accurate personality judgment is important to a large segment of applied psychology as well. For example, consider the long-term consequences of traumatic events. It has been suggested that sexually abused children grow up with lowered self-esteem, an impaired sense of control and competence, and an increase in negative emotions (Trickett & Putnam, 1993). These are important consequences. How do we know they occur? Only because somebody has somehow made a personality judgment. Accurate judgment of personality is required to even begin to study how people are affected by important life events. More broadly, any assessment by a counselor, probation officer, or clinical psychologist involves one person trying to accurately judge some attribute of the personality of another.

Recall the reader of those letters of recommendation. In organizational settings, people often must decide who they should hire, train, or promote. A member of an admissions committee reading a packet of letters of recommendation, a personnel officer reading an employment file, and a supervisor filling out a performance appraisal are all trying to judge general aspects of a person. The accuracy of the judgment is crucial to the quality of an important decision that will affect both the individual and the organization.[3]

Theoretical Considerations

The accuracy of personality judgment is also important for several issues within theoretically oriented psychology, including sources of data, the relations between personality and behavior, and the conceptualization of individual differences.

Source of Data

The human judge has long been an important data-gathering tool for personality, developmental, and clinical psychology (Funder, 1993a). In the typical application, a judge becomes acquainted with a subject, watches a subject's behavior, or peruses a file of information and then renders judgments of various personality attributes. A widely used technique, the California Q-sort, requires the judge to rate 100 attributes such as "Is critical, skeptical, not easily impressed," "Has a wide range of interests," and "Is a genuinely dependable and responsible person" (Block, 1978/

---

[3]Accordingly, even while so-called mainstream social psychology ignored accuracy issues for almost three decades, industrial/organizational psychology maintained a steady interest (Funder, 1987; Jackson, 1982; Kane & Lawler, 1978; Lewin & Zwany, 1976.).

1961). Research using this technique has been widespread in studies of adult personality (e.g., Bem & Funder, 1978; Wiggins, 1973, chap. 4) and child and adolescent development (see Funder, Parke, Tomlinson-Keasey & Widaman, 1993).

As an instrument for gathering data, the human judge has some attributes that are distinctive and other attributes that are shared by all data–gathering methods. Distinctive attributes of the human judge include the way the distinction between the source of data and the person who reads the data can become blurred and the way that many sources of bias possible with a human judge are different from those associated with more mechanical measures. A nondistinctive attribute is that the same considerations of precision, calibration, and fidelity to underlying reality are exactly as relevant for appraising human judgments of personality as the output of any measuring device, and a science built on the output of this measuring device can be no better than the quality of the data the device yields.

The accuracy of personality judgments is therefore critical for personality, developmental, and clinical psychology. A reasonable evaluation of much research in these areas depends on understanding how accurate the judgments on which it is based are likely to be. As Ozer and Reise (1994) pointed out, "Understanding the processes that create accurate observer evaluations [of personality] is thus a key methodological concern of personality psychologists" (p. 370). To do better research, it would be helpful to know when and under what circumstances personality judgment is likely to be more accurate (Funder, 1993a).

Links between Personality and Behavior

The study of personality entails the study of the links between personality and behavior. Given that someone has a particular level of a personality attribute, what can we expect him or her to do? This kind of behavioral prediction is the basic business of personality assessment (Wiggins, 1973). The study of person perception, as it has evolved within social psychology over the past several decades, studies the same link in the reverse direction. Given that somebody has performed a particular behavior, what will the observer infer about the personality attributes he or she might possess? This process of inference is the basic topic of the study of person perception as well as the more fine-grained field of "social cognition" that grew out of it during the 1980s (Fiske & Taylor, 1991).

Although traditionally examined in literatures that are almost perfectly insulated from each other, these two topics—the relationship between personality and behavior, on the one hand, and between behavior and personality, on the other—are at their roots the same. Knowledge of one of them entails knowledge of the other and, equivalently and perhaps more tellingly, ignorance of one of them entails ignorance of the other. Knowledge about how people infer personality from behavior could tell us much about how individuals' characteristic behaviors will come across in and affect their social worlds. Likewise, knowledge about how personality is manifest in behavior could tell us much about how personality is and should be inferred *from* behavior. The issue of accuracy subsumes both of these topics. It is concerned with the path between an attribute of someone's personality, on the one hand, and accurate judgment of that attribute, on the other.

Conceptualization of Individual Differences

Beyond the quality of particular judgments of personality lies the further issue of how individual differences should be conceptualized in the first place. The proverbial person-on-the-street is well accustomed to thinking about himself or herself and others in terms of personality traits. In a classic exercise, Allport and Odbert (1936) found that an unabridged dictionary contained 17,953 different personality traits, a sufficient indication of how prevalent such terms are. But more recent writers have claimed, sometimes forcefully, that trait terms do not refer to anything real or useful and should either be abolished from use or replaced by narrower, more scientifically respectable substitutes (Shweder, 1975). So a crucial issue for psychology concerns the appropriate units for the conceptualization of individual differences in personality (Jackson, 1982). Are the terms of ordinary language sufficient? Or should they be discarded or replaced? Serious study of the accuracy of personality judgment must attend to these questions as well (see Chapter 2).

Intrinsic Considerations

The accuracy of personality judgment is directly relevant to some age-old philosophical issues and to the ordinary curiosity most people have about each other. Although neither of these concerns may be directly practical, both have proven to be powerful motivators to human thought over the years.

Philosophical Issues

Perhaps the oldest and also most timeless questions in philosophy concern the relationship between perception and reality. Plato likened our perceptions to shadows on the walls of a cave—related to reality but not directly descriptive of it. His analogy also reflected the eternal uncertainty about how the subjective world inside the head might be related to the objective world outside.

This uncertainty is fundamental. If two dozen centuries of hard philosophizing has determined nothing else, it has decisively confirmed that we can never be certain about anything (except that very conclusion). This uncertainty includes our most basic assumptions. For example, perhaps you are not really sitting in a chair reading this book. Perhaps you are tied to a gurney in a dark room somewhere with fluids dripping into your veins, the effect of which is to cause you to *hallucinate* that you are sitting in a chair reading this book. Or consider the people you know and perhaps can see (or think you see) if you look up from this book. Perhaps you are the only thinking, feeling, human being in the bunch. Perhaps the rest are all robots, cleverly programmed to resemble people just like you (Perry, 1975)!

Fortunately, no sane person believes either of these possibilities. This is interesting, because philosophy has concluded that neither can be excluded on purely logical grounds. Each of the arguments that you are perceiving reality rather than a hallucination, or that other people are like you and not robots, has been painstakingly examined by professional philosophers, and found wanting. Some of these arguments—such as the observation that other people probably are not robots because their responses and nervous systems are similar to yours—are helpful, to be sure. But none of them, nor all of them together, is sufficient to prove either that reality in general or other people in particular really exist.

So why isn't anybody paralyzed by this uncertainty? Or, to amend slightly, why are *sane* people not paralyzed by this uncertainty? There are two reasons. First, the evidence that reality and other people exist, while *not* conclusive, does seem to point in that direction. Second, to believe and act on either of these skeptical propositions is tantamount to suicide. Someone who really believed that his or her perceptions were all hallucinations or that other people did not exist would become apathetic, asocial, and perhaps literally suicidal. So even though neither skeptical proposition can be disproved, the wisest course seems to be to think of them as interesting possibilities that are almost surely false, and live one's life accordingly.

I belabor this point a bit because it is important to realize that even our most fundamental orienting beliefs require a leap of faith (Funder, 1995a; James, 1915). There must always be a small but real gap between what is surely true and what we choose to believe is true. The most basic issue underlying a concern with accuracy in personality judgment is the question of in what ways, and to what degrees, our perceptions of ourselves and each other match what *is* actually true about each other and ourselves. The problem with this obviously important question, as many commentators have observed, is that it is impossible to find a perfect, infallible indicator of what is "actually true" about ourselves and each other. This impossibility has led more than a few influential psychologists to suggest that the topic of accuracy therefore may not be worth investigating, and would better be ignored (Cook, 1984; Jones, 1985; Schneider et al., 1979).

What such suggestions fail to appreciate is that uncertainty is not a problem that uniquely plagues the study of accuracy in personality judgment; it is a basic fact of life. The consequences of nihilistically asserting that accuracy can never be meaningfully assessed are similar in kind—if not in degree—to the consequences of nihilistic points of view concerning the existence of reality and other people. Such an overly skeptical view produces a chaotic, self-defeating interpretation of social judgment, forecloses action that might allow such judgments to be evaluated and improved, and rules out accuracy as a topic of research.

The point of view taken in the present treatment is that, for the reasons summarized, accuracy is too important of a topic to be avoided or finessed. To insist on knowing the true nature of reality "for sure" before investigating accuracy is too strict of a standard, because we *never* know for sure. The objective of accuracy research should be to attempt to determine the actual nature of reality using the widest possible range of evidence (see Chapter 4). Then it becomes possible to study accuracy through research that explores the circumstances under which judgments most closely match reality, as best as it can be determined on the basis of that evidence.

Curiosity

A good part of the way in which psychology earns its keep is by addressing the practical, methodological, and philosophical issues outlined earlier. But beyond all of the pragmatic and academic reasons for being interested in accuracy, the most important reason remains intrinsic. As was mentioned at the outset of this chapter, it is part of the human condition to care about what other people are like, including how they differ from each other and ourselves.

On most college campuses, psychology is either the first or second most popular major subject. This popularity is surely not due to students' perceptions of wide-open career prospects for holders of bachelor's degrees in psychology.[4] Rather, in many cases, it is because of the naïve hope, too often dashed, that in psychology courses they might learn something *interesting*. Among the population at large, people follow with rapt attention the personality quirks and marital problems of sportscasters and the royal family, among many other psychological topics with no possible relevance to their own actual lives. This interest is perhaps as pure an illustration of intrinsic motivation as can be imagined: The only reward for knowing about a princess's personality quirks is that you get to know about her personality quirks!

The great perceptual psychologist J. J. Gibson and his modern-day "Gibsonian" counterparts have argued cogently that all "perception is for doing" (e.g., Gibson, 1979; McArthur & Baron, 1983; Zebrowitz & Collins, 1997). By this they mean that people perceive not abstract qualities of things or people, but "affordances" or potentials for use or interaction. The partial truth of this observation should not obscure the way that much perception—perhaps especially social perception—is of abstract qualities and is emphatically *not* for "doing." People are interested in sights (like a golden sunset) that do not contain useful affordances and are even more interested in people (such as celebrities) who they will never meet and who cannot affect them in any way.

It could be argued that all perception is *potentially* for doing, in the sense that all perception absorbs information that might eventually or under some unforeseen circumstances prove to be of use. But if this is granted, then Gibson's statement

---

[4]Nor, contrary to what some might say, is it because psychology is the easiest major on campus. Other subjects—not to be named here—do not require statistics, biology, computer literacy, or rigorous analytic training, as psychology does, and are therefore much easier.

degenerates from a truly provocative idea to one that is much less powerful. If the dictum "perception is for doing" means anything interesting, it means we perceive only aspects of use, which seems to be false.

Psychology can justify its existence—and indeed probably came into existence in the first place—by virtue of the way it attempts to satisfy intrinsic interest. Like all other sciences, in the final analysis psychology is an expression of curiosity (Funder, 1998). While there is surely room in psychology for investigators who spend all their time addressing topics too esoteric for nonpsychologists to comprehend, unless somebody is willing to address the ingenuous and naïve questions of common curiosity then the very existence of the field is imperiled (Block, 1993).

There are two reasons. First, if taxpayers and students lose interest in psychology, then they will become unwilling to support it with tax dollars and enrollments. Second and perhaps even more important, vacuums never persist for long. If research psychologists will not address issues of common interest, you may be sure that somebody else will. And if a credulous public then comes to believe the pronouncements of untrained, irresponsible, or demagogic "pop psychologists," the field of scientific psychology, in its dignified silence, will have only itself to blame.

THREE PROPOSITIONS

The present approach to the study of accuracy in personality judgment is organized by three commonsense propositions. Indeed, if these propositions are not accepted, then the study of accuracy cannot even begin. The propositions are as follows:

1. Individual differences in personality (personality traits) exist and are important.
2. People sometimes make judgments of these traits.
3. These judgments are sometimes accurate.

These propositions may seem fairly innocuous, but all three are (or have been until recently) highly controversial. Because they must be granted before accuracy research can begin, their controversiality has served to make accuracy research itself problematic.

The first proposition was for more than two decades the subject of the person-situation debate (Kenrick & Funder, 1988). This extraordinarily bitter and persistent debate, not quite over even yet, concerned whether individual differences in personality, expressed in the everyday colloquial terms of personality traits, exist to a sufficient degree as to be important. The feasibility of accuracy research hinges on the outcome, because if personality does not exist, then it makes no sense to assess the degree to which judgments of personality are accurate—all judgments of personality are simply wrong. This debate is reviewed in Chapter 2.

The second proposition has been considered doubtful by some psychologists, otherwise allied with accuracy research, who espouse "pragmatic" or "ecological" approaches to human judgment identified with the writings of J. J. Gibson (1979). As was mentioned earlier, the "Gibsonians" argue that people judge not abstract qualities such as traits but only more immediately utilitarian "affordances" such as the degree to which somebody likes them or is threatening to them (Zebrowitz & Collins, 1997). This is an interesting idea and is surely true to some extent, but it too obviates the study of how accurate I am if I *do* conclude that somebody is honest or sociable or even neurotic. All these traits are much too abstract, say the Gibsonians, and people never really think that way. This idea was discussed briefly earlier and will receive further attention in Chapter 5.

The third proposition has been the most controversial of all. For almost three decades the psychological literature has been filled with insult after insult directed at the capacities of ordinary human judgment. The insults have been both broad and specific. Some researchers have concentrated on putative demonstrations that people are unable to understand or correctly employ the most elementary, fundamental canons of logic. But nowhere has the attack on human judgment been more vehement than in the specific domain of person perception. We are *characteristically* wrong in our judgments of other people, research in this domain has claimed again and again.

The most basic putative flaw in social judgment is the "fundamental attribution error" (Ross, 1977). This error is the human being's characteristic tendency to see personality where none exists or, more precisely, to think that the behavior of others is relevant to the kind of people that they are (instead of just the situations they are in). Yet again, we see that the outcome of this argument is crucial to accuracy research, for if human judgment is permeated by the fundamental attribution error, then accurate personality judgment becomes nearly oxymoronic. The research on this point is evaluated in Chapter 3.

A large part of this book is devoted to a detailed exposition of the controversies concerning each of these propositions, along with my own take on them. For now, to make a long story short, I will simply claim that controversies notwithstanding all three propositions are true. The latter part of this book will proceed as if the controversies were over and that all three of these propositions could be accepted: Personality exists, people judge it, and these judgments are sometimes right. Chapters 5 through 8 will endeavor to show how accepting these three propositions opens a new paradigm for the study of person perception and illuminates new insights and research directions.

The propositions imply that it is important to know when (i.e., under what circumstances) personality judgment is accurate, and how accurate judgment can be achieved. These issues, in turn, require attention *both* to processes of social perception, on the one hand, and the actual nature of the personalities of the persons who are perceived, on the other. Without attention to both, the connection between actual personality and judgments of personality—accuracy—cannot be examined. Thus, as we will see in subsequent chapters, accuracy research necessarily crosses a hazardous frontier, between personality psychology and its study of properties of individuals, and social psychology and its study of the processes of person perception.

   This necessity to travel between two subdisciplines creates an extra difficulty for accuracy research, because social and personality psychologists have not always gotten along well in recent years. Before embarking on the quest for accuracy in personality judgment, therefore, it might be useful to take a short side journey to consider how and why these two fields have become disconnected and to look at some of the consequences. These consequences have had wide impact, and none are more powerful and important than the way the separation between social and personality psychology has inhibited the development of research on accuracy in personality judgment.

SOCIAL AND PERSONALITY PSYCHOLOGY: SEPARATION AND INTEGRATION

Social psychology and personality psychology were born at about the same time, and of the same parents. Only later did they become strangely estranged. Gordon Allport was one of the founders, and perhaps the founder, of both fields in their current form. In the 1930s, he more or less single-handedly wrested the study of personality away from the exclusive hands of the psychodynamic clinicians and refocused attention on the nature of normal personality (Allport, 1937). The topic of this new field was the psychological variation across individuals, none of whom were necessarily neurotic or abnormal in any way.

   Allport thought that although every individual's psychological makeup is unique, certain general patterns or "personality traits" could be useful in describing the ways in which people differed from each other. So Allport became interested in the means by which personality traits could be accurately evaluated. For example, with Paul Vernon he investigated how people who walked about the room with long strides tended to be perceived as extraverted and dominant, and he found that such perceptions tended by and large to be accurate (Allport & Vernon, 1933). This interest in how personality is perceived led him in a number of directions, one of the most important being his path-breaking work on racial prejudice, a phenomenon in which normally accurate processes of social perception tragically and dangerously break down (Allport, 1950).

   Allport's work on the conceptualization and measurement of personality is today regarded as definitive of mainstream personality psychology; his work on prejudice is one of the cornerstones of modern, mainstream social psychology. And Allport's 1937 textbook, often credited with inventing the modern field of personality psychology, contains an entire chapter on the perception of personality traits (Chapter 20), a topic now usually found only in social psychology textbooks (but see Funder, 1997a, chap. 6). Allport saw the two fields of social and personality psychology as inseparable; in fact, it is not clear he saw any real distinction between them (Funder,

1993b). This integration came naturally from how he thought about person perception: each person has certain traits that a perceiver must try to accurately judge somehow. To Allport, the study of traits included trying to understand how they are manifest in nonverbal as well as verbal behavior and therefore making an effort to enumerate the cues that others could use to judge these traits accurately. The behavioral manifestations of personality and the processes of personality judgment are in that way two sides of the same coin.

Half a century later, however, researchers interested in personality and in personality judgment had somehow become not only separated but also alienated. The study of individual differences had come to belong exclusively to personality psychologists, whereas the study of personality judgment—now called "person perception"—belonged to social psychologists. Worse, these two camps rarely communicated in any positive manner.

Reasons for the Separation

It is easier to describe what the current differences between the approaches of social and personality psychology are than it is to explain how they arose. The latter issue is one for historians and sociologists of science—not that they have said much of use on this topic yet. The origins may lie partially in the way personality psychology became reentangled with clinical psychology despite Allport's own best efforts otherwise. The separation may also have been influenced by the way American social psychology was changed in the 1930s and 1940s by prominent European psychologists who espoused an experimental tradition that led away from correlational designs or the study of individual differences.

Personality psychology also developed some bad habits over the years. The field became distracted by self-defeating issues such as a long and ultimately pointless debate about "response sets" (Hogan & Nicholson, 1988; Rorer, 1965). It became increasingly insular in its interests and narrow in its methods. In the hands of some investigators, personality psychology was transformed from a broad and exciting area of theory and research to the study of the properties of self-report questionnaires. It has only recently begun to recover, broadening its research methods and topics of concern, but with a much-reduced base of researchers and resources.

At the same time personality psychology was self-destructively narrowing, social psychology was broadening. It took on major topics such as attitudes, prejudice, conformity, obedience, altruism, and many more. Social psychology may have failed to attain theoretical coherence, being characterized by a large number of independent "minitheories" developed to explain specific phenomena. But there is no denying that at the same time—and perhaps concomitantly—it addressed an extraordinarily wide range of important and interesting topics. It should be no surprise, therefore, that when the two fields began to battle both for research resources and the interest of the next generation of psychologists, it was social that won on both fronts. There are vastly more active social than personality psychologists now doing research, more social psychology training programs, and more grant money for social psychology research.

Differences between Social and Personality Psychology

Regardless of the reasons for the separation of these two fields, their current differences in approach are plain to see.

Experimental versus Correlational Methods

Perhaps the most obvious difference between modern social and personality psychology is that the former is based almost exclusively on experiments, whereas the latter is usually based on correlational studies.

Social psychologists experimentally vary the stimuli they provide their subjects, and then they observe how the subjects respond. Sometimes these stimuli are vivid minidramas, involving shock generators, smoke pouring under doors, or confederates apparently passed out in the street. More often, the stimuli are words printed on a form. Subjects in one condition read one set of words while subjects in the other condition read another set of words. The behavioral dependent variable, in turn, may occasionally be what the subject does, but more often it is what he or she writes or which response option he or she checks on a questionnaire.

The advantages of this latter, frequently used procedure are ease of use and experimental control; the disadvantages—entailed by a profound lack of realism—should be obvious. In the field of person perception, thousands of studies have been conducted in which subjects *read* descriptions of *hypothetical* stimulus persons: "Bob is kind, gentle, cold, honest, and friendly." The subjects write their resulting impressions, or complete a checklist or attribution questionnaire, on a further page. Some interesting findings concerning the processes of impression formation (in this limited context) have been obtained from studies like this, but notice how the accuracy issue is completely avoided. There is nothing *accurate* you can say about Bob, because Bob never existed.

The typical independent variable for personality psychology is an individual's score on a dimension of personality. Such a score cannot be experimentally manipulated, so research typically consists of correlating personality trait scores with various dependent variables of interest. The personality trait score may come from self-report questionnaires or from peers' or experts' ratings. As in social psychology, the dependent variable sometimes is a behavior, observed and measured directly in the lab or in real life. More often, also as in social psychology, the dependent variable is derived from marks on a page, questionnaire responses. But the variable is at least associated with some attribute of a person that the researcher has reason to believe the person actually possesses.

Constructivist versus Realistic Assumptions

Social and personality psychology have also come to differ profoundly in the positions they take (usually implicitly) in the debate between constructivist and realistic interpretations of reality.

The Route of Social Psychology

The social psychological study of person perception has been undergirded by constructivist assumptions from its early days. It has concentrated on how person perceptions are cognitively constructed and socially influenced and has largely ignored the relationship—if any—between social perceptions and social reality. This tendency was evidenced in one of the earliest books ever published that collected research on person perception (Tagiuri & Petrullo, 1958). It drew heated complaint from Allport who feared—correctly as it turned out—that this approach would inhibit the study of the accuracy of personality judgment, as the study of person perception nearly became permanently estranged from the study of persons (Allport, 1958, 1966). One of Allport's prescient remarks on this point is worth quoting in full:

> Skepticism [about personality] is likewise reflected in many investigations of "person perception." To try to discover the traits residing within a personality is regarded as either naïve or impossible. Studies, therefore, concentrate only on the process of perceiving or judging, and reject the problem of validating the perception and judgment (Allport, 1966, p. 2, emphasis in the original).

In more recent years the tendency noted by Allport has only become exaggerated. "Deconstructivist" ideas have swept the literature departments of universities around the world, claiming that "texts" (works of literature) have no inherent meaning beyond that given to them by each individual reader. Perhaps not many social psychologists are even aware of these ideas, but they have had a subtle influence nonetheless. There is a remarkable parallel between the arguments in the English Department that a Shakespeare play means nothing beyond what you (solipsistically) read into it, and that the persons you encounter have no inherent qualities beyond those you (solipsistically) perceive. On an even more subtle level, there is a visible parallel between Jacques Derrida's famous dictum that "there is nothing outside of the text" and cognitive social psychology's implicit assumption that there is nothing outside of the mind. Both act as if reality (the text) has no inherent meaning beyond what each reader or perceiver idiosyncratically attributes to it.

This point of view has had a profound and pervasive influence on how social psychologists view person perception. For example, as Jussim (1993) has pointed out, research showing a small (but real) tendency for people to live up or down to the expectations we have of them has been translated, in many textbooks, as indicating that all evaluative judgments are self-fulfilling and otherwise fictitious social constructions. The most stunning apotheosis of this viewpoint was the widespread and surprisingly ready acceptance of Lee Ross's (1977) idea that essentially all perceptions of stable personality qualities in others derived from a "fundamental attribution error."

It must be admitted that person perceptions do seem like particularly good candidates for constructivist interpretation, because the qualities we perceive in others, such as their sociability, honesty, or dominance, are not palpable entities and cannot be seen directly but only inferred. And there is no denying that a vast amount of valuable and useful research has grown out of treating person perceptions as interesting phenomena in and of themselves, quite separate from the reality of the stimuli to which they refer. For example, Asch's brilliant, pioneering program of research showed how perceivers manage to integrate disparate information about a person into a coherent overall impression (Asch, 1946). Several decades of subsequent research on "social cognition" examined in detail the cognitive processes by which social information can be selectively perceived, interpreted, remembered, and recalled (Fiske & Taylor, 1991).

Yet to regard social perceptions solely as social constructions imposes an important limit on the topics that can be examined. Years ago Allport, in yet another prescient comment, observed that astronomers regard stars as real objects and not as interesting hypothetical entities (Allport, 1958, p. 246). Yet nobody has ever touched a star and everything we know about stars is the product of long and elaborate chains of questionable inference. Imagine the damage that would be done to astronomy if its wiser heads decided that it was therefore naïve to regard stars as real and began to regard them as interesting but constructed celestial ideas instead. A constructivist astronomy might discover all sorts of intriguing things about the perceptual and inferential processes of astronomers, but would very probably stop learning any more facts about stars! In the same vein, to regard social perceptions as social constructions might lead to many insights about the mental processes of social perceivers (as it has) but nothing about the properties of the persons who are perceived, or the relationship between social perception and social reality.

The Route of Personality Psychology

At the constructivism–realism crossroads, personality psychology went the opposite route. In part this may have been because of Allport's strenuous arguments, but another important influence came from outside of psychology—World War II. Many prominent psychologists joined the American war effort, leading among other consequences to the founding of the Institute of Personality Assessment and Research (IPAR) at Berkeley. The military was understandably concerned with the selection and placement of its millions of recruits, and personality psychologists were enlisted to develop instruments to aid in this process. These efforts spurred progress in psychometrics and test development during the war and after, in much the same way (though of course on a vastly smaller scale) that the Manhattan Project spurred progress in physics.

Accordingly, the primary focus of personality psychology since the 1940s became personality assessment, the enterprise of locating individuals as precisely as possible along one or more dimensions of individual difference. This focus entailed a narrowing of the concerns of personality psychology, which in the hands of theorists such as Freud, Jung, Adler, Horney, Kelly, Rogers, and others addressed a much wider range of issues. At the same time, the concentration on individual differences succeeded in generating a vast amount of productive research over the next several decades, including the development of a sophisticated psychometric technology and the introduction of several state-of-the-art personality assessment instruments. Most of these were self-report questionnaires, and included the Minnesota Multiphasic Personality Inventory (MMPI) (Hathaway & Meel, 1951), the California Psychological Inventory (CPI) (Gough, 1990), and 16PF (Cattell & Cattell, 1995). Another important development was Jack Block's California Q-sort (Block, 1978/1961), an instrument for thoroughly and precisely capturing the personality judgments of clinical judges and other observers (Bem & Funder, 1978). On the downside, as was mentioned earlier, much of the field's energy became absorbed during the 1950s and 1960s by an unproductive technical debate concerning the effects of response sets on questionnaire responses. This inwardly focused debate may have helped drive away young researchers and others who might otherwise have been attracted to the field.

In summary, over the past 50 years social psychology has concentrated on the perceptual and cognitive processes of person perceivers, with scant attention to the persons being perceived. Personality psychology has had the reverse orientation, closely examining self-reports of individuals for indications of their personality traits, but rarely examining how these people actually come off in social interaction.

The "Counter-intuitive Result" versus Psychometric Rigor and Normal Science

The research emphases of social and personality psychology have importantly differed in another way as well. For much of the past several decades (until about 1980), social psychology steadily expanded the range of issues it attempted to address. A glance at any social psychology textbook will reveal a dizzying array (even hodgepodge) of topics including attitudes, prejudice, influence, conformity, attraction, altruism, and many more. As was mentioned earlier, although social psychology never succeeded in sorting these topics into any kind of order, their sheer range and variety was extremely attractive to students, funding agencies, and prospective researchers.

A particular goal of social psychologists throughout the late 1960s and 1970s was the counter-intuitive result, by which a researcher manages to show that something the person-on-the-street might have expected to be true is actually wrong. The attraction of the counter-intuitive result includes both its surprise or news value and the way it obviates complaints that so much social psychology seems intuitively obvious. Examples have included findings that intervening in an emergency is less likely when more bystanders are present (Darley & Latane, 1968), that higher incentives produce less rather than more attitude change (Festinger & Carlsmith, 1959), and that ordinary citizens will obey orders to give innocent people apparently fatal electrical shocks (Milgram, 1975). But the granddaddy of all counter-intuitive results was offered by the literature on judgmental error (e.g., Nisbett & Ross, 1980; Ross & Nisbett, 1991), when it argued that essentially *all* ordinary intuitions about other people are wrong (Funder, 1992).

Again, personality psychology went the opposite route. Rather than broadening its realm of application or chasing surprising findings, it narrowed its concern to the development and refinement of self-report personality instruments. A few personality psychologists, such as Jack and Jeanne Block, still dared to develop theoretical ideas of wide relevance (Block & Block, 1980), but most of the field's energy went into the development of psychometric technology and new self-report tests. True innovation was rare and "exciting" findings were not even sought; rather, the inventory of self-report instruments steadily expanded and statistical methods became ever more sophisticated. A surprising number of these methods, once developed, were never actually applied to substantive issues.

By the late 1970s, the result of these two contrasting trends was the evolution of two very different fields of research. Social psychology was still on the chase of exciting and surprising findings but had done little to assimilate what it had learned. Its methodology was relatively primitive—it primarily consisted of simple 2 x 2 experimental designs—and the result was deemed important if it was statistically significant. Personality psychology, methodologically and statistically much more sophisticated—it routinely employed complex multivariate analyses—was focused on a narrow set of issues many of which were more methodological than truly substantive.

Behavioral Observations versus Questionnaires

The databases of social and personality psychology also came to differ. Sometimes, social psychologists have used observed behaviors as their dependent variable. For example, Darley measured whether and how quickly a bystander intervenes in an emergency; Milgram measured how much shock a subject would administer to a victim. Surprisingly often, however, the dependent variable in social psychological experiments has been a mark on a questionnaire intended to measure the subject's attitude, intention, or impression. For its part, personality psychology came to be based almost *entirely* on questionnaires. A few investigators, such as the Blocks and Walter Mischel, have included direct observations of performance in their research. Much more often, entire research programs have consisted of the construction, administration, comparison, and intercorrelation of questionnaires.

Behavioral and questionnaire measures, while both useful, raise the same problem: The meaning of neither can be taken for granted. The seemingly straightforward measurement of how long a child waits for a reward might reflect the child's tendency to obey adult authority as much as his or her degree of self-control (Bem & Funder, 1978). And it is obvious that people at least sometimes describe themselves in the way they would like to be seen or as they wish they were, rather than as they really are (Hogan, 1983). Unfortunately, this lack of transparency of methods has not always been noticed or acknowledged by researchers in either field. Too often it has been assumed that a behavioral measure taps exactly the psychological attribute or process that would superficially appear the most relevant and that a questionnaire offers direct and immediate insight into an individual's nature.

Consequences of the Estrangement of Social and Personality Psychology

The estrangement that developed over the years as social and personality psychology traveled their divergent paths has had many consequences, none of them good.

Mutual Ignorance

The most obvious and perhaps most dangerous consequence of the estrangement is that individuals trained in either social or personality psychology are often more ignorant of the other field than they should be. Personality psychologists sometimes reveal an imperfect understanding of the concerns and methods of their social psychological brethren, and they in particular fail to comprehend the way in which so much of the self-report data they gather fails to overcome the skepticism of those trained in other methods. For their part, social psychologists are often unfamiliar with basic findings and concepts of personality psychology, misunderstand common statistics such as correlation coefficients and other measures of effect size, and are sometimes breathtakingly ignorant of basic psychometric principles. This is revealed, for example, when social psychologists, assuring themselves that they would not deign to measure any entity so fictitious as a trait, proceed to construct their own self-report scales to measure individual difference constructs called schemas or strategies or construals (never a trait). But they often fail to perform the most elementary analyses to confirm the internal consistency or the convergent and discriminant validity of their new measures, probably because they do not know that they should.

It is my impression that the ignorance by social psychologists of personality psychology is more profound than the other way around. I suspect two reasons. The first is the institutional reason that because social psychology won the contest in most minds as to which is the more interesting field, it has more practitioners, journals, and graduate training programs.[5] Every year, it seems, the faculties of fewer universities include someone who can teach psychometrics, and students are exposed to fewer examples of psychometrically competent research either by their own faculty or in the journals. The second reason is that the person-situation debate and Mischel's influential claim that personality does not exist led many social psychologists to believe they were not missing much if they failed to learn the substance or methods of personality assessment (Zajonc, 1976). When later some decided to develop measures of individual difference variables such as schemas, strategies, or competencies, they failed to realize that psychometric technology was just as relevant to their enterprise as to that of someone who is trying to measure a trait by name.

Topical Neglect

The scientific result of all this mutual estrangement and ignorance is that researchers in each field concentrated on topics that seemed to require no reference to the other field (or that could be studied long periods of time without referring to the other field, which is not quite the same thing). As both personality and social psychology retreated to safe distances from their borders, the end result has been an astonishing *lack* of investigation of certain key issues in the two fields that happen to lie in the no-man's-land near their borders.

This is a startling outcome. When one contemplates the size and accelerating growth of the research literature of psychology in general, it seems difficult to believe that *anything* could possibly have been left out as a topic of investigation, let alone anything important. Yet such is the case. Consider two prominent examples:

Personality and Behavior

Personality psychology owns an embarrassingly small inventory of information concerning the ways in which people who differ on the thousands of traits that have been measured actually differ in what they *do*. As will be discussed in Chapter 2, this is an important reason the field was so vulnerable to Mischel's (1968) critique. When he challenged personality psychologists to show their evidence that traits were related to behavior, nearly all they could respond with was a vast body of studies showing how questionnaire responses were interrelated. For evidence concerning relations between personality and behavior, the same decades-old studies (e.g., Hartshorne & May, 1928) were dragged out again and again. Why were more recent studies examining individual differences in behavior not available? The reason is not far to seek. Such studies are extraordinarily difficult. The setting up of experimental settings in which sufficient numbers of subjects can be induced to

[5] This reason is parallel to the reason why people in New Zealand know much more about America than Americans usually know about New Zealand.

perform behaviors at least somewhat revealing of their personalities presents daunting logistical difficulties, especially for those investigators who lack generous grant support (see Chapter 4). It is much easier to make up questionnaires asking people what they usually do, or would do under various circumstances, than it is to observe what they actually do in any circumstance. Indeed, given the limits on the resources of the typical psychological researcher, this usually may be all that is possible. The difficulty and sometimes sheer impossibility of observing behavior directly has not only made research incorporating such measures exceedingly rare, but in some cases seems to have caused whatever skills personality psychology might have had for the observation of behavior to atrophy. The necessity of so often limiting one's methods seems to have created a larger and even more consequential failure of imagination, such that even when resources become available, the only thing researchers can sometimes think to do is to hand out more and longer questionnaires.

It is interesting to contrast this situation in the study of adult personality with developmental and comparative psychology. Psychologists who study small children and animals find that neither kind of subject is cooperative about completing questionnaires. So they have developed imaginative and useful methods for observing and recording behavior directly (Cairns, 1979).[6] But these methods appear only rarely in the personality literature.

Perception and Reality

In the typical social psychological study of person perception, the stimuli presented to subjects are experimentally manipulated. Actual persons, and especially actual persons who have had their personalities assessed, are seldom if ever employed as stimuli. The experimentally manipulated stimuli almost always consist of words (usually typed on a questionnaire) rather than observations, even simulated, of people or their actions. Therefore, the research may be informative about how people interpret collections of descriptive words (e.g., Asch, 1946), or other written stimulus materials (e.g., Jones & Harris, 1967), but not how people observe, parse, and interpret action. More important, in research of this kind nothing is learned about the connection—indeed if any—between person perception and actual properties of persons perceived.[7] The persons perceived *have* no actual properties.

The Ironic Reunification

There is one domain in which the concerns of social and personality psychology have been reunited, but that domain is an ironic choice. Mischel's famous 1968

---

[6]It is probably not accidental that the few personality psychologists who have routinely included behavioral measures are those with a deep background in and who are major contributors to developmental psychology as well (e.g., Block & Block, 1980).

[7]An exception is the work of Paul Ekman on the detection of deception (Ekman, 1991). Instead of experimentally manipulating the stimuli that make people infer lies, Ekman often investigates how subjects perceive stimulus persons who really are or are not lying.

book argued two theses: (a) personality traits do not exist to any important degree and (b) people perceive such traits in each other not because such traits exist, but because they are biased to perceive traits even in the absence of sufficient evidence. This joining of assertions foreshadowed the subsequent alliance between behavioristically inclined researchers who doubted the existence of meaningful individual differences in personality, and social psychologists obsessed with documenting the inadequacy and "shortcomings" (Ross, 1977) of the lay judge of personality.

Although I believe both of Mischel's theses are incorrect in their strong (and often propounded) form, he and subsequent researchers were onto something important when they drew a connection between the existence of personality and layperson's judgments of it. Mischel realized that to fully conceptualize the relationship between personality and behavior it was necessary, as well, to account for the connections that laypersons perceive. To make his argument that personality did not exist, Mischel had to account for why most people believe that it does. The fact that he immediately saw this implication and tried to deal with it is to his profound credit—others have not been so prescient.

The present treatment of accuracy will take the connection Mischel identified and reverse only its evaluative tone. The present treatment assumes that personality *does* exist, then tries to understand how people manage to judge it accurately, when they do. As Mischel clearly saw, to examine the connection between the way personality is and the way it is perceived requires an investigator to cross repeatedly the traditional boundary between topics in personality and social psychology.

RENEWED RESEARCH ON ACCURACY

The modern approach to accuracy in personality judgment comprises a renewed attempt to address a long-neglected topic and to reunite two fields of research that have been separated for too long. Although the approach is new, it has deep historical roots.

Historical Roots

Many years before Mischel, Gordon Allport (1936) clearly saw the very same connection between the concerns of personality and social psychology that was just discussed. As already mentioned, the difference is that he probably never saw them as separate in the first place (Funder, 1993b). With particular reference to person perception, the concerns of personality and social psychology are mirror images of each other. My own attempt to bring these together—the Realistic Accuracy Model (Funder, 1995)—is strongly influenced by Allport's perspective (Funder, 1991) and by the approaches to perception and judgment pioneered by Egon Brunswik (1956) and James J. Gibson (1979).

Both of these latter psychologists theorized about the connection between perception (or judgment) and reality. Gibson argued forcefully that to understand perception it was absolutely crucial to inventory the "stimulus array" that exists in nature. He proposed that the perception of reality did not need to be constructed by the mind, but was rather "directly" perceived.[8] Therefore, research on perception should concentrate on trying to figure out how the physical world is revealed through the information available to the senses.

Brunswik's views were similar to Gibson's insofar as he also argued that one needed to understand how nature is revealed through stimuli in order to understand perception and judgment. But rather than view perception as "direct," he tried to understand the processes of uncertain inference that connect perceptions to judgments. He described how stimuli that are probabilistically connected with various properties could be used as "ecologically valid" cues to those properties by a perceiver.[9] The perceiver then needs to detect those cues and to interpret them correctly. For example, a twitching foot might usually indicate that a person is nervous, and so be an ecologically valid cue to anxiety. But it is not infallible, because sometimes people twitch their feet when they are not nervous. This uncertainty or probabilism is an important if unfortunate fact of life, which Brunswik acknowledged by referring to the process of judgment as "probabilistic functionalism."

The Realistic Accuracy Model shares with Gibson and Brunswik an emphasis on the actual properties of the stimulus but leans more heavily toward Brunswik. I believe Brunswik's probabilistic functionalism is more appropriate than Gibson's approach for explaining perceptions and predictions of phenomena that can at best only partially and probably be known. It is particularly well suited to weather forecasting, for example (Lusk & Hammond, 1991), and seems appropriate as well for person perception and attempts to predict behavior. Gibson's approach seems better suited for object perception in the here and now. This situation is not greatly analogous to the task of figuring out what someone's personality is like, a task where so much is *not* here, now.

The Realistic Accuracy Model

The Realistic Accuracy Model (RAM) is considered in detail in Chapter 5 (see also Funder, 1995). Briefly, it begins with the assumption that accurate personality judgment occurs at least sometimes, then attempts to explain how this outcome could ever be possible. It argues that the process must go like this: First, a person emits some sort of cue—usually, by performing a behavior—that is relevant to or diag-

---

[8]Even writers friendly to Gibson's approach have confessed failing to understand exactly what he meant by "direct perception" (Neisser, 1976).

[9]This term refers to how a cue is valid only in a given context or "ecology." The term ecological *validity* has been redefined by social psychology and now is usually used to refer to experimental realism, a very different (and almost wholly unrelated) concept (Hammond, 1996).

nostic of some attribute of his or her personality. Second, this cue must emerge in some way and some place that is visible, or available to a perceiver. Third, the perceiver must detect this cue. Fourth, the perceiver must utilize or interpret this cue correctly as to its meaning for personality.

Notice that accurate judgment will fail to occur if any of the four steps is not successfully traversed. If the stimulus person never does something relevant, if the behavior occurs somewhere inaccessible to the judge, if the judge fails to perceive or misperceives the behavior, or if the judge fails to interpret it correctly, accuracy will fail. To the extent the traversal of any or all of these four stages is imperfect, the ultimate judgment will also be imperfect in a way that multiplies the imperfections at each stage.

A full understanding of the relevance and availability stages ultimately requires a full understanding of personality and how it affects what people do and under what circumstances. These are traditional concerns of personality psychology. A full understanding of the perception and utilization stages ultimately requires a full understanding of the processes by which people perceive and interpret social stimuli. These are traditional concerns of social psychology, in particular the subfield of social cognition.

It is time to begin filling in both lacunae of knowledge. We need to learn more about how people parse observed behaviors into cues they then interpret in terms of their implications for personality. Even more critically, we need to learn more about what people with different levels of personality traits do and the circumstances under which they do it. In early work on this latter issue, we must forgive ourselves (and perhaps those authors whose work we review) for not using huge ranges of contexts, or behavior. Let us do what we can, rather than worry overmuch about how limited our efforts necessarily are, and permit others to do so too. Then psychology can begin to accumulate knowledge about what people with certain personality traits do, what behaviors lead us to infer the presence of certain traits, and thus how we can learn to better connect perception and reality.

THE AGENDA OF ACCURACY RESEARCH AND PLAN OF THE BOOK

In pursuit of this goal, the last two decades of accuracy research have passed through four overlapping stages.

1. *The defense of personality.* Before accuracy research could begin, it had to deal with the widespread belief that personality traits are essentially fictitious constructs. Such a belief stops accuracy research before it begins, for it makes no sense to study the accuracy of the judgment of a phenomenon that does not exist. Chapter 2 begins with a reconsideration of the "person-situation debate" and the work that was done to reaffirm the existence of personality.

2. *The defense of the human judge.* In close partnership with the attack on the existence of personality was an attack on the lay judge who thinks he or she sees personality traits in the people he or she knows. Proponents of the fundamental attribution error implied that essentially all judgments of personality were intrinsically erroneous. Chapter 3 considers the arguments made in defense of the lay judge of personality and the evidence that lay judgments of personality are correct often enough to make it worthwhile to study (a) when correct judgment is most likely and (b) how correct judgment ever occurs.

3. *Moderators of accuracy.* With those two issues out of the way, accuracy research can begin in earnest. Chapter 4 considers some of the many methodological and philosophical issues that arise in any attempt to study the accuracy of personality judgment, and Chapter 6 surveys some of the studies that have addressed moderators of accuracy. These moderators can be organized into four categories: properties of the judge (the "good judge"), the target (the "judgable" target), the trait judged, and the information on which the judgment is based.

4. *The process of accurate judgment.* The Realistic Accuracy Model was developed in an attempt to explain the four moderators of accurate judgment, and to suggest new directions for research. This model, described briefly here, is discussed in detail in Chapter 5. The order of Chapters 5 and 6 is the opposite of the historical order of the development of their topics. The Realistic Accuracy Model described in Chapter 5 was actually developed after and as a result of much of the research on moderators described in Chapter 6. But I believe the presentation is more coherent if the topics are introduced the other way around. By beginning with the theoretical model, the presentation of moderator variables can occur in a theoretical context.

5. *New issues in the "normal science" of accuracy.* Research on accuracy in personality judgment can be regarded as having entered the phase of what Kuhn (1962) called "normal science," in the sense that the paradigm is no longer regarded as radically new and the legitimacy of the topic of accuracy is less often questioned. This development allows new areas of research to open. Some early speculation on two such areas is presented in the final two chapters. Chapter 7 addresses the applicability of the Realistic Accuracy Model to the problem of self-knowledge. Chapter 8 addresses the prospects for improving the accuracy of interpersonal judgment, and draws some general conclusions concerning the future of research on accuracy in personality judgment.

CHAPTER 2

The Very Existence of Personality

DOES PERSONALITY EXIST?

It would make little sense to study the accuracy of personality judgment if personality did not even exist. A controversy on just this point preoccupied the research literature for more than two decades. An astonishingly influential book by Walter Mischel (1968) argued that behavior is inconsistent: Only a small relationship, if any, exists between the way an individual behaves in one situation and the way he or she behaves in another. Concomitantly, there is only a small relationship between any measurement of any aspect of an individual's personality and his or her behavior in any given situation. These two assertions, Mischel argued, imply that personality traits are of extremely limited use for predicting or explaining behavior.

Implications for Accuracy Research

The widespread acceptance of these conclusions, especially by social psychologists, created a formidable obstacle to the investigation of accuracy for years. In the views of many, personality became the unicorn of psychology, and the quest for accuracy in personality judgment seemed about as promising as a hunt for a mythical beast. So the very existence of personality is an issue that needs to be addressed before consideration of the accuracy of personality judgment can begin in earnest.

The Accuracy Issue and Common Sense

The debate over the existence and consistency of personality can be and has been framed in numerous ways (Kenrick & Funder, 1988; Funder, 1997a). For present purposes the issue boils down to this: Do the ordinary, commonsense terms used by laypersons to describe personality refer to anything real and important?

Esoteric redefinitions or reconceptualizations of personality, even to the extent they might be correct, are not really relevant to the accuracy issue. The accuracy issue relates to the everyday terms people naturally use to describe each other (Kenny, 1994). The conceptualization of personality in commonsense terms is what makes it possible to compare the scientific evidence on the personality attributes that people possess, on the one hand, with lay judgments of those attributes, on the other hand (Funder, 1991).

The use of commonsense conceptualizations of personality has two other advantages. One is that the practice allows psychology to address and take advantage of the vast reservoir of implicit knowledge about personality that laypersons possess, but may not always know they possess. The ordinary meaning of terms like *extraversion, sociability, reliability,* and so on is quite complex and tied to a wider variety of behavioral manifestations in a wider range of contexts than formal psychology has ever managed to systematize. A second advantage is that lay conceptions of personality go to the heart of what makes personality important. When one is assessing the results in adulthood of having been abused as a child, one wants to know whether the formerly abused adult is insecure, unhappy, unsociable, isolated, untrusting, and so forth. If one is assessing the effects of a therapeutic intervention, one wants to know whether they include the client becoming more trusting, sociable, and secure. All of these outcomes are ultimately rooted in common sense rather than anything esoteric; it is their common, "surplus" meaning that makes them important.

THE SITUATIONIST ONSLAUGHT

Bowers (1973) characterized the basic theme of the assault on personality as "situationist." Situationism is the belief that personality and individual differences have little or no effect on what people do. Instead, only situations matter: What a person does depends on the exact circumstances at the moment of action. Usually, this argument has been based on evidence concerning small effects of personality, rather than on any evidence concerning large effects of situations. Indeed, the nature of the variables that characterize situations has never been clearly enunciated (Bem & Funder, 1978; Goldberg, 1992). So instead of directly showing situational variables to be important, situationist argument has instead relied on showing personality variables to be unimportant, awarding the remainder of psychological causality to situations by subtraction.

The summary of the personality literature on which Mischel based his original, situationist critique of commonsense views of personality has sometimes been cited as a "comprehensive" review. In fact, it was quite brief. Mischel's review of the literature on behavioral consistency and personality occupied pages 20–36 of his 1968 book, about the length of a typical undergraduate term paper. In the course of this brief essay, he summarized several studies that showed the consistency across different manifestations of the same trait in the same individuals to be at a level he considered low. By low, he meant that correlations among different behavioral indicators of the same trait—in one example, attitude toward authority—were generally smaller than about .30. Out of a vast literature, he addressed just a few traits and a few studies, some of which were less than exemplary (see Block, 1977). So it is worth pondering why the impact of this small essay, contained within a by no means large book, was so devastating.

The Vulnerability of Personality Psychology

One factor can be found in the receptive biases of social psychology. Social psychology has long held a basically constructivist orientation, tending to focus on the way perceptions are socially influenced or perceptually biased rather than how they might ever be based in reality. In 1968 the very tendency to perceive personality traits had yet to be named the "fundamental attribution error," but the social psychological study of attitudes and perceptions was already focused on the ways both could be based partly or wholly on error. At the same time, a neo-behaviorist orientation was becoming more widespread in some parts of clinical psychology, where it was argued that changing a client's environmental circumstances was vastly more powerful and helpful than attempting to change or even to understand his or her personality.

Another contributing factor was that the social psychologists who turned out to be Mischel's most receptive audience tended to be unfamiliar with the implications of measures of effect size, such as the .30 correlation that Mischel so tellingly dubbed the "personality coefficient" (1968, p. 78). All most knew was the standard practice of squaring correlations to yield "percentage of variance explained," a practice that transforms a .30 correlation into a seemingly paltry 9% of variance "explained."

In this context, the 9% figure is not as directly informative as it might seem. It actually reflects a doubling of predictive validity over random selection (Rosenthal & Rubin, 1982). Moreover, it is no smaller than several of the most important findings in social psychology (Funder & Ozer, 1983). But most readers at the time did not, and perhaps today still do not, appreciate either of these points.

Other reasons for the effect of Mischel's critique can be found within personality psychology itself. As was noted in Chapter 1, the field had developed some self-defeating tendencies that made it vulnerable. Perhaps the worst of these tendencies was that in the years after Allport (1937) essentially invented the modern field of personality psychology, the research done within it had become progressively less interesting. That is, it had less to say to psychology in general, which caused its own existence to be valued less by psychologists in fields outside of personality.

Many empirically inclined personality psychologists turned inward, devoting vast amounts of research time and journal pages to technical issues related to the use of self-report questionnaires. In particular, the "response set" controversy occupied large segments of the careers of several talented investigators. This controversy concerned the possibility that questionnaire responses were based on various tendencies or "sets" to respond to items that were independent of the items' content (see Hogan & Nicholson, 1988; Rorer, 1965; Wiggins, 1973, chap. 9). This is an interesting possibility, and certainly deserved some examination. But notice how this issue is specifically relevant only to questionnaire methods. Assessments of behavior or real-life outcomes are not subject to this artifact, to the extent it exists.

This point was clearly perceived by Jack Block, who in an exhaustive analysis of response set interpretations of the MMPI showed that people who earned pathological scores on their questionnaires really were worse off as independently evaluated by clinicians and in terms of their capacities to deal with the world (Block, 1965). But although his specific conclusion and defense of the MMPI was widely accepted, the wider implication of Block's research seemed lost on much of his audience of personality psychologists. The wider implication was that a field of research based exclusively on one kind of data source—such as self-report questionnaires—is a field of research that is forever vulnerable to any criticism of that data source. As a whole, personality psychology failed to appreciate this implication as it continued to develop and refine questionnaires, while neglecting to engage in serious efforts to develop other kinds of methodology.

This failure is, in my opinion, the main reason personality psychology was so vulnerable to Mischel's seemingly simple challenge. When he demanded evidence that responses to self-report questionnaires were relevant to *behavior,* not just responses to other self-report questionnaires, the field was caught embarrassingly flat-footed. Almost no one had gathered such data. When Mischel demanded evidence that behavior in one situation was related to behavior in another situation, the situation was even worse. For years, the only relevant study anybody could seem to find was one conducted five decades earlier by Hartshorne and May (1928)! This study of children at a summer camp in the 1920s was analyzed, reanalyzed, and re-reanalyzed, all in pursuit of indications that behavior in one situation was related to behavior in another.

The results of these analyses of elderly data tended to depend on the predilections of the analyst: Mischel (1968) found evidence for gross inconsistency; other reanalysts such as Burton (1963), Conley (1984) and Epstein and O'Brien (1985) found evidence of an impressive degree of consistency in the very same data (and other data of similar vintage). In my own opinion, the latter investigators conducted a sounder reanalysis but the larger point is that such extensive reanalysis of very old data should not have been necessary in the first place. If the field had developed properly all along, Mischel's critique might never have arisen. If a "situationist" critique had arisen, personality psychology would have been able to respond instantly with vast amounts of contemporary data showing the relations between personality and behavior, and between behaviors in one situation and behaviors in another.

Consequences of the Situationist Onslaught

The consequences of the situationist onslaught on personality were widespread and serious. On a scientific level, many psychologists became convinced that personality psychology was to a large extent an exercise in mythology. This is not to say that many or any personality psychologists changed their minds about the fundamentals of their field. But many cognitive, biological, and social psychologists were quick to accept the secondhand news that personality had been proved nonexistent or, at very least, unimportant. The situationist viewpoint crept into several introductory psychology textbooks, one of the most influential routes by which psychological knowledge is communicated to the public at large, and became conventional wisdom within much of psychology.

The consequences were just as serious on an institutional level. Personality research became increasingly difficult to publish. The *Journal of Personality and Social Psychology*, then and now the most visible and prestigious publication outlet in both fields, closed its doors to most personality research for several years. Every issue carried a statement that "Low priority is given to papers concerned with personality assessment or the development and validation of assessment instruments" (frontispiece, August 1976). Long standing and important personality research projects, such as the Berkeley study of creative architects, suddenly found themselves without funding. Newly trained personality psychologists found jobs almost impossible to come by. And one after another, graduate training programs in personality psychology were formally abolished or simply melted slowly away at former strongholds such as Berkeley, UCLA, Harvard, and Illinois.

These institutional effects, in turn, had a profound effect on the infrastructure of personality science, some of which were noted in Chapter 1. Fewer new personality psychologists came to be trained, and fewer universities even offered appropriate training in basic psychometric technology (Aiken, West, Sechrest & Reno, 1990). As a consequence, an astonishing number of research articles currently published in major journals demonstrate a complete innocence of psychometric principles. Social psychologists and cognitive behaviorists who overtly eschew any sympathy with the dreaded concept of "trait" freely report the use of self-report assessment instruments of completely unknown and unexamined reliability, convergent validity, or discriminant validity. It is almost as if they believe that as long as the individual difference construct is called a "strategy," "schema," or "implicit theory," then none of these concepts is relevant. But I suspect the real cause of the omission is that many investigators are unfamiliar with these basic concepts, because through no fault of their own they were never taught them.

Over the long term, one has to be optimistic about the survival of personality psychology and its methodological tools. The basic phenomena of personality will continue to exist whether anybody studies them or not, and eventually if not soon research attention will swing back toward addressing them. As social and cognitive-behavioral psychologists continue to study traits by other names, they will eventually find themselves reinventing the concepts of reliability and validity.

THE RESPONSE

In a review unsympathetic to personality psychology, Ross and Nisbett (1991) correctly noted that the initial response of personality psychologists to Mischel's critique was a "stony silence" (p. 105). Surprisingly little reaction was evinced at first. The article that came to be regarded as the definitive early defense of personality was not published until almost a decade after Mischel's book appeared (Block, 1977). The first article to announce that the debate was finally over and resolved in personality psychology's favor did not appear for more than a decade after that (Kenrick & Funder, 1988).

Why was the reaction so slow? One reason seems to be that some personality psychologists failed to take Mischel's threat seriously at first. Deeply familiar with the subject matter, they felt they learned little from Mischel's brief review and polemical comments and failed to realize how persuasive they could seem to those outside the business. Another and perhaps more important reason is that personality psychology actually had embarrassingly little ammunition stockpiled with which to reply. As was noted earlier, the database for much of the argument was a study by Hartshorne and May conducted a half century before, precisely because so little relevant contemporary data was available.

This situation is all the more embarrassing for personality psychology because once a serious effort was begun to gather relevant data outside the realm of questionnaires, they were readily (if not inexpensively) obtained. A major effort to gather much of this evidence was an article by Douglas Kenrick and the present author published in *American Psychologist* in 1988, exactly 20 years after Mischel's book. The Kenrick-Funder article was written with two intentions. The first was to help to at last end the consistency controversy by declaring it over, and by writing a comprehensive retrospectively toned review. The second was to line up the various hypotheses, some of which in retrospect appeared to be almost like straw men, that had been advanced in the assault on the existence of personality and to deal with each of these hypotheses in turn.

Kenrick and Funder began with the first and most radically skeptical of these hypotheses, that perceptions of personality reside solipsistically solely in the eye of the individual beholder, and have no reality beyond that. This hypothesis had been advanced by serious writers and occasionally is sighted still, but it is easily dealt with. Many studies over a period of several decades have shown that the impressions others have of your personality agree to an impressive extent both with each other and with your impression of yourself. So although personality judgments may or may not often be wrong, they are not typically solipsistic.

The remaining six hypotheses can be dealt with in a similar manner. The second grants that impressions of personality are not solipsistic, but insists that they arise through artifacts of semantic similarity among trait terms rather than any relation with reality. The third hypothesis claims that such accuracy as arises is not due to any correct judgment of any individual, but only to judges correctly describing the "base-rate" or "stereotype" profile that characterizes people in general. The response to these hypotheses is that semantic similarity and stereotype accuracy can explain only relations among trait judgments, not discriminations between targets or relations between trait judgments and external criteria. The fourth, fifth, and sixth hypotheses all claim that observers' shared discriminative judgments are the result of one or more artifacts, such as the use of invalid stereotypes, discussion among observers, or the viewing of targets within a limited (and misleading) range of situations. But none of these hypotheses is sufficient to explain how personality judgments by different observers who have never met can tend to agree, or how personality judgments can be used to predict the future behavior of the person who is judged.

The Size of the Effect of Personality on Behavior

The seventh and final skeptical hypothesis is probably the most serious and interesting contender. This hypothesis accepts that observers tend to achieve consensus in their judgments of personality, and even grants that these judgments can to some extent serve as valid predictors of behavior. But the seventh hypothesis claims that when compared with the effect that situations have on behavior, cross-situational consistencies and the effect of personality on behavior are too small to be important.

This hypothesis echoes Mischel's coining of the phrase "personality coefficient," meant to refer to the putatively maximum correlation of $r = .30$ ever found between a personality measurement and a behavior or between a behavior in one situation and behavior in another. This claim that .30 is the ceiling originally hit the field of personality psychology with devastating force because of two separable assumptions. The first assumption was that the coefficient of .30 was not simply an artifact of poorly developed research tools but is the true upper limit for the degree that behavior can be predicted from personality. The second assumption was that this upper limit is a small upper limit. Acceptance of both of these assumptions is necessary for the situationist critique to have a major impact, and many psychologists initially did accept them.

Questioning the Limit

Several writers disputed the first of these assumptions, in various ways. Some argued that Mischel's initial literature review did not give a fair hearing to the better studies in the personality literature. Several studies have found higher correlations between personality and direct observations of behavior (e.g., Albright & Forziati, 1996; Block, Buss, Block, & Gjerde, 1981; Block, von der Lippe & Block, 1973; McGowen & Gormly, 1976; Moskowitz, 1982) and consensus across personality judgments made by observers from different, nonoverlapping contexts (Borkenau & Liebler, 1992a; Funder & Colvin, 1991; Malloy, Albright, Kenny, & Agatstein, 1997). Moreover, very recent research using sophisticated data analyses has shown that the consistent effect of the person is by far the largest factor in determining behavior, overwhelming more transient influences of situational variables or person-by-situation interactions (Kenny, Mohr, & Levesque, 1998). Finally, in an important and influential series of articles, Seymour Epstein made the further point that correlations between personality and behavior are particularly high when the predictive target is aggregates or averages of behavior rather than single instances (Epstein, 1979, 1980).

Epstein's point is more than merely technical. It points toward the proper standard by which predictive accuracy should be evaluated. In everyday life what we usually wish to predict on the basis of our personality judgments are not single acts but aggregate trends. Will the person we are trying to judge make an agreeable friend, a reliable employee, or an affectionate spouse? Each of these important outcomes is defined not by a single act at a single time, but by an average of many behaviors over a diverse range of contexts. The classic Spearman-Brown formula shows how even seemingly small correlations with single acts can compound into high correlations with the average of many acts. For example, Mischel and Peake (1982) found that inter-item correlations among the single behaviors they measured were in the range of .14 to .21, but that the coefficient alpha for the average of the behaviors they measured was .74. That is, a similar aggregate of behaviors would be expected to correlate .74 with that one. In the same vein, Epstein and O'Brien (1985) reanalyzed several classical studies in the field of personality and found in each case that although behavior seemed situationally specific at the single-item level, it was quite consistent at the level of behavioral aggregates. This issue now seems resolved. Protagonists on both sides of the controversy now seem ready to allow that the putative .30 ceiling applies only to behavior in unaggregated form.

The Effect of the Situation

Even if it were accepted that correlations larger than .30 or .40 are rarely found, it might be a mistake to accept—as so many psychologists were quick to do—that such correlations are "small." The word *small,* after all, is a relative term. Small has to be evaluated in comparison to something that is regarded as large. In psychology, what is large?

For many social psychologists inclined to doubt the importance of personality, what is large is the effect of situations on behavior. Indeed, as noted earlier, the position skeptical of the existence of personality has sometimes been called situationism, which refers to the expressed belief that situational variables overwhelm personality variables in the determination of behavior (Bowers, 1973). To evaluate the degree to which a behavior is affected by a personality variable, the routine practice is to correlate a measure of behavior with a measure of personality. But how does one evaluate the degree to which behavior is affected by a situational variable?

As I have noted elsewhere (Funder, 1997a), this question has received surprisingly little attention over the years. Where it has been addressed, the usual practice is rather strange: The power of situations is determined by subtraction. Thus, if it is found that a personality variable correlates .40 with a behavioral measurement and that it therefore "explains 16 percent of the variance," the other 84% is assigned, by default, to the situation (e.g., Mischel, 1968).

Of course, this is not a legitimate practice, though it has been frequently employed. Even if one unquestioningly accepts the "percentage of variance" terminology, it would be just a reasonable to attribute the "missing" variance to other personality variables that you did not measure as it would be to attribute it to situational variables that you also did not measure (Ahadi & Diener, 1989). Moreover, assigning variance by subtraction in this way tells you nothing about *which* aspects of the situation might be important, in a way parallel to how trait measures tell you which aspects of personality are important.

It seems remarkable that the situationists have argued that situations are overwhelmingly important, while at the same time they have remained seemingly unconcerned with measuring situational variables in a way that indicates precisely how or how much situations affect behavior. Moreover, there is no good reason for this vagueness about what specific aspects of situations can affect behavior. There is a large and impressive body of psychological research that *does* specify the effects of situations: nearly the entire corpus of research in experimental social psychology.

In the typical social psychological experiment, two (or more) separate groups of subjects are placed, randomly and usually one at a time, into one or another of two (or more) different situations. The dependent variable is some aspect of the subject's behavior, measured fairly directly.[1] If the average behavior of the subjects who are

---

[1] Sometimes, this "behavioral" dependent variable is actually a mark the subject makes on some sort of response questionnaire.

placed in one situation (experimental condition) turns out to be significantly different from the average behavior of subjects placed in the other condition, then an effect of an aspect of a situation on a behavior has been specifically identified.

For example, one might be interested in the effect of the level of incentive on attitude change. In an experiment, you could ask subjects to express a point of view they do not actually hold, such as that a dull game was really interesting. One group of subjects could be offered a large incentive for expressing this counterattitudinal view, and another group could be offered a smaller incentive. Then the subjects' final real attitude toward the game could be measured. If the average final attitude in the two groups is different, then one has successfully demonstrated the effect of an important situational variable, incentive, on an important behavior, attitude change.

The experiment just described is one of the classic illustrations of the workings of cognitive dissonance, conducted by Leon Festinger and J. Merrill Carlsmith in 1959 (as is well known they found that less incentive produced *more* attitude change). And the social psychological literature is a treasure trove of studies that are just as interesting. John Darley and his colleagues investigated how likely people were to help someone in distress as a function of how many other people were present or how much the potential helper was in a hurry (Darley & Batson, 1973; Darley & Latane, 1968). Stanley Milgram demonstrated that the likelihood that an ordinary person would obey orders to administer severe shocks to an innocent victim was affected by the proximity of the victim and of the experimenter (Milgram, 1975).

Each of these studies demonstrated effects of specifically identified and manipulated situational variables on behavior, and as far as I know nobody has ever expressed doubts that they are important. But it was left for Dan Ozer and I to reanalyze some of the data in these articles and report the size of the effect of these situational variables on behavior (Funder & Ozer, 1983). As is traditional within social psychology, the original researchers had been largely content to report that the effects were statistically significant, without reporting any actual effect sizes.[2, 3] But, because there is a precise mathematical relation between measures of effect size and of statistical significance, given certain other information (such as N's and variances) one can derive one from the other. For our purposes we transformed the significant effects found by Festinger, Darley and Milgram on attitude change,

[2]Effect size and statistical significance are independent, because significance depends on the number of subjects in the study, whereas effect size does not. Thus measures of effect size, such as r (the correlation coefficient), report the size of the effect of the independent variable on the dependent variable. Measures of significance report the probability that the difference between conditions could have arisen from chance alone. With a large number of subjects, very small effect sizes are significant; with a small number of subjects, even large effect sizes are not significant. In general, therefore, measures of effect size are more informative than measures of statistical significance.

[3]Darley and his colleagues did include several analyses that yielded effect size estimates (e.g., multiple regression) in their studies of bystander intervention.

bystander intervention and obedience, and found their sizes to be (in terms of r, the usual effect size in personality research) to be in the range of .30 to .40.

Two possible conclusions could be drawn from these results. The first, expressed in some textbooks, is that we have shown that neither personality *nor* situational variables have strong effects on behavior. But Ozer and I prefer to point out that until our reanalyses came along, nobody doubted that each of these studies demonstrated a powerful, important influence of a situational variable. Each of these studies is one of the classic building blocks of social psychology. Our interpretation, therefore, is that these situational variables *are* important determinants of behavior, but so might be personality variables that generate effect sizes in about the same range. When they were at last put on a common scale for comparison, the effects of the situation and of the person turned out to be much more similar than had been previously imagined. In this light, the labeling of a correlation of .30 or .40 as a "personality coefficient" loses a little of its pejorative glow.

Predictive Accuracy

There is yet another reason to reevaluate the traditional evaluation of correlations in the range between .30 and .40. Rosenthal and Rubin's (1982) Binomial Effect Size Display (BESD) reveals the important fact that a correlation of .40 means that a prediction of behavior based on a personality trait score is likely to be accurate 70% of the time (assuming a chance accuracy rate of 50%). If the correlation between personality and behavior is .30, you can expect 65% accuracy in your predictions. These percentages are far from perfect, of course, but enough to be useful for many purposes. For example, an employer choosing who to put through an expensive training program could save large amounts of money by being able to predict with 70% accuracy who will or will not be a successful employee at the conclusion of the program.

Consider a hypothetical example.[4] Say a company has 200 employees being considered for further training but only has resources to train 100 of them. Let's further assume that, overall, 50% of the company's employees could successfully complete the program. The company picks 100 employees at random and spends $10,000 to train each one. But, as we said, only half of them are successful. So the company has spent a total of $1 million to get 50 successfully trained employees, or $20,000 each.

But consider what could happen if the company used a selection test to decide who to train—a test that has been shown to correlate at .40 with training success. (Notice that by common practice this test would be said to "explain only 16% of the variance" in outcome.) If it selects the top half of the scorers on this test for training, the company will get 70 successful trainees (instead of 50) out of the 100 who are trained, still at a total cost of $1 million but now only at about $14,300 per

---

[4]This example is taken from the discussion in Funder, 1997a (p. 69).

successful trainee. In other words, using a test with .40 validity could save the company $5700 per successful trainee, or about $400,000. That will pay for a lot of testing.

It is possible to quibble with minor aspects of the interpretation of the correlation coefficient and its expression in the BESD, but not the basic arithmetic. I believe the BESD reveals that the traditional language of "percent of variance explained" has led to a widespread misunderstanding of effect sizes in psychology. For me, the most vivid illustration occurred when I was giving a colloquium talk at a major research university in the United States. For fun, I put the 50-50 predictive accuracy figures derived from a correlation of .00 on the board. Then I asked the assembled faculty, who included several renowned experts on data analysis and research methods, to guess how that figure would change if the correlation were .40. One of them simultaneously revealed both his courage and ignorance by confidently proclaiming, "about 52-48." I do not know exactly how he arrived at this answer, but I suspect it resulted from his awareness that, in conventional terminology, a .40 correlation "explains only 16% of the variance," "leaves 84% unexplained," and therefore is seemingly very small. All this led to a drastically wrong answer. The correct figures, easily calculated in a moment by anyone who understands the BESD, are 70-30.

Entrenched practices die hard, and students in statistics classes around the world are still being taught that to understand the size of a correlation coefficient you must square it to find out how much variance it explains. These unfortunate students do not really understand what the phrase "percent of variance explained" means. But they know how it sounds. Until this situation is somehow someday corrected, psychologists and semitrained laypersons alike will continue to misunderstand the effect sizes associated with the results of correlational research in personality and experimental research in social psychology.

Empirical Assessments of Cross-Situational Consistency

For an astonishing length of time, the principal evidence for the consistency or inconsistency of behavior across situations was drawn—by advocates of each side— from the study by Hartshorne and May (1928), who observed the behavior of children attending a summer camp. Among other procedures, these investigators observed the degree to which children cheated at various games and found that a child who cheated at one did not necessarily cheat at another. This finding led them to the rather sweeping conclusion not only that the trait of honesty did not exist, but that moral behavior, rather than stemming from consistent attributes of character, was simply a product of specific situations.[5]

---

[5] This conclusion has been disputed in reanalyses by Burton (1963), Conley (1984), and others.

The second major investigation of behavioral consistency did not appear until the publication of a study by Mischel and Peake (1982). This study of students at a small college in Minnesota yielded a large number of results. A typical finding was that an aggregated measure of the thoroughness of students' class notes correlated only $-.03$ with an aggregated measure of their punctuality to lectures (p. 735)— both behaviors being putative manifestations of conscientiousness. This single study, being in some ways only the second of its kind in 60 years, evoked so much interest that it managed to spawn a small literature devoted solely to arguing about its findings (Bem, 1983; Epstein, 1983; Funder; 1983; Mischel & Peake, 1982). Its principal conclusion— which did not go undisputed—will sound familiar to anyone who remembers Mischel (1968): "It is . . . clear from these results that behavior is . . . highly discriminative and . . . broad cross-situational consistencies remain elusive" (Mischel & Peake, 1982, p. 735).

The subsequent literature review by Kenrick and Funder (1988) yielded a more optimistic overall view of behavioral consistency and the importance of personality. But a thorough and successful empirical demonstration had yet to be conducted. This was the purpose of the large study reported by Funder and Colvin in 1991.

A New Investigation of Consistency

The Funder-Colvin study examined the behavior of 164 Harvard undergraduates in each of three videotaped experimental settings. In the first, a male and female student who had never previously met were shown immediately into a small room, seated on a couch in full view of an unconcealed video camera, invited to talk about whatever they liked, and left by themselves for 5 minutes. In the second experimental setting a few weeks later, each subject returned and was paired with a different opposite-sex partner. They too were then left alone to chat. In the third setting, which occurred a few minutes after the second, the subjects were induced to debate briefly about the issue of capital punishment.[6]

Notice the many ways in which these three situations are different from each other. The first two are similar in that both are almost completely unstructured, but the subject interacts with different partners. Perhaps just as importantly, in the first situation the subject is naïve and a bit uncertain as to what is to happen but has "been there and done that" by the time of the second situation a few weeks later. The second and third situations are similar in that both involve interacting with the same partner on the same day, but the second is unstructured whereas the third requires the subjects to debate about a specified topic.

The differences between these situations make this study a true, repeated-measures experiment. Each subject is exposed to three experimental conditions that differ in specific, predesigned ways. Conventional analyses can be employed to verify that the experimental manipulations indeed had an effect on behavior.

---

[6]This issue was chosen because most people are familiar with the basic arguments on both sides.

TABLE 2-1 Significant Behavioral Mean Differences between Sessions 1 and 2

Behavioral Q-sort item	Session 1 M	Session 2 M	t
Higher Session 1 means			
18. Talks at rather than with partner (e.g., monologue).	3.98	3.51	4.96***
14. Exhibits an awkward interpersonal style.	4.19	3.60	4.50
23. Shows physical signs of tension or anxiety.	5.19	4.66	3.76
61. Shows lack of interest in the interaction.	3.98	3.55	3.33
41. Keeps partner at a distance.	4.81	4.40	2.97**
22. Expresses insecurity or sensitivity.	4.77	4.49	2.93
37. Behaves in a fearful or timid manner.	3.98	3.64	2.85
24. Exhibits high degree of intelligence.	5.39	5.24	2.24*
12. Physically animated; moves around a great deal.	3.85	3.56	2.14
32. Acts in an irritable fashion.	3.76	3.60	1.95
Higher Session 2 means			
8. Exhibits social skills.	5.94	6.46	−4.65***
7. Appears to be relaxed and comfortable.	5.56	6.13	−3.98
44. Says or does interesting things (from partner's point of view).	5.78	6.08	−2.79**
38. Is expressive in face, voice, or gestures.	5.11	5.42	−2.68
2. Interviews partner (e.g., asks series of questions)	5.83	6.21	−2.56*
54. Speaks fluently and expresses ideas well.	5.98	6.25	−2.38
21. Is talkative (in this situation).	5.73	6.05	−2.33
60. Engages in constant eye contact with partner.	6.08	6.37	−2.32
43. Seems genuinely to enjoy interaction with partner.	5.90	6.14	−2.00
50. Behaves in a cheerful manner.	5.89	6.11	−1.94

Note. $N=140$, $df=138$. All tests were two-tailed. Items are arranged according to the significance of their mean difference across sessions.
*p <.05 for absolute value of t = 1.94 to 2.56. **p <.01 for absolute value of t = 2.68 to 2.97. ***p <.001 for absolute value of t = 3.33 to 4.96.
From Funder, D. C., & Colvin, C. R. (1991). Explorations in behavioral consistency: Properties of persons, situations, and behaviors. Journal of *Personality and Social Psychology, 60,* 780, Table 5. Copyright 1991 by the American Psychological Association. Reprinted by permission of the publisher.

Through a painstaking process that took several years to complete, we gathered ratings from independent observers of the videotapes as the degree to which each subject manifested each of 62 different behaviors.[7] (No rater coded the behavior of a subject in more than one setting to keep estimates of differences and consistencies across settings uncontaminated.)

One set of relevant results is reproduced in Table 2-1 (this was Table 5 in Funder & Colvin, 1991). The analysis is simple. We simply performed a t-test examining

[7]The data gathering for this project took about 2 years, and the behavioral coding took about 3 years of steady effort. After completing this project we came to a better understanding as to why studies like this, which gather direct observations of behavior in multiple settings, are so rarely conducted.

the mean level of each behavior in each of the first two conditions (the unstructured interactions with the two different partners). Of the 62 behaviors coded, 20 yielded significant change across the situations (at p < .05, two-tailed). For example, in the first situation subjects were relatively awkward, tense, disinterested, distant, insecure, fearful, agitated, and irritable. But in the second situation they became more socially skilled, relaxed, comfortable, interesting, expressive, fluent, talkative, and in general seemed to have a much better time. It seems clear that the fact the second situation was a revisit to a now familiar setting had an important effect. The subjects were no longer strangers to the laboratory, the situation, or to the experimenters (even though they still were strangers to each other), and this familiarity allowed them greatly and visibly to relax.

This is precisely the kind of data analysis so often used in experimental social psychology to demonstrate the power of the situation to effect behavior. A seemingly subtle change in experimental context had rather large and quite noticeable effects on behavior. What people did clearly depended to a large extent on the situation they were in.

But this kind of analysis says nothing about behavioral consistency in the sense personality psychologists use the term. The relevance of personality for behavior is revealed not by a lack of change across situations but by the maintenance of individual differences. Such maintenance is indexed by the correlation coefficient, which reflects the degree to which subjects who perform a given behavior more than others do in one situation also do so relatively more in a second situation. Of the 62 cross-situational consistency correlations calculated across the same first two situations just examined, fully 45 were significant at $p < .05$, and 37 or more than half were significant at $p < .001$. These correlations are reproduced in Table 2-2 (Funder & Colvin's original Table 2).

Some of these cross-situational consistency correlations are large by any standard. For example, 8 of them are larger than .60, and the largest ("Speaks in a loud voice") achieved an impressive .70. If the putative upper limit for the consistency of behavior across situations is held to be .40, it can be noted that 26 behaviors exceeded it; if the limit is held to be .30 then 35 exceeded it. And this point needs to be reiterated: The two situations have already been shown to be psychologically different in ways that revealed powerful effects on behavior. So these behavioral consistencies are in no sense limited to holding across "the same" or even "highly similar" situations; they hold across two situations already demonstrated to be consequentially different.

Two conclusions can be drawn immediately. The first is that it is perhaps unfortunate these data were not available in 1968. If they had been, the whole person-situation debate might never have taken hold and the conventional wisdom and even basic infrastructure of psychological science might look very different today.

A second, more subtle conclusion is that the two sides of the person-situation debate have in an important way been talking past each other for a couple of decades. For the cognitive behaviorists, significant differences in behavior across

TABLE 2-2   Cross-Situational Consistency Correlations across Sections 1 and 2 for Total
Sample and by Sex of Subject

Behavioral Q-sort item	Total sample	Total sample (disatten.)	Women	Men
57. Speaks in a loud voice.	.70	.89	.74	.67
14. Exhibits an awkward interpersonal style.	.60	.88	.67	.62
37. Behaves in a fearful or timid manner.	.65	.84	.68	.62
10. Laughs frequently (whether genuine or nervous).	.63	.80	.56	.63
38. Is expressive in face, voice, or gestures.	.63	.93	.65	.58
9. Is reserved and unexpressive.	.62	.77	.64	.57
11. Smiles frequently.	.60	.81	.39	.60
50. Behaves in a cheerful manner.	.60	.81	.52	.60
16. High enthusiasm and high energy level.	.59	.72	.55	.59
62. Speaks quickly.	.59	.88	.55	.60
8. Exhibits social skills.	.58	.88	.56	.59
60. Engages in constant eye contact with partner.	.57	.78	.59	.53
22. Expresses insecurity or sensitivity.	.56	.86	.52	.60
31. Appears to regard self physically attractive.	.55	.92	.55	.53
61. Shows lack of interest in the interaction.	.54	.73	.44	.62
7. Appears to be relaxed and comfortable.	.48	.71	.48	.48
28. Exhibits condescending behavior.	.47	.78	.56	.40
23. Shows physical signs of tension or anxiety.	.45	.69	.40	.50
36. Is unusual or unconventional in appearance.	.45	.73	.29	.55
24. Exhibits high degree of intelligence.	.44	.70	.39	.48
32. Acts in an irritable fashion.	.43	.94	.35	.48
52. Behaves in a masculine or feminine style or manner.	.43	.65	.39	.45
43. Seems genuinely to enjoy interaction with partner.	.42	.65	.27	.53
54. Speaks fluently and expresses ideas well.	.42	.79	.40	.41
26. Initiates humor.	.41	.60	.40	.40
20. Expresses skepticism or cynicism.	.40	.67	.34	.43
12. Physically animated; moves around a great deal.	.39	.56	.34	.43
41. Keeps partner at a distance.	.39	.57	.29	.48
5. Tries to control the interaction.	.38	.67	.41	.33
18. Talks at rather than with partner (e.g., monologue).	.38	.72	.24	.48
19. Expresses agreement unusually frequently.	.38	.61	.40	.35
21. Is talkative (in this situation).	.38	.54	.46	.32
42. Shows genuine interest in intellectual matters.	.36	.54	.22	.46
4. Seems genuinely interested in what partner has to say.	.34	.53	.27	.40
35. Expresses hostility.	.30	.56	.31	.25
53. Offers advice to partner.	.29	.37	.41	.20
48. Expresses self-pity or feelings of victimization.	.28	.56	.37	.22

Note. $N = 140$. Items with consistency correlations of $p < .001$ (two-tailed) or better are listed. Items
are arranged in order of their cross-situational consistency. Disatten. = disattenuated.

From Funder, D. C., & Colvin, C. R. (1991). Explorations in behavioral consistency: Properties of
persons, situations, and behaviors. *Journal of Personality and Social Psychology, 60,* 780. Table 2. Copyright
1991 by the American Psychological Association. Reprinted by permission of the publisher.

conditions has been taken as conclusive proof that behavior is situationally determined and otherwise inconsistent. For personality psychologists, the maintenance of individual differences in behavior across situations demonstrates the importance of stable aspects of personality for determining what people do.

It turns out that these two conclusions are not in the least incompatible. Indeed, a further analysis by Funder and Colvin examined the relationship between the behaviors that were inconsistent in the experimental sense and consistent in the correlational sense and found its size to be near zero. The correlation between the average size of the difference in mean behaviors across the three experimental settings and the average correlations across those same settings, calculated across the 62 behaviors measured, was $-.02$, *ns*. Behavior in general changes with the situation, and the behavior of individuals is impressively consistent across situations. These statements are not incompatible; they are both true, in a way that psychologists are perhaps just beginning finally to understand clearly (Ozer, 1985).

Consistent and Inconsistent Behaviors

As my collaborator Randy Colvin and I perused the complex results of our investigation of behavioral consistency, a further important and wholly unanticipated finding emerged. For each of the 62 behaviors assessed in each of the three experimental situations, three cross-situational consistency correlations could be computed.[8] When one studies the three tables of correlations (Tables 2, 3, and 4 in Funder & Colvin, 1991), it becomes apparent that the same behaviors that show high consistency across one pair of situations also tend to show more consistency across the other pairs.

This is more than an illusion. We calculated the correlations between the cross-situational consistency scores (correlations) earned by each behavior in the three comparisons (these correlations between patterns of correlations are sometimes called "vector correlations"). The results astonished us. The same behaviors that were highly consistent across one pair of situations tended to be highly consistent across the other two pairs as well. The cross-situational consistency correlations between Sessions 1 and 2 correlated .73 with those calculated between Session 2 and the debate. The correlations between Session 2 and the debate correlated with .75 with the correlations between Session 1 and the debate. And the cross-situational consistency of behavioral items between Session 2 and the debate correlated .84 with the consistency between Session 1 and the debate. These are high correlations! The consistency of behavior is itself a highly consistent attribute of particular behaviors.

Despite its strength, this is an effect that to our knowledge had gone unnoticed in a half century of prior research on consistency and a decade of more recent

---

[8] That is, correlations could be computed between behavior in Situation 1 and Situation 2, between Situation 2 and Situation 3, and between Situation1 and Situation 3.

research searching for moderators of consistency (e.g., Bem & Allen, 1974; Mischel & Peake, 1982). The data reported by Funder and Colvin (1991) were gathered from Harvard undergraduates; the phenomenon was replicated by the even more extensive data set that constitutes the Riverside Accuracy Project. The latter research employed six experimental situations, creating 15 unique cross-situational comparisons and 105 correlations that index the consistency of consistency itself across these comparisons. These 105 correlations ranged from .81 down to .13, with an average of .48 ($p < .001$).[9]

Explaining the Consistency of Consistency

This newly discovered, strong, and replicated effect clearly requires further investigation and explanation. The first step is to see which behaviors are the most and least consistent. The 15 most and least consistent in the Harvard data set are shown in Table 2-3 (taken from Funder & Colvin, 1991, Table 8). The reader is invited to invent his or her own characterization of the characteristics that distinguish the items at the top and bottom of this table. A preliminary observation is that whatever the difference is, it is subtle. Nothing obvious (at least, nothing obvious to us) discriminates between the most and least consistent behaviors, despite the power of this property.

Psychometric Explanation

Before thinking too hard about what the difference might be, it is important to rule out the possibility that a relatively uninteresting artifact lies behind the apparent consistency of consistency. An elementary principle of psychometrics is that the size of a correlation coefficient (including a consistency correlation) is constrained by the reliabilities and variances of the variables that go into it. Hence, one possible explanation for the difference between behaviors we uncovered is simply that some of them were coded more reliability, or exhibited wider variance across subjects, than did others, and so were able to manifest larger cross-situational correlations.

Some evidence can be found to support this possibility. The average variance of the 62 Behavioral Q-sort (BQ) items (that is, the average of the three between-subjects variances calculated within each of the three laboratory situations) correlated .75 ($p < .001$) with the average consistency of these items across the three situations. These findings raise the plausible and psychometrically sound possibility that BQ items with larger within-session variances yielded greater reliabilities, as would be expected on purely statistical grounds, and accordingly manifested higher correlations across the lab situations.

This psychometric effect is part, but only part, of what is going on. If we partial both item variance and reliability from the correlations that index the stability of

[9]These data are undergoing further analysis and are as yet unpublished.

TABLE 2-3   Most and Least Consistent Behavioral Q-Sort Items, Averaged Across 3 Situational Comparisons

Behavioral Q-sort item	Average r	Operant/respondent score
15 most consistent		
57. Speaks in a loud voice.	.65	67
37. Behaves in a fearful or timid manner.	.57	41
38. Is expressive in face, voice, or gestures.	.56	74
62. Speaks quickly.	.56	67
60. Engages in constant eye contact with partner.	.54	38
16. High enthusiasm and high energy level.	.53	67
9. Is reserved and unexpressive.	.52	56
36. Is unusual or unconventional in appearance.	.51	72
52. Behaves in a masculine or feminine style or manner.	.48	65
31. Appears to regard self physically attractive.	.47	56
10. Laughs frequently (whether "genuine" or "nervous").	.46	44
50. Behaves in a cheerful manner.	.44	66
11. Smiles frequently.	.44	50
14. Exhibits an awkward interpersonal style.	.44	62
22. Expresses insecurity or sensitivity.	.42	46
M	.51	58.07
15 least consistent		
39. Expresses interest in fantasy and daydreams.	−.01	50
2. "Interviews" partner (e.g., asks series of questions).	.01	45
49. Seems interested in partner as member of opposite sex.	.04	14
47. Seems to view interaction as sexual encounter.	.05	17
34. Tries to sabotage or obstruct experiment or partner.	.06	44
33. Expresses warmth.	.06	49
58. Demonstrates interest in topics related to power.	.08	43
55. Brags.	.08	47
51. Discusses philosophical issues with interest.	.08	51
17. Discusses unusually large number of topics.	.09	35
3. Volunteers unusually little information about self.	.10	43
40. Expresses guilt (about anything).	.10	41
46. Displays ambition.	.11	55
30. Seeks advice from partner (low=*partner seeks advice from subject*).	.11	27
15. Interrupts partner (low=*partner interrupts subject*).	.12	38
M	.07	39.93

From Funder, D. C., & Colvin, C. R. (1991). Explorations in behavioral consistency: Properties of persons, situations, and behaviors. *Journal of Personality and Social Psychology, 60,* 787. Table 8. Copyright 1991 by the American Psychological Association. Reprinted by permission of the publisher.

the difference between behaviors across the three laboratory situations, the correlations that were .73, .75, and .84 remain the still sizable (and statistically significant) .40, .51, and .71, respectively.[10]

Breadth of Situational Relevance

A second perusal of the items in Table 2-3 reveals that the more consistent items might describe behaviors that are observed more often than the less consistent items. For example, items such as "speaks in a loud voice" and "behaves in a fearful or timid manner" describe behaviors that are relevant to a broader range of situations in real life than items such as "expresses interest in fantasy and daydreams" or "demonstrates interest in topics related to power."

To check this hypothesis, we gathered ratings of each of the 62 BQ items in response to the question, "In how many situations can each behavior occur?" To provide their answers, a group of six raters, working independently, sorted the 62 BQ items into a forced, nearly rectangular, 9-step distribution ranging from *very few situations in real life* to *most or all situations in real life.* The aggregate reliability of these ratings was .79.

Across the 62 BQ items, these breadth ratings correlated .50 ($p < .001$) with the items' variability and .53 ($p < .001$) with the items' reliability. More to the point, they also correlated .55 ($p < .001$) with the average consistency of these behaviors across the three laboratory situations. Thus, one property of the content of the BQ items that underlies item variability, reliability, and cross-situational consistency is the range of the situations to which they are relevant. A further pair of questions follows close on the heels of this finding: Why should more broadly relevant behaviors be more variable? And what does the breadth of a behavior's relevance have to do with its cross-situational consistency?

Operants versus Respondents?

A few years ago, David McClelland suggested a difference between behaviors that he would and would not expect to be consistent across situations. In an intriguing article titled "Is personality consistent?" McClelland (1984), borrowed a couple of well-known (but perhaps widely misunderstood) terms from Skinner (1931, 1938/1966). He argued that it was important to distinguish between "respondents," defined as "responses having clearly identified stimuli," and "operants," defined as

---

[10] A further issue could be raised at this point as to whether these psychometric analyses really explain, or explain away, anything at all. If items differ in their reliability and variance, this difference is more than a statistical artifact. It is a psychological fact that ultimately demands a psychological explanation. Thus, I actually believe the unpartialled correlations more faithfully reflect the phenomenon of the "consistency of consistency," because it is they that index the actual difference between behaviors as empirically manifested. Be that as it may, a skeptic can be reassured that the basic phenomenon is only slightly attenuated after partialling.

"thoughts or actions the stimulus to which cannot be readily identified" (1984, p. 194). McClelland pointed out that according to these definitions, one would expect operant behaviors to express aspects of personality that are generally influential across diverse situations and expect respondent behaviors to more responsive to the specific stimuli present in each setting. Therefore, he argued, it would be through operant behaviors that cross-situational consistency, and personality itself, would be more clearly manifest.

Perhaps McClelland (and Funder and Colvin after him) would have been wiser to avoid using these terms. Over the years since Skinner (1931) proposed the distinction between respondents and operants, a great deal of excess baggage attached itself to them. For instance, in "two-factor theory" respondents took on connotations of being innate, unconditioned, and physiologically based, and operants were viewed as those that were under more "voluntary" control (Bower & Hilgard, 1981, p. 200).

The original distinction carried none of these implications, however. Skinner specifically decried "the unfortunate historical definition of the [respondent] as a form of movement unconscious, involuntary, and unlearned" (1931, p. 455). His preferred definition was more simple and, as one might expect, more directly observable. "The kind of behavior that is correlated with specific eliciting stimuli may be called *respondent* behavior . . . The term is intended to carry the sense of the relation to a prior event." About the other class of behavior, Skinner wrote, "An operant is an identifiable part of behavior of which it may be said, not that no stimulus can be found that will elicit it, but that no correlated stimulus can be detected upon occasions on which it is observed to occur" (1938/1966, p. 21). Skinner further observed that "the original 'spontaneous' activity of the organism is chiefly of this sort, as is the greater part of the . . . behavior of the adult organism" (p. 19).

This last-quoted sentence from Skinner implies that operants occur across a wider range of situations than do respondents. McClelland claimed that operants are performed more consistently than respondents are. Perhaps this is the basis of the relationship between behavioral variability, breadth of situational relevance and cross-situational consistency.

To explore this possibility, we asked nine raters to evaluate the degree to which each of the 62 BQ items described an operant as opposed to respondent behavior.[11] We did not use these esoteric terms, however. Instead, we asked our raters to judge each item in relation to the essence of the distinction, the degree to which each behavior tends to occur in response to a specific, identifiable stimulus. The raters sorted the 62 items into a nearly rectangular distribution ranging from *stimulus bound (i.e., having a clearly identifiable stimulus) (1) to stimulus free (i.e., are a characteristic style*

---

[11] In defense of rating the distinction along a continuous scale, Skinner himself can be quoted to the effect that "although a distinction may be drawn between the operant and the respondent field, there is also a certain continuity" (1938/1966, p. 439).

that people possess) (9). The aggregate reliability of these ratings was .86. Three items that received particularly high operant ratings was "speaks fluently," "is expressive in face, voice, or gestures," and "is unusual or unconventional in appearance." Three relatively respondent items were "seems interested in partner as a member of the opposite sex," "seems genuinely interested in what the partner has to say," and "expresses sympathy towards partner."

The final step was to integrate these ratings with the analyses of cross-situational consistency. The results were striking. Higher scores reflected a rating of the behavior as being more operant, and lower scores reflected a rating of the behavior as being more respondent, as we have defined the terms. The 15 most consistent behaviors, as listed in Table 2-3, were rated significantly higher (more respondent) than the 15 least consistent behaviors (t (28) 4.17, $p < .001$). Across all 62 behavioral items, the operant/respondent score correlated .51 ($p < .001$) with the average consistency of these items across the three experimental situations.

Toward a More Complete Explanation

Stripped of excess baggage acquired over the years, Skinner's original (1931) distinction was between respondent behaviors *elicited* in obvious and direct response to specific situational stimuli and operant behaviors *emitted* by the organism across wide range of contexts. If this simple and basic distinction is accepted as valid, then the findings of Funder and Colvin (1991) leap into clear focus. Behaviors that occur in response to specific stimuli are stimulus specific and therefore narrowly situation specific, by definition. Similarly, behaviors that are not dependent on specific, eliciting stimuli are more likely to occur across a broad range of situations that might differ in their stimulus properties, and therefore reflect characteristics—such as personality dispositions—of the people who emit them.

At rock bottom, the results of Funder and Colvin (1991) show that naïve raters can identify, a priori, differences between behaviors that are and are not elicited by specific situational stimuli, as opposed to being emitted by and expressing psychological characteristics of the behaving person. These ratings, in turn, powerfully predict which behaviors (in a set of 62) will manifest the least and greatest cross-situational consistency correlations.

But an unsolved puzzle remains. Like Skinner himself, we have said almost nothing about why this difference between behaviors should exist, or how it arises. A reading of the behaviorist literature of a half century ago reveals a variety of attempts, none really successful, to develop a theoretically reasoned distinction between operants and respondents. In the end, the community of researchers of that era took the lead of Skinner himself, and eschewed further attempts to distinguish between the two kinds of behaviors on principled grounds. Instead, true to the behaviorist tradition, they accepted the distinction as descriptive rather than explanatory and proceeded with their research from there.

And that is where the matter roughly stands today. Funder and Colvin in a sense rediscovered an old Skinnerian phenomenon, that some behaviors are more dependent on the situation than are others. They have further found that naïve raters can identify with impressive accuracy just which those behaviors are. But a complete understanding of this important and powerful phenomenon awaits not just further empirical research but progress in the currently neglected area of personality theory.

Redefinitions of Personality

For research on the accuracy of personality judgment to be meaningful, the conceptualization of personality to which judgments are compared must basically match the way laypersons tend to think of it. Some seemingly promising reconceptualizations of personality that have been proposed over the past few years are more esoteric and differ fundamentally from the way laypersons think of personality. Their complete acceptance would make accuracy research difficult, because the psychological model of personality they propose, and the data research on them would yield, could not be directly compared to laypersons' judgments. Therefore, each of these reconceptualizations needs to be considered briefly.

Situationism

The first of these, sometimes called "situationism" (Bowers, 1973), was the idea that complex human behaviors are driven by aspects of the situations rather than by any stable intrinsic characteristics of persons. As we have already seen, this was an enterprise that was nearly bankrupt on its opening day. One reason is that cross-situational consistencies in behavior are in fact often strong and pervasive. Another reason is that for all the advocacy it received, situationism never really comprised a coherent point of view. The specific situational variables that were supposed to be so powerful were never identified, named, or organized into a taxonomy. As a result, as one critic tellingly wrote,

> Situations turn out to be "powerful" in the same sense as Scud missiles (the erratic weapons used by Iraq during the Persian Gulf war) are powerful: They may have huge effects, or no effects, and such effects may occur virtually anywhere, all over the map. (Goldberg, 1992, p. 90)

Act Frequencies

A second reconceptualization of personality is less threatening to the idea of accuracy in personality judgment but is still worth addressing. The "act frequency approach" (Buss & Craik, 1983) maintains that personality trait terms refer not to determinative or causal structures within individuals but only to frequencies of relevant acts performed in the past. In this view, sociability refers not to an individual's inherent tendency to be sociable but to the number of sociable acts he or she has performed in the past.

This conceptualization preserves the relevance of trait judgment for behavioral prediction, because future acts can be predicted—on "actuarial grounds" (Buss & Craik, 1983, p. 106)—from past acts. In other words, what you have done before you are likely to do again. But it loses nearly everything else. Personality traits no longer explain why people act as they do; such a role is explicitly abdicated. Nor do they interact with each other, or even develop. As Avshalom Caspi has pointed out, "because this conception [the act frequency approach] bypasses the explanatory work of psychology, it is unlikely, by itself, to yield theoretical insights about personality development" (1998, p. 322).

For purposes of accuracy research, I think it is useful to maintain the idea that personality judgments try to describe not just other people do, but what they are like. As was argued at the outset of Chapter 1, personality judgment is motivated not just by a desire to predict others' behavior but by an intrinsic desire to understand them. Such understanding is deliberately precluded by conceptualizing personality traits as no more than act frequencies.

Social Intelligence

Several influential writers have advocated a reconceptualization of personality that entails a deliberate narrowing of individual difference constructs. Instead of conceptualizing personality in terms of broad motivational, emotional, and behavioral propensities, personality is regarded as a collection of relatively discrete, independent, and narrow social capacities, each relevant to performance only within a specific domain of life.

A prominent example of this viewpoint is the "social intelligence" theory of Nancy Cantor and John Kihlstrom (1987). They have explained how their approach "guides one away from generalized assessments [of personality or behavioral tendencies] . . . towards more particular profiles about the individual's profile of expertise in the life-task domains of central concern at that point in time" (Cantor & Kihlstrom, 1987, p. 241). This narrowing of the relevance of individual difference constructs is of course portrayed as good thing.

At the same time, the constructs are nonintuitive; they are not well captured by the terms laypersons ordinarily use to describe each other. For instance, Walter Mischel's cognitive theory of personality, drawn on heavily by Cantor and Kihlstrom, includes person variables such as "self-regulatory systems," "encoding strategies," and the like (Mischel, 1973).

The Advantages of Breadth

The use of narrow constructs may well increase correlations when predicting single behaviors, just as at the same time (and equivalently) it decreases the range of behaviors that can be predicted (Fishbein & Ajzen, 1974). But this predictive advantage does not always hold. For example, we saw earlier, in the summary of Funder and Colvin's 1991 study, that it was the broader behaviors, those relevant to the widest range of situations, which also exhibited the most consistency across situations. The same point was made in a different way by Chapdelaine, Kenny, and LaFontana (1994), who showed that people could more accurately predict an individual's *general* popularity than they could the degree to which he or she would be liked by a particular person. The reason seems to be that to predict a person's general popularity requires only knowledge about that person, but to predict a person's popularity with a specific other person also requires knowledge about that other person. As Chapdelaine et al. pointed out, this is what makes matchmaking so difficult. More broadly, general attributes of personality might be easier to judge than context-specific attributes because the latter require possibly-fallible inferences about the context—such as attributes of an interaction partner—as well as about the person who is judged (Kenny & DePaulo, 1993; Levesque and Kenny, 1993).

Moreover, beyond whatever advantages narrowly construed variables may or may not have for purposes of prediction, they are often presented as if they were somehow *conceptually* similar as well. They are not. Indeed, explaining behavior on the basis of a narrow trait relevant to it and little else represents an extreme case of the circularity problem sometimes (unfairly) ascribed to trait psychology in general. If "social skill at parties" is a narrowly construed individual difference construct assessed by measuring social skill at parties, then is seen as a *predictor* or even *cause* of social skill at parties, it is obvious that psychological understanding is not really getting anywhere.

Broader traits, however, have real explanatory power. The recognition of a pattern of behavior is a *bona fide*—albeit incomplete—explanation of each of the behaviors that comprise it, especially if the pattern is identified at a broad level of generality far above that of the behaviors it is mean to explain. The more global a trait is, the more real explanatory power it has, because connections between apparently distal phenomena are the most revealing about the deep structure of nature. For instance, if a general trait of social skill exists (see Funder & Harris, 1986), then to explain each of various, diverse behavioral outcomes with that trait is not circular at all. Instead, such an explanation relates a specific behavioral observation to a complex and *general* pattern of behavior. Such movement from the specific to the general is what explanation is all about.

This is not to say the explanatory task is then finished, because it never is. The general pattern of behavior—the trait—itself will require further explanatory efforts. One might want to examine the developmental history of a trait, its dynamic mechanisms, its interactions with other traits, or the way it derives from even more general personality variables. But such general traits (in Funder, 1991, I called them "global traits") remain important stopping points in the explanatory regress. To any explanation, one can always ask "why?" (as every 4-year-old knows). Still, between each "why" is a legitimate step toward understanding.

The Advantages of Intuitive Accessibility

I would argue further that personality constructs need to be not only reasonably broad but also intuitively accessible. Traits of the sort used by and understandable to laypersons have at least three advantages. First, intuitively discernible traits are likely to have greater social relevance and utility. Many such traits—such as the ones found in ordinary dictionaries—describe directly the kinds of relationships people have or the impacts they have on each other. More esoteric variables, by and large, do not.

Second, psychology's direct empirical knowledge of human social behavior incorporates only a small number of behaviors, and those only under certain specific and usually artificial circumstances. Restricting the derivation of individual difference variables to the small number of behaviors that have been measured in the laboratory (or the even smaller number that have been measured in field settings) adds precision to their meaning but inevitably fails to incorporate the broader patterns of behaviors and contexts that make up daily life. Ordinary intuitions, by contrast, sometimes leapfrog ahead of painstaking research. If we were to restrict our understanding of the term "sociable," for example, to include only its manifestations as have been so far observed in psychological laboratories, much of common knowledge would be missed and our understanding would be seriously distorted. The range of behaviors and social contexts implicit in the meaning of common trait terms goes far beyond anything research could address directly in the foreseeable future. Of course, common intuition is unlikely to be completely accurate, so traits as we think of them informally and as they actually exist in nature are surely not completely identical. However, to be useful in daily life our intuitions must provide at least roughly accurate organizations of behavior and a logical starting point for research (Clark, 1987). Corrections and refinements can come later, but to begin analysis of individual differences by eschewing intuitive insights and the rich terms of ordinary language seems a little like beginning a race before the starting line.

Third, and most important for present purposes, the omission of intuitively meaningful concepts from personality psychology makes study of the *accuracy* of human judgments of personality almost meaningless. As has already been observed several times, people make global trait judgments of each other all the time, and the accuracy of such judgments is obviously important. Unless one wishes to finesse the issue by studying only agreement between *perceptions* of personality (Kenny & Albright, 1987), research on accuracy requires a psychology of personality assessment to which informal, intuitive judgments can be compared. In a somewhat different context, Gibson (1979) persuasively argued that the study of perception cannot proceed without knowledge about the stimulus array and, ultimately, the reality that confronts the perceiver. The point applies with equal force to the study of person perception. A theory of personality will be helpful in understanding judgments of people for the same reason that a theory of physics of light is helpful in understanding judgments of color.

DO PERSONALITY TRAITS EXPLAIN ANYTHING?

A persistent criticism of personality traits over the years has been that they do not actually explain anything. They are merely labels for consistent patterns of behavior that restate the phenomenon without getting us any closer to understanding what is going on. The distinction underlying this criticism is that used in modern philosophy between two kinds of explanation, vertical and horizontal (Haig, 1998).

Vertical explanation pertains to the possibility of an underlying entity that exists at a different level than the phenomenon itself or the entity's evidential base. For example, a mechanism of repression might underlie the phenomenon of a person's forgetting an appointment, or a trait of extraversion might underlie the phenomenon that the person goes to many parties. The key here is that something is posited that operates underneath the surface manifestations of the psychological entity.

Horizontal explanation, sometimes called "conciliance," pertains to the extent to which a concept unifies at least two overt phenomena, preferably phenomena that are distant from each other. So if we find that people who go to a lot of parties also express a good deal of positive emotion, the idea of extraversion provides a "horizontal" explanation, in that it claims both are manifestations of the same trait.

The issue here is the degree to which these two kinds of explanation are truly different. Sometimes they are. An act frequency approach, for example, is purely horizontal. It ties together different behavioral observations but does not go "under the hood" for a deeper explanation. Sometimes traits have a vertical component too, though. For example, the recent writings of McCrae and Costa (1995) attempt to provide dynamic mechanisms underlying their favored five basic traits of personality.

In my own writing, and in this book, I generally employ traits as explanatory in a horizontal sense. I have left the job of explaining psychological dynamics, genetic components, and developmental histories of traits to others. Instead, I have concentrated on the sense of trait explanation that I believe is most relevant for a lay perceiver for his or her usual purpose, which is to decide what to do next.

For example, a person treats me in a mean manner. Is he mean otherwise, or was it me or something I did? This is an important question, and its answer is an extremely useful explanatory step. To answer it, as the attribution theorist Hal Kelly explained (Kelly, 1973), I need some more horizontal-type information. Is this person mean to everybody, or just me? And does everyone treat me this way, or just him?

Once I have the answers to these questions I can decide whether or not the mean behavior came from this person's personality. Let's say I ask around and find out this person is mean to nearly everybody, all the time—a purely "horizontal" kind of information. But I now have accomplished much of the work of what one ordinarily needs an explanation for—that is, to decide what to do next. In this case, my decision is to avoid this person whenever possible.

And that is not all. Having identified the source of behavior in the person, I am also embarked on the first step toward vertical explanation. If sufficiently interested, I might ask why this person has this trait of meanness, how it functions, and so forth. I might inquire as to what in this person's past experiences has made his personality so mean. Or perhaps I could explore his genetics, or psychodynamic mechanisms, if so inclined. All of these attempts at explanation are along the vertical explanatory axis, and all of them are initiated by the horizontal conclusion that something about the individual's personality was the source of his or her behavior.

The importance of horizontal explanation—the tying together of one behavioral observation with another through the supposition of a common trait to them both—should not be underestimated therefore. Horizontal explanation is important because it is useful, because it gets you started toward the enterprise of vertical explanation, and because in itself it is the very first step in vertical explanation.

PERSONALITY REAFFIRMED

The history of science has included several interesting periods where it was unclear whether a key concept would be redefined, replaced, or declared not to exist. For instance, more than a century ago Lavoisier convinced the scientific community that phlogiston did not exist and that the phenomena phlogiston was meant to explain were better accounted for by his new concept called "oxygen." But later observers have noted that he could almost as well have argued that phlogiston simply had some properties not hitherto recognized, and kept the old term (Stich, 1996).

The term "personality trait" may be undergoing a similar crisis at present. Some psychologists are eager to discard the term altogether, doing research on individual differences that in principle is little different from trait research (including the widespread use of self-report questionnaires) except that it avoids like the plague any use of the term "trait." Thus the literature has filled with questionnaires to measure any number of "schemas," "strategies," "implicit theories," and other putatively nontrait individual difference variables.

This shift in terminology is not completely empty; it gives investigators a fresh empirical and theoretical start. But it also loses much. The empirical and theoretical fresh start is so fresh that it has led some researchers to neglect elementary principles of reliability, homogeneity, and convergent and discriminant validity that apply to individual difference constructs no matter what they are called (recall the discussion in Chapter 1). And it has led to a neglect of the possibility that some and perhaps many of these new constructs are simply relabelings of constructs that have been around a very long time. For instance, Fuhrman and Funder (1995) showed that the procedures used by Markus (1977, 1983) to identify individuals with "sociability schemas" were equivalent to identification of high scorers on the sociability scale of the California Psychological Inventory (CPI; Gough, 1990). Specifically, individuals who scored high on CPI sociability manifested the same patterns of self-descriptive reaction time Markus found for her so-called schematic individuals.

The newer constructs of cognitive personality psychology include some properties not always included in older conceptualizations of traits, such as imputed processes of perception and cognition. But to the extent these properties prove to be useful they can of course be incorporated into our understanding of the nature of personality traits, an understanding that has been evolving for most of the 20th century. So I end this chapter with a conservative conclusion, not that phlogiston be revived as a viable concept for chemistry, but that the ordinary terms of personality description be broadened in their meaning and application to include new properties as they are discovered and understood. For only if we keep in our scientific lexicon terms like sociability, conscientiousness, and impulsiveness will we be able to assess the degree to which we are accurate—or inaccurate—when we think we perceive these traits in the people we meet and get to know.

CHAPTER 3

Error and Accuracy in the Study of Personality Judgment

In 1979, the leading textbook on person perception included a statement that was as astonishing as it was revealing:

> "The accuracy issue has all but faded from view in recent years, at least for personality judgments. There is not much present interest in questions about whether people are accurate. . . . There is, in short, almost no concern with normative questions of accuracy. On the other hand, in recent years there has been a renewed interest in how, why, and under what circumstances people are inaccurate." (Schneider, Hastorf, & Ellsworth, 1979, p. 224; see also Cook, 1984)

The astonishing aspect of this quotation is the way in which, at least to an uninitiated reader, it seems blatantly self-contradictory. As a bright undergraduate student (who was majoring in physics) asked me several years ago, aren't accuracy and inaccuracy essentially the same topic? How can research simultaneously manifest a disappearing concern with accuracy and an enhanced concern with inaccuracy?

The authors of the quote never acknowledged or resolved this apparent contradiction. Their book goes on to review a large number of studies of "attribution error" without ever coming back to explain how studies of error can be irrelevant to the topic of accuracy. Yet the quote is revealing of the state of the literature at the time (and to some extent even now). Despite the apparent contradiction, research on error—on "how, why, and in what circumstances people are inaccurate"—*is* irrelevant to "normative questions of accuracy." An entirely different kind of research has turned out to be necessary to address the topic of accuracy.

EVOLUTION OF RESEARCH ON ACCURACY AND ERROR

Research on accuracy in personality judgment has a complex and ironic history. After a lively beginning, it fell into disrepute and was replaced by research that addressed the process rather than content of social judgment. This research on process gradually came to address issues of *in*accuracy, as it increasingly focused on errors of interpersonal judgment. Finally, by the late 1980s this research on error was beginning itself to be eclipsed by a renewed program of research on the circumstances that promote accurate judgment of personality.

The Fall of Accuracy

From the 1920s into the early 1950s, a lively field of research addressed the accuracy of personality judgment. A variety of studies directly assessed the accuracy of subjects' judgments by comparing them to external, more or less realistic criteria. For example, Vernon (1933) assessed how well subjects were able to predict the performance of themselves, friends, and strangers on various tests of intelligence, personality, and artistic tendency. Estes (1938) had subjects judge stimulus persons viewed on film, and evaluated the accuracy of their judgments by comparing them with judgments made by trained clinicians. Yet the most common sort of criterion by far was that used by Adams (1927), Dymond (1949, 1950), and many others, who assessed the accuracy of judgments made by group members about each other in terms of how well they agreed. In many studies, judgments were deemed accurate to the degree they agreed with the judgments the targets made about themselves. When Taft reported a comprehensive review of the accuracy literature in 1955, nearly every study he summarized used self–other agreement as the criterion for accuracy.

This research activity came to an abrupt and nearly complete halt after the publication of a methodological critique by Lee Cronbach (1955, see also Gage & Cronbach, 1955). Cronbach demonstrated how the criteria used in studies of interjudge and self–other agreement, typically profile-similarity scores, were contaminated to an unknown degree by influences such as "stereotypic accuracy," "elevation," and "differential elevation" (Funder, 1980a, pp. 479–482). Few if any critiques in the history of psychology have had such a powerful and immediate impact. The reaction of accuracy researchers could best be described as panic, followed by fleeing. Accuracy quite suddenly became a disreputable topic, and most of the former experts soon found other, less risky issues to address.

This outcome was unfortunate because it was needless. Read closely and decoded, Cronbach's critique did *not* imply that research accuracy is impossible or even exceptionally difficult compared with other topics in psychology. Rather it addressed some complexities of data interpretation that most researchers had neglected up to that time but that could be dealt with given reasonable care and sophistication. Most centrally, Cronbach's critique highlighted the need to keep the components of judgment due to various nonsubstantive response sets separate from those components truly relevant to several different types of accuracy (see Chapter 4). A few investigators took heed of his suggestions and pressed on. Notably, industrial/organizational psychologists, who typically are quantitatively sophisticated and whose applied issues concerning selection and placement simply could not be ignored, maintained research on judgmental accuracy. This work was not widely read by social and personality psychologists, however, and so it developed on an isolated track.

The Shift to Process

As research on accuracy and the *content* of judgments fell off dramatically within personality and social psychology, research attention shifted to the *process* of judgment. The advantage of this shift was that process could be addressed while bypassing or finessing the difficulties entailed by external criteria. Instead of assessing the relation between a subject's judgments and the real attributes of the person who was judged, psychologists could present information—usually in written form—about a *hypothetical* target of judgment and investigate how subjects perceived, categorized, and interpreted that information. The transformation that occurred between input and output could be presumed to reflect judgmental processes, but accuracy issues did not arise because there was no real stimulus person for these processes to be accurate (or inaccurate) about.

Thus, psychologists soon found that research could be conducted with relative ease in the laboratory, using hypothetical targets of judgment and wholly artificial stimuli. A pioneer in this kind of research was Solomon Asch (1946). Asch showed his subjects lists of personality trait terms said to characterize a hypothetical stimulus person, then asked the subjects to draw an overall impression. The data he obtained supported an interesting holistic (or Gestalt) view of impression formation. At the same time, as E. E. Jones noted years later in an historical review, "Asch solved the accuracy problem by bypassing it" (Jones, 1985, p. 87).

Gordon Allport (1958) was quick to notice this shift. He wrote:

> Recently I attended a conference of psychologists working on the problem of the "perception of persons" (see Tagiuri & Petrullo, 1958). At this conference one heard much

about perception but little about persons, the object of perception. The reason, I think, is that the participants . . . much preferred to . . . evade the question of what the person is really like. (Allport, 1958, p. 243)

The trend Allport identified only accelerated after he made this comment. As the fields of person perception, attribution theory, and social cognition developed over the next 30 years, the predominant issue changed from whether judgments were right or wrong to how they were made. Studies in all three of these closely interrelated fields eschewed the use of real persons as targets of judgment. Instead, subjects were presented with artificial stimuli, typically in written form, and asked for their judgments. The resulting data led to models of the relation between proximal stimuli and judgments but contained no information about the relations between distal stimuli—that is, actual attributes of persons—and proximal stimuli, or between distal stimuli and judgments.

Whatever its virtues, this basic change in the approach of social psychology entailed at least one important cost. As the field turned from studying the relations between properties of actual people and social judgments to the study of perceptual and cognitive processes of judgment, social psychology became much less social (Neisser, 1980). Suddenly the process of acquaintance and interaction between people, and the development of relationships over time and across contexts, became treated (or not treated) as if they were irrelevant to interpersonal judgment. Models of social judgment described processes going on within the heads of social judges rather than anything involving either the stimulus person or the way information is conveyed from the stimulus person to the perceptual apparatus of the judge. It is this increased neglect of events and processes in the interpersonal world that made "social" psychology become less social as it became more cognitive.

The Rise of Error

At the same time social psychology was increasingly seeking to emulate cognitive psychology, an important new program of research was beginning to develop within cognitive psychology itself. This new research became known as the "error paradigm" or the "heuristics and biases approach." Originally identified with the groundbreaking work of Daniel Kahneman and Amos Tversky (e.g., 1973), the research had two aims.

The first aim was to reveal the "heuristics" or cognitive shortcuts people ordinarily use to process complex information. Theorists acknowledged that the stimuli that people confront are ordinarily just too complex and the time and cognitive resources available to process these stimuli are too limited for the use of logical, thorough, step-by-step, mathematical or algorithmic processing to be possible. Instead, people need to use cognitive shortcuts or "heuristics."

Perhaps the most pervasive of the cognitive shortcuts identified by Kahneman and Tversky was the "representativeness heuristic." As was pointed out by Nisbett and Ross (1980), this heuristic is extremely difficult to define precisely. But it roughly has to do with a tendency to predict outcomes that are in some way similar to or "representative" of the information used to predict those outcomes. An example of the misleading way this heuristic is used is that apparently dice players throw the dice harder when they wish to obtain a high number. More reasonably, perhaps, people assume a person with a grouchy facial expression is a grouchy person and that someone who has cheated them is dishonest.

Errors in Cognitive Psychology

The second aim of the heuristics-and-biases approach was to compile a vast catalog of the many different ways in which human judgment is faulty (Lopes, 1991). Surprisingly often, authors slid easily from describing heuristics as useful and even necessary components of human judgment under heavy cognitive load to characterizing them as woeful ways in which otherwise rational thinking too often goes astray. This is an important change of emphasis. By itself, the study of judgmental heuristics comprises a fairly simple, loose, and even vague way of characterizing human cognition, compared to more complex and finely tuned characterizations elsewhere in cognitive psychology such as associative memory or parallel distributed processing (PDP) models. But its impact on psychology was dramatically increased by its transformation into a critique of the accuracy of human judgment (Christensen-Szalanski & Beach, 1984). As one writer commented:

> Mistakes are fun! Errors in judgment make humorous anecdotes, but good performance does not. It is fun to lean back in our chairs and chuckle about our goofs. (Crandall, 1984, p. 1499)

The emphasis on mistakes—however much fun it may have been—had a deep and pervasive influence throughout psychology and even beyond. Over the 20-year reign of the error paradigm, a conventional wisdom became established that people were—not to put too fine a point on it—stupid. Examples of the expression of this point of view in the literature are nearly unlimited, but perhaps one will suffice.

The following illustration is interesting because the conventional wisdom is casually invoked in a way that leads to an extreme and implausible conclusion. It appears as a passing remark in a review of a book on cognitive psychology, in a reference to the "Turing test" of artificial intelligence (AI). In a Turing test, a judge is shown productions of a computer program and productions of a real human being, which might include various typed statements and replies to questions. If the judge cannot tell which replies come from the computer and which come from a person, according to the Turing test the computer has successfully modeled human intelligence. Although this test has been a staple of AI theorizing for years, the author of the review finds reason to doubt its utility:

> Considering what we know about the foibles of human judgment, how will the hapless judge be able to differentiate between communicative patterns of a real person and even

> a poor imitation? . . . The last four decades of research in cognitive psychology suggest
> that a human judge could be easily fooled. (Shaklee, 1991, p. 941)

Of course, this statement is absurd, and it is hard to doubt that its own author would not realize this with a moment's thought. The vast literature on human error does *not* imply that a judge would not be able to tell the difference between the output of a computer and of a real person—and in all demonstrations to date, judges have found this distinction quite easy. The literature even more emphatically does not suggest that "even a poor imitation" could fool a human judge where the best ones have not yet succeeded. The author's judgment was itself misled by a not-really-incorrect reading of the conventional wisdom that resulted from error research, "four decades" of research the author describes as having demonstrated so many "foibles" of human judgment that the typical person should be described as "hapless."

The Importation of Error into Social Psychology

It did not take long for this research approach and its associated general point of view to be imported into the increasingly cognitive-oriented field of social psychology. The most successful importers were Lee Ross and Richard Nisbett, who in their influential 1980 book drew many connections between the heuristics-and-biases research of Kahneman and Tversky and processes of interpersonal judgment.

The most important of these imports was Ross's translation of the representativeness heuristic into what he called the "fundamental attribution error" (Ross, 1977). The fundamental attribution error, another term for what Jones (1990; Jones & Harris, 1967) preferred to call the "correspondence bias," is evidenced by the tendency to infer personality attributes on the basis of seemingly relevant behaviors. In general, Ross argued, if you see a person act in a compliant, sociable, or grouchy manner, and then infer that he or she is a compliant, sociable, or grouchy *person,* you have committed the fundamental attribution error.

This imputation of error had two bases. One basis was a set of studies by Ross, Jones, and others that showed people to be willing to infer the presence of personality traits or attitudes on the basis of behavior that was controlled by situational forces. For example, Jones and Harris (1967) had shown how people assumed that essays were diagnostic of essay writers' attitudes even when the writers had no choice about what to write. Ross (1977) observed that most students who view films of the Milgram (1975) obedience study believe that the people who obeyed the experimenter's instructions to harm an innocent victim were themselves unusually obedient or cruel.

The second, more indirect but perhaps more important basis for the imputation of error was the influential situationist argument by Walter Mischel (1968), discussed in Chapter 2. Ross, Nisbett and other authors favorably cited Mischel to the point that behavior is inconsistent and dependent solely on the stimulus situation and that personality has a negligible influence on what people do. Therefore, they inferred, *any* inference of the existence of a personality characteristic on the basis of *any* behavioral observation was ipso facto erroneous. Because people in fact *do* make judgments of the personalities of themselves and others all day long, the implications for the quality of human reason were even graver than portrayed by Kahneman and Tversky.

Some of the rhetoric deployed while touting these implications made Kahneman and Tversky seem tame by comparison. The later book by Ross and Nisbett (1991) claimed that the typical person is "guilty" of being "naïve" (p. 119), "oblivious" (p. 124), and "insensitive" (p. 82). It also stated that the typical person suffers from "ignorance" (p. 69), "lack of awareness" (p. 82), "dramatic . . . overconfidence," "general misconceptions," and a "whole range" of other "shortcomings and biases" (p. 86). The only question left to ask about accuracy, it seemed, was "How could people be so wrong?" (p. 139).

Despite these heated words, the single most brilliant and effective rhetorical maneuver was the renaming of Jones's relatively pallid "correspondence bias" as the "fundamental attribution error." This label, which quickly caught on, drove the point home: People see the influence of personality on behavior where none exists. Therefore, any investigation of the *accuracy* of personality judgment would be intrinsically—"fundamentally"—oxymoronic.

Shortcomings of Error

The error paradigm thoroughly dominated the study of human judgment for about two decades, but inevitably it eventually came in for its own share of criticism. Critics made several observations. First and perhaps most obviously, whatever the merits of this research might be otherwise, the rhetoric deployed by researchers who focus on error has been embarrassingly excessive. For Jones to identify a "correspondence bias" was one thing; for Ross to repackage it as the "fundamental attribution error" was clearly another (see Jones, 1990, p. 139, for agreement on this point). When research psychologists start tossing around words like *hapless, oblivious, ignorant, insensitive,* and even *guilty* to characterize their fellow humans, it may be wise to worry about whether they have succumbed to hubris. Indeed, the very inappropriateness of its rhetoric has helped to motivate other psychologists to develop thorough critiques of the whole heuristics-and-biases approach (see Lopes, 1991).

It could be argued that—other than the blow to collective human pride and dignity—it really does no harm to characterize human judgment as inept. One writer, for example, suggested that a seeming overemphasis on error could be a good thing:

> Although it is nice to know that people are reasoning well or making good decisions in some contexts, it is much more important to know when they are not. . . . Surely, the

imperative message for us to impart to decision makers is that of their proneness to error. (Evans, 1984, pp. 1500–1501)

However, it might not necessarily be helpful to make one's judgments while afflicted by the kind of self-doubt a reading of some researchers on error would inflict. According to the social behaviorist Albert Bandura:

> People who believe strongly in their problem-solving capabilities remain highly efficient in their analytic thinking in complex decision-making situations, whereas those who are plagued by self-doubts are erratic in their analytic thinking . . . Quality of analytic thinking, in turn, affects performance accomplishments. (Bandura, 1989, p. 1176; see also Bandura & Wood, 1989; Wood & Bandura, 1989)

Furthermore, some writers have noted that the heuristics-and-biases approach, as typically employed, has a direct and powerful implication that seems to be quite false. The implication is that if we could eliminate all heuristics, biases, and errors from our judgment, our judgments would become more accurate. In fact, the reverse seems to be the case. Researchers on artificial intelligence find they must build heuristics and biases into their programs to allow them to function at all in environments that have any degree of complexity or unpredictability—environments, in other words, like the real world (Lopes & Oden, 1991).

For example, successful elimination of the "halo" effect has been shown to make judgments of real individuals less accurate (Bernardin & Pence, 1980; Borman, 1975, 1979a). This is probably because socially desirable traits really do tend to co-occur, making the inference of one such trait from the observation of another—the halo effect—a practice that ordinarily enhances accuracy (Funder & West, 1993). Other heuristics have also been found to enhance accuracy (e.g., Kenny, Bond, Mohr & Horn, 1996). The fundamental attribution error itself will lead to correct judgments to the extent that Mischel is wrong and personality really does have an effect on behavior (Funder, 1987, 1993a; Jussim, 1993).

A related reason why instruction to "avoid error" seldom increases accuracy is that it is aimed solely at analytic rather than intuitive processes of judgment (Hammond, 1996). The relative advantages of and tradeoffs between these two modes of judgment are discussed in Chapter 8 (Brunswik, 1956; Epstein, 1994).

The Fundamental Error of Error Research

A further critique of the error paradigm is at once more specific and more wide-ranging. Many and perhaps nearly all of the studies that purport to demonstrate incorrect human reasoning can be criticized on grounds that are highly ironic: Interpretations of studies of error themselves usually commit the fundamental attribution error as defined by Ross (1977). That is, they place the cause of the error in the person rather than in the situation.

As we have seen, the individuals who have been subjects in error experiments have been characterized as hapless, naïve, oblivious, and worse. The fault, it is assumed, lies in their poor judgment. But error research seldom examines the opposite possibility, that the experimental situations in which subjects make errors are specifically and powerfully designed to elicit them. In other words, perhaps the cause of inferential errors lies not in the person but in the situation.

This general critique can be instantiated through close analyses of particular experiments. Each experimental demonstration of error in the literature leads its subjects down the path of wrongness in a different way and so requires a separate examination. Of course there are thousands of such experiments. Rather than attempt to describe large numbers of them, in what follows I will describe a general demonstration of one way to produce and misinterpret an error. Then I will describe how error was produced and interpreted in two well-known studies. One of them was among the first demonstrations of error in social judgment; the other is more recent and seemingly—but perhaps not really—more sophisticated. The critique of each is fairly close and detailed, but I submit that such a close examination should be required whenever psychologists presume to tell their fellow human beings that their thinking is incorrect.

Count the Fingers

I once saw Robert Zajonc conduct the following entertaining and useful demonstration of how error can be produced at will. It goes like this: Ask your audience to tell you how many fingers you are holding up, and reassure them that a thumb counts as an ordinary finger. Raise your fingers one at a time until both your hands are outstretched with all 10 fingers showing. Then ask, "quick, how many fingers in *10* hands?" In my experience, about 80% to 90% of any audience (even one primed to expect a trick) will call out "100." Only about 10% to 20% will give the alternative answer, which is 50.

What can be made of this little demonstration? If it were an experiment on error in judgment interpreted in the standard way, it might be used to argue that people cannot correctly multiply 10×5! At very least, it would be pointed out that people have been led to commit what they themselves will readily admit was a mistake. The victims of this demonstration usually feel quite sheepish indeed.

But this demonstration does not show that people are poor mathematicians, mistake-prone, or anything else of this sort. It is a demonstration of something else entirely. Communication between two people, here the trickster and the tricked or (in many cases a close analogy) between experimenter and subject, proceeds on multiple channels and by generally agreed-upon rules (Grice, 1975). One of these rules is that the listener is entitled to assume that the speaker is cooperative, providing relevant information in a coherent and nonmisleading fashion. For example, if more than one channel of communication is employed, the messages on the different channels should be consistent with one another. If this or any other rule is violated, communication rapidly becomes impossible.

This is precisely the implicit rule violated by the finger-counting trick. The speaker is holding up *two* hands, when asking how many fingers are in 10 times *one* hand. The nonverbal "illustrator," as such communicative gestures are called, is inconsistent with the verbal statement.[1] Such gestures are ordinarily so vivid and clear that a listener can safely not pay much attention to the literal words that accompany them. That is the fatal "error" of the victims of this demonstration: They respond to the nonverbal message, which asks "how many fingers in 10 of these" (pairs of hands) and give the *correct* answer to that question, which indeed is 100. They fail to notice the paradoxical and contradictory message on the verbal channel, which refers instead merely to *hands* of five fingers each.

This demonstration yields several interesting implications. The first and most obvious is simply that it is fun to fool one's audience, as Crandall noted in the quote presented earlier. This fun should not be underestimated as part of the widespread appeal of the error paradigm. Demonstrations of error can be enjoyable to conduct and to report, and can provide a good way to jazz up an otherwise dull lecture about the processes of human judgment (Funder, 1987).

A second implication is that on full reflection it is not clear what the correct answer really is. Two different questions are asked on two different channels, and each has a different answer. The answer of 50 is correct only if one regards the literal content of the verbal message as having priority over the more vividly expressed content of the nonverbal message.[2] So individuals who give that answer should perhaps not be so smug; the correct answer is legitimately debatable.

A third implication is that this demonstration shows how easy it is to draw inappropriate inferences about the basis of subjects' responses to situations deliberately designed to fool them. It illustrates the tactic of sending subjects contradictory messages on different channels and lambasting them for responding to one channel rather than the other. This tactic is utilized *throughout* the error literature and characterized one of the first studies of error in social judgment ever reported, a study that influenced a generation of subsequent research.

Overattribution

One of the pioneering studies of error in social judgment, and perhaps still the most widely cited, is the demonstration of "overattribution" by Jones and Harris (1967). This is the famous study in which subjects were given essays to read that either favored or opposed the regime of Fidel Castro. Some subjects were told that the essays were written by individuals who had free choice as to what position to take (the "choice" condition). Other subjects were told that the position expressed had been assigned to the writers (the "no choice" condition). All subjects were then

---

[1] This is equivalent to saying "it was really enormous!" while holding thumb and forefinger close together. A listener will be confused, because the consistent gesture in this case would be to hold one's arms outstretched to each side.

[2] Indeed, it is my informal observation that literal-minded people such as engineers and cognitive scientists are more likely to give the answer of 50. More interpersonally and subjectively inclined people, such as clinical psychologists, nearly always give the answer of 100. A study should be done to check this impression.

TABLE 3-1   Imputed Attitudes toward Castro in Jones and Harris (1967)

Attitude expressed	Condition	
	Choice	No choice
Pro-Castro	59.6	44.1
Anti-Castro	17.4	22.9

Note. Higher numbers reflect a more "pro-Castro" position imputed to the essay writer. All pairwise comparisons are statistically significant ($p <.01$). This table was adapted from Jones and Harris, 1967. From Funder, D. C. (1993). Judgments as data for personality and development psychology: Error versus accuracy. In D. C. Funder, R. D. Parke, C. Tomilson-Keasey, & K. Widaman (Eds.), *Studying lives through time: Personality and development* (Table 1, p. 128). Washington, DC: American Psychological Association. Copyright 1993 by the American Psychological Association. Reprinted by permission of the publisher.

asked to estimate the writer's "true attitude toward Castro" (Jones & Harris, 1967, p. 5) on a scale where higher numbers reflected a more pro-Castro position. The results are reproduced in Table 3-1.

As Jones and Harris pointed out, one aspect of these results is unsurprising almost to the point of being boring. Subjects made less strong inferences about attitudes on the basis of the essay-writing behavior when that behavior was constrained. The imputed pro-Castro position was more than 15 points less strong in the no-choice (44.1) than in the choice condition (59.6), and the imputed anti-Castro position was more than 5 points less strong in the no-choice (22.9) than in the choice condition (17.4). Both of these comparisons were statistically significant (at $p < .01$), providing a good demonstration of what Jones had earlier named the "discounting principle" in attribution, that the imputation of a given cause for a behavior becomes weaker to the extent that other causes become plausible. In this case, the assignment of the author's position is an alternative possible cause for the essay writing, which quite reasonably makes it less diagnostic of the writer's true attitude in the subject's eyes.

It was a different aspect of these results, however, that really captured Jones and Harris's attention and, even more so, the attention of a generation of subsequent researchers. Jones and Harris were deeply startled by the observation that subjects differed in the attitudes they attributed to the essay writers even in the no-choice condition. There was a 22-point difference between the attitudes imputed to the pro-Castro and anti-Castro authors, even when subjects were told neither author had a choice about which position to take. As Jones and Harris put it:

> Perhaps the most striking result of [this] experiment was the tendency to attribute correspondence between behavior and private attitude even when the direction of the essay

was assigned. . . . [T]heir tendency . . . would seem to reflect *incomplete or distorted reasoning*. (p. 7, emphasis added)

The italicized passage in this quote is among if not the very first instance of subjects being accused of faulty reasoning on the basis of how they responded to misleading or confusing stimuli provided to them by an experimenter. It marks an important turning point in the history of social psychology. For the next two decades, a large number of researchers would increasingly occupy themselves designing studies where subjects could be given stimuli that they could be counted on to misinterpret. They did this by repeating, again and again, a bad mistake in the Jones and Harris design.[3]

The mistake was this: The communication between experimenter and subject was uncooperative in the Gricean sense discussed in the previous section. Different messages were simultaneously conveyed on different channels. On one channel, subjects were told "the essay writer had no choice about what to write." But on another channel of sorts, subjects were *also* given the essays to read and were asked to estimate their writers' "true attitudes." Notice that if subjects take their verbal instructions literally, the provision to them of the essays must be seen by them as pointless, and the request to estimate their writers' true attitudes, absurd. In a cooperative communication, why would someone be given irrelevant information and then asked to make a judgment for which no other possible basis is provided?

These observations clarify what Jones and Harris's subjects were guilty of, exactly. As we have seen, they were *not* guilty of ignoring or being "oblivious" to the choice manipulation, although some secondary texts (not the original Jones–Harris article) summarize the results in just that way. The choice manipulation affected subjects' judgments to a significant degree; the study was a *successful* demonstration of Jones' discounting principle. What they were precisely guilty of was of *not completely ignoring* the attitude manipulation. The fact is that the only way they could possibly have avoided having error imputed to them would have been for the two numbers in the right-hand column of Table 3-1 to turn out exactly equal. The only way subjects could have achieved this equality would have been by ignoring the most prominent stimulus in the experiment, the essay whose writer they were asked (based on no other information) to judge.

Assuming the experimenter to be a cooperative communicator, they assumed the information provided in the essay was relevant and that the task they were set was reasonable. What they failed to bargain on was that the experimenter was a deliberately deceptive communicator. They were guilty of misplaced trust, not inferential error.

The mistake in the Jones-Harris study was repeated many times over the years. In study after study, the stimulus that if properly attended to would have led to the

---

[3]This mistake of design was committed by those who followed Jones and Harris, but not the original investigators. Their study was designed to demonstrate the discounting principle (and did so), and a rereading of their article makes it clear that they were genuinely surprised by their results.

response the experimenter would have treated as correct was hidden or drastically de-emphasized. The stimulus leading to the "wrong" inference, however, was always front and center. It was presented vividly, loudly, and sometimes repeatedly. Then, precisely as in the finger-counting trick, an answer based on the emphasized information was treated as wrong, and only the answer to the nearly hidden information—the answer few subjects reached—was treated as right. Indeed, in many other studies besides Jones-Harris, subjects are deemed wrong if they pay *any attention at all* to the misleading stimulus.

Such studies of inferential error are like magic shows. In stage magic, the whole art lies in directing the audience's attention away from what is really going on and toward some interesting but irrelevant stimulus. Magicians are uncooperative communicators and not above the use of a little deception. Some social psychology is "magic" in precisely the same way. Like magic tricks, they demonstrate only that people can be fooled, not that their inferential processes are fundamentally or ordinarily erroneous.

Imputed Consistency

Most of the demonstrations of error in social judgment—especially those focused on the fundamental attribution error—are of the type described here, in which an informative but disguised stimulus is presented alongside an uninformative but prominent stimulus. A few other studies have been more complex. One of the most interesting and widely cited of those was a psychometrically oriented study by Kunda and Nisbett (1986).

The intention of this study was to go to the heart of the putative nature of the fundamental attribution error by demonstrating the degree to which people believe behavior to be more consistent than it really is. (Despite the status of this claim as a widely accepted cliché, surprisingly few studies attempt to address it directly, and this study is probably the most widely cited.) Although the data analysis in this study was complex, its procedural design was not. Subjects were simply asked a series of questions like the following:

> Suppose you observed Jane and Jill in a particular situation and found that Jane was more honest than Jill. What do you suppose is the probability that in the next situation in which you observe them you would also find Jane to be more honest than Jill?" (Kunda & Nisbett, 1986, p. 210)

Subjects were asked to provide written, numeric answers to a series of questions like this one, and their average response turned out to be 78%.

In their summary of this study, Ross and Nisbett (1991) drew a strong interpretation. The 78% figure, they asserted, shows how people "dramatically overestimate" (p. 124) behavioral consistency. Specifically, they claim, this 78% figure can be translated to an imputed cross-situational consistency correlation of .80, obviously much higher than typically found in the research literature. Because real behavioral consistency is lower, they argued, when subjects provide a probability of 78% they reveal how little they understand about the inconsistency of behavior and also reveal the mechanism by which overestimates of behavioral consistency can produce the fundamental attribution error.

Their source for their claim that real behavioral consistency is much lower is the same evidence that was cited by Mischel (1968) in his original review, discussed in Chapter 2. The specific empirical study on which they based their estimate of actual consistency, to which subjects' estimates were compared, was the famous and oft-cited summer camp study by Hartshorne and May (1928).

Each step of their reasoning deserves a closer look, for two reasons. First, even setting aside any qualms about what how subjects interpret probability questions like this or what they mean by their numeric answers, a close examination of the logic of the data analysis will provide ample reasons to doubt the appropriateness of the strong conclusion reached by Nisbett and Ross. Second, the study is one that many readers have found particularly persuasive and so can serve as a paradigmatic case study of the kind of reasoning by which the person-on-the-street came to be routinely portrayed as characteristically wrong.

Begin with a fairly technical but nonetheless important point. As was mentioned, Kunda and Nisbett claim that subjects' 78% estimate corresponds to a subject-estimated cross-situational consistency correlation of .80. This translation is based on a complex mathematical derivation that goes from Kendall's *tau* to Spearman's *rho*. A simpler calculation yields a different figure. One can chart the prediction situation presented to subjects, and their answers, in the manner shown in Table 3-2.[4]

The table illustrates subjects' predictions that 78 out of 100 "Janes" who were more honest than average at Time 1 would also be more honest than average at Time 2. This setup is equivalent to Rosenthal and Rubin's (1982) binomial effect size display, and a simple calculation based on the formula for the *phi* coefficient yields an imputed correlation of .56, rather than Kunda and Nisbett's figure of .80.

What accounts for the difference between these two figures? It turns out to hinge on whether one prefers to translate the subjects' average subjective probability of 78% into Kendall's *tau* or Spearman's *rho*. The former, just illustrated, yields a correlation of .56 and the latter, employed by Kunda and Nisbett, yields a correlation of .80. The difference between these two statistics is discussed in detail by Hayes (1973, pp. 788–794). Hayes characterizes them as closely related but "not identical" (p. 792). The crux of the conceptual difference is that as a measure of correlation "Spearman's *rho* places somewhat different weights on *particular* inversions in order, whereas in [Kendall's] *tau* all inversions are weighted equally by a simple frequency count" (p. 793).

---

[4]This table, taken from Funder (1993), is adapted from the method presented by Rosenthal and Rubin (1982).

TABLE 3-2   Binomial Conversion of Kunda and Nisbett's (1986)
Prediction Problem

Time 1	Time 2		Total
	More honest	Less honest	
More honest	78	22	100
Less honest	22	78	100
Total	100	100	200

Note. This is a tabular representation of subjects' responses to the prediction problem posed by Kunda and Nisbett (1986). Although Kunda and Nisbett claimed that these responses yielded an implied correlation coefficient of .80, by the method of Rosenthal and Rubin, 1982, they yielded a correlation of .56. From Funder, D. C. (1993). Judgments as data for personality and development psychology: Error versus accuracy. In D. C. Funder, R. D. Parke, C. Tomilson-Keasey, & K. Widaman (Eds.), *Studying lives through time: Personality and development* (Table 2, p. 131). Washington, DC: American Psychological Association. Copyright 1993 by the American Psychological Association. Reprinted by permission of the publisher.

Now ask yourself: Which of these statistics better reflects the impression laypersons were trying to communicate when they provided estimates of 78%? If the question strikes the reader as slightly absurd, then one is in a good position to appreciate the leaps of logic that are involved in forcing subjects to provide numeric estimates of how consistent some hypothetical Jane might be. At very least, the evaluation of subjects' responses is a complex matter of double interpretation, including both what subjects take the experimenter's questions to mean and how the experimenter then interprets the subjects' answers.

My own impression is that a conversion from lay probability judgments to *tau* is probably the more felicitous of the two, if only because the statistic is simpler and its calculation more straightforward. It is may be revealing that, presented with a choice, Kunda and Nisbett reported the statistic with the larger imputed correlation and larger imputed error. In a broader perspective, it is important to understand that the existence and exact degree of "error" subjects are interpreted as manifesting in this and many other studies depends critically on exactly which among several alternative calculations is used as the basis of comparison for their judgments.

Even an imputed correlation of .56 is one that Ross and Nisbett (1991), and other critics of human judgment, would claim is much too high. Mischel (1968) set the ceiling for cross-situational consistency at .30, a figure that was later raised by Nisbett (1980) to .40, both much smaller than .56. However, these estimates of .30 and even .40 are based on studies of single behavioral acts and typically based on the single study by Hartshorne and May (1928). The more recent study by Funder and Colvin (1991) provides an alternative benchmark.

This study, which was reviewed in Chapter 2, examined the consistency of behavior of 160 subjects across three experimental situations. Although "honesty" was not one of the behaviors in this study, 62 others at an equivalent level of generality were coded from the tapes. These included "speaks in a loud voice," "exhibits an awkward interpersonal style," "behaves in a fearful or timid manner," and "laughs frequently." Funder and Colvin found that, between the first two situations (unstructured interactions with different partners), 11 (including all those just quoted) exhibited a degree of consistency greater than the .56 benchmark. Although the degree of consistency for "honest" behavior remains unknown, in this light the estimates by Kunda and Nisbett's subjects do not seem necessarily unreasonable and are far less like a manifestation of anything that deserves to be characterized as error.

It is not clear to what extent the cross-situational consistency demonstrated by Funder and Colvin exactly matches the kind of consistency asked about by Kunda and Nisbett, or the kind to which their subjects' answers referred. I believe the approximation is reasonable, but that could be debated. But the very debatability of the data relevant to Kunda and Nisbett's assertion reveals the way in which a great deal depends on exactly how the problem is construed. Exactly what data would be relevant to assessing subjects' beliefs about consistency? Which statistics should be calculated from those data? In the present case, highly different interpretations can be derived depending on exactly how one interprets terms such as *behavior, situation,* and *probability* (and depending even on which of several formulas is used to calculate this last term). The typical practice of error research has been to choose one partic-ular interpretation of the stimulus problem and therefore one particular "right" answer, and then characterize subjects as error-prone to the extent their answers do not exactly match.

From Error to Accuracy

The Imputation of Error

The finger-counting demonstration and the detailed critique of two studies is a small response, perhaps, to almost three decades and thousands of studies devoted to demonstrating the inadequacies of human social judgment. But they encapsulate most of the major problems with this literature. In the typical study of error, subjects are provided with deliberately misleading information and their responses are deemed erroneous to the extent they are determined by this information. Or, and sometimes and, their judgments are deemed faulty to the extent they diverge in any way from the experimenter's definition of perfection. This definition may be one of several possible construals of the situation and the putatively correct answer may be one of several that might reasonably be calculated. You may be sure, however, that the one chosen will be the one that diverges the most from the subjects' judgments and therefore leads to the largest imputed error.

The Will to Believe

A further limitation of research on error is more basic than those just discussed. More than a century ago, William James (1897/1915) wrote about the difficulty of evaluating fallible evidence in order to decide what to believe. He noted with sympathy the passion many philosophers had to root out all error from human judgment. But he ruefully noted that once one had done that—had removed all possibility of error—one would be left with nothing. That is, to make any judgment at all is to risk error, and the systematic removal of possible errors tends to eliminate not just erroneous judgments, but all judgments. James was well aware of the necessity for critical examination of evidence and the elimination of error where possible, but he argued that it is also necessary to seek out ideas one can believe and to (just as importantly) have a certain sympathy for the means by which belief can be achieved. This realization sets the stage for a fundamentally different approach to human judgment, the accuracy paradigm.

ACCURACY IN HUMAN SOCIAL JUDGMENT

The accuracy paradigm is an almost exact reflection and reversal of the error paradigm. Instead of searching for what people do wrong, it looks for evidence of what they do right. Instead of using artificial stimuli to judgment, it uses real people. Instead of evaluating judgments in terms of normative models or experimenter-defined pronouncements of the right answer, it evaluates them in terms of converging data that gradually reveal the characteristics of real objects of judgment. Instead of a pessimistic approach, it employs a fundamentally optimistic one. As a result of all that, instead of generating belittling terms to refer to human judgment, it generates an appreciation of what people can accomplish and a bit of wonder about how they manage it.

The accuracy paradigm and its several variants will be described in Chapters 5 and 6, and some of its methodological and philosophical underpinnings will be discussed in Chapter 4. This paradigm is rapidly generating a large body of findings concerning the moderators and processes of accurate judgment and has already produced several competing and complementary theories of accuracy. But its first order of business, as the paradigm began to appear in the literature in the early 1980s, was to establish the evidence that human judgment was not always mistaken. This was necessary because the then-dominant zeitgeist, heavily influenced by error research and Mischel's situationist critique, was that essentially all human judgments of personality were wrong. Until this widespread view could be overcome, it would seem pointless to try to examine moderators and processes of accurate judgment.

TABLE 3-3   Some Personality Judgments with High Self-Other
and Other-Other Agreement

Item	Self-Other	Other-Other
Concerned with philosophical problems	.51	.48
Talkative	.45	.45
Self-dramatizing	.44	.47
Values intellectual and cognitive matters	.44	.43
Skilled at pretending and humor	.43	.42

Note. All correlations in this table are significant at $p < .001$. Adapted from Funder, D.
C., & Colvin, C. R. (1988). Friends and strangers: Acquaintanceship, agreement, and
the accuracy of personality judgment. *Journal of Personality and Social Psychology, 55,* 153,
Table 1. Copyright 1988 by the American Psychological Association. Adapted by permission of the publisher.

Basic Evidence about Accuracy

The evidence that human judgment is right at least sometimes is summarized in
several places, including Funder (1987), Kenrick and Funder (1988), and Funder
(1995a). Much of this evidence overlaps considerably with the evidence concerning
the existence of personality, summarized in Chapter 2. Indeed, the debates in the
literature concerning the existence of personality and concerning the existence
(ever) of accurate judgment proceeded more or less simultaneously, and much of
the same evidence and arguments appeared in each (Kenrick & Funder, 1988).

Demonstrations of accuracy in personality judgment have included studies showing how personality traits affect behavior and how laypersons can make judgments
of such traits that manifest both interjudge agreement and predictive validity (e.g.,
Ambady & Rosenthal, 1992; Cheek, 1982; Funder, 1980a, 1980b, 1982; Kenrick &
Stringfield, 1980; Malloy & Albright, 1990; McCrae, 1982; Moskowitz & Schwarz,
1982; Paunonen & Jackson, 1987). Two findings appear again and again.

First, different judges of the same individual tend to agree well in what they say
about his or her personality. This is true whether the comparison is between judgments by others and those of the person him or herself, or between different judges
of the same person.[5] As just one example, consider the findings reported by Funder
and Colvin (1988) concerning personality judgments rendered by Harvard University undergraduates. A few results are shown in Table 3-3.

The breadth of agreement between judges of personality was as impressive as its
degree in these cases. Of the 100 items (of the California Q-sort) that were judged,
fully 85 manifested self-other agreement that was significant at the $p < .05$ level,

[5]Self-other agreement is sometimes called "accuracy," and interjudge agreement is sometimes called
"other-other agreement" or "consensus."

TABLE 3-4   Some Personality-Behavior Correlations

Personality/behavioral item	r
Regards self as physically attractive/appears to regard self as physically attractive	.41
Values intellectual matters/shows interest in intellectual matters	.40
High intellect/exhibits high intelligence	.34
High aspiration level/displays ambition	.33
Sex-typed/behaves in masculine/feminine manner	.32
Has social poise/exhibits social skills	.31

Note. Item content is abbreviated. From Funder, D. C., & Colvin, C. R. (1991). Explorations in behavioral consistency: Properties of persons, situations, and behaviors. *Journal of Personality and Social Psychology, 60,* 788–789. Table 9. Copyright 1991 by the American Psychological Association. Reprinted by permission of the publisher.

and 82 manifested other-other agreement that was significant at that level.[6] Although there are many possible interpretations of these findings, the most parsimonious one is the most obvious. When different judges evaluate a stimulus person, they report that person's characteristics more or less accurately. This degree of accuracy leads their judgments to tend to agree.

A further and more demanding criterion for the accuracy of personality judgment is behavioral prediction. If a judgment accurately captures a real aspect of an individual's personality, it ought to be useful for predicting what that individual will do in the future. This is a difficult criterion to employ, because it is far from clear which behaviors one ought to try to predict from a particular personality judgment, how those behaviors might be operationalized, or in what contexts it is fair to observe them. Nonetheless, Funder and Colvin (1991) made an attempt in that direction. They videotaped 160 subjects in each of three experimental situations, coded 62 behaviors in each, and then summed these behavioral ratings across the three situations. The next step was to gather judgments of personality from close acquaintances of the subjects who had *not* viewed the behavior in the laboratory but knew them only from the ordinary encounters of daily life. Some of the items in the behavioral ratings, taken from the laboratory videos, had been deliberately written to closely match items in the personality Q-sort used by the acquaintances. Therefore, an approximate test of the predictive validity of some personality judgments can be obtained by correlating each of these behavioral items with the matching personality judgment (see Table 3-4).

These correlations are impressive considering the huge gap between the two variables correlated. One the one hand, we have ordinary undergraduates encountering their fellow students in the ordinary contexts of campus life then being asked to render a general description of what they have learned about them from those encounters. One the other hand, we have three specific behavioral measures taken

[6]Possible artifactual bases for these findings are considered—and defended against—in Chapter 4.

in brief (5-minute) laboratory contexts by entirely independent observers. Each correlation therefore must travel a route from behavior on campus, through the eyes and cognitive systems of acquaintances, onto a Q-sort description, over to other descriptions, rendered by research assistants, of brief behavioral episodes conducted under strange experimental circumstances.

As I noted a few years ago, what makes a dancing bear in a circus remarkable is not that it dances well but that it dances at all (Funder, 1989). In the present circumstances one might fault the precision of prediction, but I think it is more realistic to be surprised that our lay judges of personality managed any degree of predictive accuracy whatsoever. Certainly no computerized assessment, actuarial prediction, or other artificial system has this ability; the ordinary human judge outperforms them all.

The data presented earlier are from my own research program but are consistent with the findings of many other investigators (see, e.g., Berry, 1990, 1991; Berry & Finch-Wero, 1993; Gifford, 1994). A particularly relevant, but separate research program was conducted by Peter Borkenau and others concerning the "systematic distortion hypothesis." First vigorously advanced during the height of the Mischelian onslaught by Richard Shweder and Roy D'Andrade (e.g., Shweder, 1975; Shweder & D'Andrade, 1979), this hypothesis claimed that the intercorrelations among personality ratings found among self-ratings, informant-ratings, and stranger-ratings were the results of distortions on social perception systematically imposed by the structure of language. In a thorough review of the debate engendered by this hypothesis, Borkenau (1990) concluded that the evidence was largely incompatible with it. Ratings of semantically similar traits—such as friendly and sociable, for example—tend to be positively correlated not because of linguistically imposed distortion but because they refer to correct ratings based on overlapping "act universes." That is, they are correlated because to some degree they refer to the same real things. The bottom line of this research, then, also supports the essential validity of lay judgments of personality (see also Block, Weiss, & Thorne, 1979; Borkenau & Liebler, 1992a, 1992b; Borkenau & Ostendorf, 1987a, 1987b).

For present purposes, it is sufficient for me to draw only a very modest conclusion from the research summarized here: Human judgments of personality are not always wrong. There is enough indication from the data on interjudge agreement and behavioral prediction that sometimes, at least just sometimes, they manage to grab hold of a bit of psychological reality. I am aware that some psychologists are to this day still not willing to grant even this small point. But if you are, then we are ready to proceed in earnest with research on the moderators and processes of accuracy in personality judgment.

The Fundamental Attribution Error Revisited

Many different errors have been imputed to human judgment by a vast literature. The most influential of these, and the most important one for present purposes, is the one called the "correspondence bias" by Jones (1990) and the "fundamental attribution error" by Ross (1977). As we have seen, it is the granddaddy of all errors because it is the one that claims people have a pervasive tendency to see personality affecting behavior even when it does not, and therefore—when paired with Mischel's (1968) assault on the existence of personality—implies that *all* judgments of personality are wrong. This term—and its implication—remains firmly rooted in the literature, and it does not seem likely to fall out of common usage any time soon.

We have already seen some specific problems with some of the original demonstrations of this error. Most other demonstrations have similar problems. Although the specific details of each study of course differ, typically such studies present a very strong, vivid stimulus that implies an attribute of the (hypothetical) person being judged and another stimulus, almost hidden, that implies the first stimulus is uninformative. As we have seen, the fundamental attribution error usually occurs when subjects fail to ignore the first stimulus.

Aside from this methodological issue, the notion of the fundamental attribution error raises a key question: Procedural quibbles aside, *do* people have a tendency to make underdetermined inferences about personality, to see its influence where none exists? Some proponents surely think so. George Quattrone (1982) conducted a study that demonstrated the *reverse* effect, in which the power of the situation rather than of personality was overestimated. But even he was at pains to note that overattribution to the person "has been verified in so many studies" (1982, p. 607) that surely it was the more common tendency. But of course the number of studies is completely irrelevant; given that experiments can be shown to yield either overattribution to the person or to the situation (and the latter is what Quattrone demonstrated), then in principle any number of studies of either type could be conducted. A disproportion is as likely to reveal a bias among investigators, as among their subjects. And Quattrone's odd appraisal of his own results appears to exemplify such a bias.

Realizing that the relative frequency of studies of each type is uninformative, a few researchers have simply insisted that, in their experience, overattribution to the person happens all the time, and the reverse effect never or almost never occurs. But they may be on shaky ground even here. For example, the "false consensus effect" shows that people in general believe their own behaviors and attitudes to be more common in the population than they really are (Ross, Greene, & House, 1977). Behaviors that manifest "high consensus" in this sense are, according to attribution theory, determined by the situation, not by the person (Kelley, 1973). If everybody in a given context does the same thing, this tells you about the context, not differences among the people in it. So the false consensus bias is a robust example of a context in which people attribute more causality to the situation, and less to the person, than they should.

Other demonstrations of overattribution to the situation exist (e.g., Quattrone, 1982; Strickland, 1958). For example, many people assume that happiness is determined by the situation: The more advantages you have (e.g., money, health), the happier you will be. However, research persuasively establishes that this belief is an example of the inverse of the "fundamental" attribution error; happiness is much more a function of the person than of the situation. Even such seemingly strong situational manipulations as winning the Illinois State lottery or suffering a crippling accident has smaller effects on happiness than one might expect (Brickman, Coates, & Janoff-Bulman, 1978; for reviews see Argyle, 1987; Diener, 1984; Eysenck, 1990).

A reference to common experience might be even more persuasive. An important implication of the fundamental attribution error is too seldom noted. If behavior is really more malleable by situations than we think it is, and less determined by stable personality characteristics than we think it is, then we ought to be constantly surprised. Specifically, we ought to be surprised by how easy it is to change people! But is that the usual direction of the surprise? More often, it seems, we expect others to be more malleable than they really are. We expect children, spouses, and even coworkers to change their behaviors—and even their personalities—if we simply change their situation and treat them in the appropriate fashion. Usually we fail, and often we are surprised. This overattribution to the situation may not be *the* "fundamental attribution error," but it is pretty fundamental.

When the mythic age finally arrives when research has answered all our questions, it still might turn out that overattribution to the person is more common than overattribution to the situation. But already it is clear that both kinds of error exist, and both are important. Calling just one of them "fundamental" is probably unwise.

TOWARD A RAPPROCHEMENT BETWEEN ERROR AND ACCURACY

For the past two decades, the implicit null hypothesis underlying error research has been that human judgment is perfect, according to what Hammond (1996) calls "coherence" criteria. The coherence approach evaluates judgments in terms of the degree to which they follow the prescriptions of one or another normative model of judgment. This model may be very simple, such as the discounting principle invoked by Jones and Harris (1967). Jones and Harris posited the normative principle that the contents of an essay written under conditions of no choice are not the least bit informative about the attitudes of the essay writer. When subjects violated this principle—they provided different estimates of the essay writers' true positions when the essays were different—they were deemed in error (the "correspondence bias"). Other studies have provided subjects with inputs into attributional or even statistical models—such as Bayesian probability analysis—and found that subjects' responses did not precisely match the outputs of the models.

However, studies of error typically find—when they look—that subjects' estimates are *correlated* with the prescriptions of the normative models. For example, as we have seen, Jones and Harris's subjects did make less strong inferences under conditions of no choice, as discounting would prescribe. So they did discount, they just failed to discount *enough*; their inferences were in the direction of but not exactly what the normative model prescribed. The phenomenon of *error* is therefore typically better characterized as a *lack of perfection* (N. H. Anderson, 1990).

The approach of accuracy research is exactly opposite. The implicit null hypothesis is that human judgment is always wrong. This hypothesis generates studies that compare judgments with one or more "correspondence" criteria for accuracy, such as interjudge agreement or behavioral prediction, and then documents their attainment of some degree of accuracy, so defined.

These differing null hypotheses sometimes have served more to obscure than to clarify matters. As we have seen, error research more than once has slid from the conclusion that human judgment is not perfect to allegations that the performance of the human judge is generally abysmal. Accuracy research has sometimes fallen into an equivalent pitfall. It has occasionally slid from the conclusion that people are sometimes accurate to suggestions that human judgment is nearly infallible.

From the very beginning, it should have been obvious that human judgment is sometimes right and sometimes wrong. The further characterizations of it as pathetic or admirable are value judgments that depend more on prior expectations and perhaps on the degree of one's dispositional optimism or pessimism than on scientific evidence.

The difficult task for the next generation of research shall be to benefit from the contributions of both approaches while eschewing the more problematic tendencies of each. Error research has already provided a useful catalog of many ways in which judgment can go wrong, illuminated judgmental processes or heuristics that underlie error, and suggested ways in which errors might be avoided (Baron, 1988). The goal of accuracy research should be to provide equivalent and parallel contributions. Beyond establishing that accurate judgment sometimes occurs, accuracy research must also demonstrate the circumstances under which judgment is most likely to go right, describe the processes of accurate judgment, and provide its own suggestions for how accuracy might be improved.

CHAPTER 4

Methodological and Philosophical Considerations

The history of accuracy research teaches us that this is an area with a particular penchant for methodological difficulties. Accuracy research has the dubious distinction of having been shut down for decades by a single methodological critique, that by Lee Cronbach (1955, see Funder & West, 1993). It is also a topic where philosophical issues—in particular, those concerning the nature and knowability of reality—routinely arise, even if they are not often explicitly addressed. Some of the methodological and philosophical issues involved in the study of judgmental accuracy deserve a degree of attention, therefore, and that is the purpose of this chapter.

THE LESSON OF CRONBACH

In 1955 Lee Cronbach published a statistical decomposition of the criterion then used almost exclusively for the study of accuracy, which was self-other agreement (Cronbach, 1955; Gage & Cronbach, 1955). The usual research practice was to assume that a judge's description of another person was accurate to the extent that it matched the person's own self-description. Cronbach did *not* attack this assumption or the criterial status of self-other agreement on psychological or any other grounds. Rather, he closely criticized the way self-other other agreement was usually *calculated*. He complained that the similarity indices used to assess the agreement between self and others' views were contaminated—or, to be precise, were potentially contaminated—by several different factors. Some of these were measurement artifacts, and some could be considered either measurement artifacts or different kinds of accuracy. They included the degree to which target and judge use the response scale in a similar fashion, the degree to which the target and judge share various other response sets, the degree to which the judge assumes that the target is similar to the judge, the actual similarity between the target and judge, the judge's knowledge about people in general (as opposed to the particular target), and so forth (Funder, 1980b; Kenny, 1994).

None of these factors was fatal to the study of accuracy. Rather, the potential existence of these factors implied that the calculation of self-other agreement (and, by extension, interjudge agreement of any kind) was more complicated than it looked. Simple profile correlation or discrepancy scores are the result of numerous influences, some of which can and should sometimes be controlled, depending on how these scores are to be interpreted. Cronbach's analysis implied that one should be very careful when speaking about accuracy, because several different kinds are hidden within what is sometimes a single calculation. Cronbach observed, "investigators run much risk of giving psychological interpretation to mathematical artifacts when they use measures which combine the components [of interjudge agreement]" (p. 177).

As was mentioned in Chapter 3, the reaction of psychology at the time Cronbach's critique appeared was rather out of proportion to these implications. In retrospect and after almost half a century it is difficult to be sure exactly what happened. Apparently, contemporary psychologists were intimidated by the critical tone of Cronbach's article and, perhaps, confused by the complex arguments and unorthodox statistical notation the article employed. Whatever the exact reasons, the practical effect was clear. Accuracy research nearly stopped, and many researchers who formerly addressed the topic turned their attention to other issues. Despite its obvious importance, the topic went into virtual hibernation and did not re-emerge until the early 1980s.

Accuracy research revived only when the real implications of Cronbach's analysis were appreciated in early research by David Kenny (e.g., 1991; Kenny & LaVoie, 1984) myself (e.g., Funder, 1980b), and others (e.g., Harackiewicz & DePaulo, 1982). My approach dealt with "Cronbachian" issues by employing item analyses, forced-choice rating procedures, and other tactics to minimize or eliminate the biases he identified. More will be said about this strategy later in this chapter.

Kenny went in a somewhat different direction, himself serving the role of a latter-day Cronbach. By this I do not mean that he was critical in the way Cronbach was. Rather, Kenny developed innovative data-gathering and data-analytic techniques that allowed several potential artifacts to be not merely bypassed but directly confronted, precisely measured, and statistically controlled. More will be said about Kenny's approach later in this chapter, as well.

The general lesson to be drawn from this history is that although research on accuracy may be fraught with methodological difficulty, investigators should not allow themselves to be unduly discouraged. The complexities of the topic should be frankly acknowledged and directly addressed, with all the sophistication and ingenuity at researchers' command. Once that is done, research should proceed. As was discussed in Chapter 1, accuracy is too important of a topic to be ignored.

THE CRITERION PROBLEM

Cronbach aside, the first, most obvious, and perhaps most daunting difficulty in accuracy research is the criterion problem. To study the moderators and processes of accurate judgment, a researcher needs some sort of criterion for determining the degree to which a given judgment is right or wrong. But how can any researcher presume to do that? This question raises difficult philosophical and methodological issues.

The philosophical issues concern the relation between perception and reality. The methodological issues concern the techniques a researcher should use to assess and statistically analyze the two criteria for accuracy that are available. To make a long story (temporarily) short, these criteria are interjudge agreement and behavioral prediction. As was mentioned earlier, accuracy research fell once already because practitioners were insufficiently careful about the way they calculated self-other agreement. As we will see, the less-common use of behavioral prediction as a criterion entails difficulties that are different, but every bit as serious. These difficulties should not prevent research, but they require due attention and care.

Defining Accuracy

By what criterion can a personality judgment be evaluated as right or wrong (Hastie & Rasinski, 1988; Kruglanski, 1989)? Some psychologists believe this question to be unanswerable, because any attempt to answer it would reduce to pitting one person's judgment against another's. Who is in a position to say which judgment is right?

As we saw in Chapter 3, researchers on error share with researchers on accuracy— if they share nothing else—a willingness to answer this question. But they employ fundamentally different criteria to assess the degree to which a judgment is "right." Error researchers employ what Hammond (1996) called "coherence" criteria. These criteria include the degree to which a judgment follows the prescriptions of one or another normative model of judgment, as was discussed in Chapter 3. Accuracy researchers employ "correspondence" criteria. Correspondence criteria include the degree to which a judgment matches or corresponds with one or more independent indicators of reality.

Both criteria can be and sometimes are applied to the same judgment. For example, the process by which a weather forecaster makes his or her judgments might be compared to the inferential rules that were taught in meteorology school. If the process followed by the forecaster makes logical sense and follows the rules he or she was taught, the judgment passes the coherence criterion. Alternatively, if his or her judgment is that it will rain tomorrow, one can also wait and see if it actually rains. If it does, then the judgment passes the correspondence criterion.

The difference between these criteria is interesting and important because a judgment deemed correct by one criterion may be incorrect according the other. The forecaster may follow all the standard rules of meteorology with great precision, but make an incorrect forecast. Such an outcome—not at all rare—occurs when the normative rules taught in school are insufficient to account for a complex and rapidly changing reality. By the same token, a forecast might be correct even when the forecaster violates many of the standard rules. Such an outcome might just be a lucky accident or (if consistently obtained) might suggest that the forecaster has acquired some implicit knowledge not included in the formal rules of the trade.

Hammond has pointed out that many confusing issues and even heated debates in the literature—for example, the argument over "clinical vs. statistical prediction"—can be resolved when the distinction between these two criteria is appreciated. In an ideal world, researchers interested in accuracy would use both. Coherence criteria would apply to those aspects of judgment that can in principle be calculated with certainty or at least with statistical optimization; correspondence criteria would apply to complex stimulus situations—such as the interpersonal world—not sufficiently accounted for by normative models. At present, however, the two criteria are employed by areas of research that are quite separate. We saw in Chapter 3 how coherence criteria are employed (and mis-employed) by error research. Now it is time to turn to a consideration of how correspondence criteria are employed by accuracy research.

Three Approaches to Accuracy

The accuracy paradigm is characterized by three different approaches to correspondence. Each approach defines accuracy slightly differently, which leads it to use different kinds of correspondence criteria.

The Pragmatic Approach

The pragmatic approach to accuracy is one that can be traced back to J. J. Gibson (1979), William James (1897/1915), and probably even farther. James espoused a pragmatic approach to truth, which—to oversimplify—maintained that beliefs were best regarded as true to the degree they were useful for accomplishing worthwhile ends. Gibson, a perceptual psychologist, argued forcefully that people perceive not abstract properties of objects but their use-properties or "affordances." Thus, one perceives not the height and width of a door but whether one can fit through it. One perceives not the friendliness of another person but whether one can approach that person and not be rebuffed. This approach defines accuracy in terms of the successful accomplishment of the relevant goal. If you successfully walk through the door, your perception of it was accurate in that sense. If you successfully interact with a friendly person, your perception of him or her was accurate in that sense. As Gibsonians put it, "perception is for doing" (Zebrowitz & Collins, 1997, p. 217).

Gibson wrote almost entirely about judgments of the physical world, but pragmatically inclined psychologists such as Leslie Zebrowitz, Rueben Baron and William Swann translated his viewpoint into the domain of social psychology. These writers maintained that the essence of accurate social judgment is its usefulness for functioning adaptively in the social environment. To apply this criterion to research on accuracy, the investigator must gather information about the judgments that an individual makes in his or her natural social environment and then assess how well this individual is faring. If he or she is faring well, then his or her judgments can and perhaps must be regarded as accurate.

As Swann (1984) pointed out, this perspective seems to relieve some of the demands that are otherwise made on judgment. To interact successfully with someone you really need to know accurately only about those aspects of the person that are relevant to his or her behaviors in the environments you share. Thus, a "circumscribed accuracy," as Swann has called it, that characterizes how the person acts at work with you might be entirely sufficient to fulfill your pragmatic needs, even if the same judgment were to be grossly inaccurate as a characterization of how the person acts at home.

This approach is useful, but its implications are limited in two ways. First, research seems to show, perhaps surprisingly, that circumscribed accuracy is no better and is sometimes worse than generalized accuracy (Kenny, Kiefer, Smith, Ceplenski, & Kulo, 1996). For example, people are better at judging another person's general degree of talkativeness than at judging how talkative he or she will be specifically with them (Levesque & Kenny, 1993). Circumscribed accuracy might be more difficult than generalized accuracy because it requires knowledge of (at least) two people, not just one. For circumscribed accuracy you need to understand not just the target person, but the particular person with whom he or she is interacting, along with the particular context. For generalized accuracy the target person is all you need to focus upon. Circumscribed accuracy might be all we need, but generalized accuracy might in some cases be easier.

A second limitation to the pragmatic approach is that, contrary to Gibsonian doctrine, all perception probably is *not* just for "doing." To some degree—and this degree might vary across individuals (Neuberg & Newson, 1993)—the perception of other people is motivated by an intrinsic desire to know them and the social world. To claim that all perception is for doing is a bit like claiming that all research is applied. Perhaps all research has potential application (this is a debatable claim), but the motivations of many researchers are certainly not to produce useful findings. Rather, they seek to satisfy their curiosity. To some degree social perceivers are like this. As was discussed in Chapter 1, we seem to be *intrinsically,* not just pragmatically, motivated to understand other people.

The Constructivist Approach

The constructivist point of view, which has lately become widespread throughout recent, "post-modernist" intellectual life, is that an external reality of objects does not exist (e.g., Gergen, 1985, 1994; Gergen & Semin, 1990; for critiques see Stanovich, 1991; Wilson, 1998). Or, in a slightly milder version, the nature of the world can never be known with any degree of certainty; in principle all guesses have equal status. All that does exist—or all that can be known—are human ideas or *constructions* of reality.

The constructivist view finally provides an answer to the age-old question, "If a tree falls in the forest with no one to hear, does it make a noise?" The answer is, "No." A more important implication of the constructivist view is that there is no real way to regard one interpretation of reality as accurate and another interpretation as inaccurate, because all interpretations are mere "social constructions" (Kruglanski, 1989), and the only criterion for anything like truth, under these circumstances, is the collective point of view of a community of judges.[1]

Although constructivism might seem like a radical position, historically it has been an implicit underpinning of most research on person perception within social psychology. As was mentioned in Chapter 3, some social psychologists took pride in the way research on attributional processes could solve the accuracy problem by bypassing it. Because they assumed there was no way to show one personality judgment to be any more accurate than another, some researchers were positively relieved to find a research strategy that allowed them to ignore the issue.

When the constructivist approach does not lead to bypassing accuracy issues altogether, it typically yields research that focuses on interjudge agreement as a topic of interest in its own right. An example is the prolific and influential research program of David Kenny (e.g., 1994). For operational purposes, Kenny has defined an accurate personality judgment as the consensus or averaged view of all possible

---

[1] It might be noticed that constructivism has here slipped from a solipsistic to a collectivist view of reality. That is, it supports the integrity and incontrovertibility of each individual's point of view, but also argues that the difference between good and bad points of view is evident only through the degree they gain acceptance in the community. This slip may be a subtlety of constructivism, but some have argued it is in fact an internal contradiction (G. Thomas, personal communication, 1998; Strongman, 1998). Or it may be a difference between extreme (solipsistic) and more moderate "social contructivist" views such as that of Gergen (B. Haig, personal communication, 1998).

observers of a person, in all possible situations. This is truly a "man is the mea-sure of all things" criterion. In postmodernist fashion, it definitionally bypasses the possibility that a reality exists beyond the consensual opinion of a community of judges.

This approach allows several important issues to be addressed. Kenny's program has yielded a useful analytic technology and valuable insights about the degree to which and circumstances under which people agree with each other in their judg-ments of personality. However, a definition of reality limited to the consensus of all possible observers neglects the implications of a reality that might exist apart from what people currently perceive it to be. On a purely philosophical level, one might wish to hold open the possibility that everybody might be wrong at once, as difficult as ascertaining such collective error would of course prove to be.[2]

A second problematical aspect of a constructivist point of view is that defining social reality solely in terms of the perspectives of social perceivers can lead a re-searcher to neglect other evidence that might be brought to bear. For example, if a large group of social perceivers agrees about some aspect of this individual's person-ality, can this collective judgment be used to accurately predict his or her future behavior? Constructivism—or a definition of reality that refers only to interjudge agreement—provides no reason why such prediction should necessarily be possible. But if you assume the existence of a psychological reality that extends beyond the consensus view of observers, then it is this reality—the traits the target person *really* has—that affects his or her future behavior and allows it to have some degree of predictability. It is the potential failure of such predictability that opens the possibil-ity of someday demonstrating that the current collective view is wrong.

The Realistic Approach

Both the pragmatic and constructivist approaches provide an important step beyond the error paradigm by attending to theoretical considerations, sources of data, and correspondence criteria that go beyond the cognitive process by which judgments are made. Still, each has the net of effect of narrowing what accuracy means and simplifying how it can be evaluated. The result of this relative narrowing and sim-plification is to limit the range of data that are sought.

The Demanding Nature of Realism

A realistic perspective is more demanding. The postpositivist philosophy of sci-ence variously called *fallibilistic realism, scientific realism,* or *critical realism* maintains that truth exists, but there is no single, sure pathway to it (see Bhaskar, 1978; Cook & Campbell, 1979; Manicas & Secord, 1983). There are a wide variety

---

[2]In later writings, Kenny (1997) has acknowledged this point and discussed definitions of accuracy that go beyond consensus.

of alternative pathways, each of which is extremely unsure. This point of view also characterizes Egon Brunswik's (1956) "probabalistic functionalism," which emphasizes how reality can only be perceived via multiple cues, each of uncertain validity.

For the study of accuracy in social judgment, realism demands that a portrayal of the actual psychological attributes of the target person be sought though the combination of a wide range of information. The accuracy of a judgment of the target's personality is then evaluated in terms of its congruence with this portrayal. The information about the target can and should take many forms. It might include self-ratings of personality, inventory scores, ratings by knowledgeable informants, direct observations of the person's behavior (e.g., in a laboratory), and reports of the person's behavior in daily life, perhaps gathered using diary or "beeper" methods (Csikszentmihalyi & Larson, 1992; Funder, 1993a; Spain, 1994).

The Duck Test

Consider how we might go about deciding whether something is a duck (this example is adapted from Block, 1989, pp. 236–237). The first question we might ask is, does it look like a duck? Let's say it does. Are we safe in concluding it is a duck? Not so fast. Perhaps it is merely a duck decoy or a high-quality toy duck. So go on. Does it quack like duck? Does it walk like a duck? Say the answers are again yes. Now is it a duck? We still cannot be sure, because it might be some sophisticated audio-animatronic imitation. But a reasonable person might be fairly sure it is a duck. Say we observe now that the ducklike object swims, migrates to warmer climates in the winter, and lays eggs. At some point, as the evidence accumulates, it becomes absurd to think the stimulus is anything but a duck. But it is important to realize that this transition point between reasonable and unreasonable skepticism is neither obvious nor clearly labeled, and the point of absolute certainty beyond that is *never* attained. It is also important to note that no single piece of evidence clinches the deal—duckiness simply becomes more likely as the evidence accumulates.

In personality psychology, the procedure equivalent to the duck test is called *convergent validation*. The convergent validity of a personality test, for example, lies in the diversity of evidence—peer's reports, behavioral observations, life outcomes, and so forth—that indicate the test measures what it purports to measure (Cronbach & Meehl, 1955; Messick, 1989). The accuracy of a personality judgment can and should be evaluated the same way (Funder, 1995a; Funder & West, 1993). An acquaintance's personality judgment of dominance might be evaluated in terms of the extent to which it can (a) predict the target's dominant behavior, (b) *not* predict his or her friendly behavior, and (c) agree with the judgments provided by another peer or the target himself or herself. Each of these two principal criteria for accuracy, interjudge agreement and behavioral prediction, entails important complications that require close attention.

INTERJUDGE AGREEMENT

Research on accuracy in personality judgment has gathered data concerning two kinds of interjudge agreement. The first kind is the agreement between a judge's description of an individual's personality and that individual's description of himself or herself. One label for this phenomenon is "self-other agreement," but it sometimes also goes by the (potentially misleading) term of "accuracy." (It is potentially misleading because self-other agreement is only one of many possible indicators of judgmental accuracy.) The second kind of interjudge agreement is between the descriptions of personality provided by two different "other" judges. This could be called "other-other agreement" but the label might lose in awkwardness what it gains in clarity. Kenny (1994) and Funder and West (1993) have used the term "consensus" to refer to the degree of agreement among different judges of the same person.

The relationship between accuracy and agreement of either sort is asymmetric. Agreement is necessary for accuracy, but not vice versa. If two judges disagree about the *real* nature of a criterion, they cannot both be right.[3] But if they both agree, they might both be wrong. Our faith that agreement is a reasonable proxy for accuracy can be enhanced by findings (reviewed in this book and elsewhere) that many of the same variables that reasonably *ought* to affect accuracy *do* affect agreement. For example, more visible traits ought to be easier to judge accurately, and they are judged with better interjudge agreement (Funder & Dobroth, 1987). Likewise, knowing someone longer ought to cause someone to judge him or her more accurately, and increased acquaintance also increases interjudge agreement (Funder & Colvin, 1988). Still, it is important to remember that agreement and accuracy are not the same concept, and criteria beyond agreement should be sought when possible (Funder, 1987, 1995a; Kenny, 1994).

Self-Other Agreement

Examination of self-other congruence requires, of course, that the self and others be asked for personality descriptions. The precise way this request is made reveals something subtle but important concerning the interests of the investigator and has important consequences for interpreting the answers that will be obtained (Funder & Colvin, 1997).

---

[3] Arguments can arise on this seemingly obvious point if it is overlooked that the reference here is to the real nature of a stimulus. Different judges might disagree because they both are accurately reporting the evidence available *to them*. So they are both accurate in this subjective sense. But they cannot both be accurate in a realistic sense. (Perhaps one of them received misleading information.)

Asking the Other about the Target's Perceptions

One way is to ask the other judges to describe, not the personality of the target, but how the target *perceives* or *would describe* his or her own personality. From about the 1930s to the early 1960s, this was the traditional method for research on accuracy. In a typical early study, Bender and Hastorf (1950) asked students to describe themselves on three measures: one on behavior in social situations, another on dominance, and another on empathic ability. Another group of students, composed of acquaintances of these targets, then completed the same three measures *as they thought the targets had answered them*. For two of the three measures, significant agreement was found between targets' and acquaintances' responses. Early researchers regarded this sort of ability to predict targets' self-judgments as an indicator of social sensitivity or empathy (e.g., Gage & Cronbach, 1955; Taft, 1966).

Asking the Target about the Other's Perceptions

When research on self-other agreement reappeared in the mid-1980s after its 30-year hiatus, a methodological approach opposite to that used during the earlier incarnation became typical. Instead of asking the *judge* to predict the target's self-description, many latter-day investigators asked the *target* to predict how others would describe him or her. This is an interesting change in focus. Between the 1950s and 1980s researchers' interests seem to have shifted from the ability of others to characterize what a person thinks of herself to the person's ability to characterize what others think of her.

The reason for this shift is not obvious, and the shift itself seems to have been almost invisible. But the shift constitutes a subtle change in focus from a concern with what other people are like to a concern with how one appears to others. Instead of "What are you like?" the question becomes "What do you think of me?" (Funder, 1997b). As Bette Midler once said, "That's enough about you. Let's talk about me." This change in emphasis seems consistent with the increasingly narcissistic cultural tone of the 1980s compared with the 1950s (Fine, 1986).

Advantages and Disadvantages

An advantage of both of these approaches, one older and one newer, is that both are designed to neatly finesse the whole issue of accuracy. They do this by giving accuracy an operational definition that is not quite the same as its ordinary, realistic meaning, but that has the advantage of being directly measurable (see Cronbach, 1955). If one is asked to predict what a person will say about himself or herself, the accuracy of this prediction can be directly assessed: if the prediction matches the self-description, the prediction was accurate by definition. In the same way, if one is asked to predict what others will say about one, the accuracy of this prediction can also be directly assessed.

These two methodologies are perfectly appropriate, even necessary, for the study of mutual perception. For example, if one is interested in the ontogeny of the self-concept from a sociological perspective, then it is important to find out whether people see themselves in the way they *think* others see them (Shrauger & Schoeneman, 1979).

The use of operational definitions to finesse a conceptual issue often seems attractive, but it always carries a cost (Bronfenbrenner, Harding, & Gallwey, 1958; Cronbach, 1955). In this case, the cost is that no information is gathered relevant to the ordinary, realistic meaning of accuracy. This is because, in both methodologies, *one member of the self-other dyad is not asked to describe a person.* In the older research the other judge, and in the newer research the target, is asked to describe merely the *judgments* rendered by the other member of the dyad.

It is easy to imagine cases where this seemingly subtle difference might prove to be important. Imagine trying to describe someone you think is intelligent but who appears to have extremely low self-esteem. If asked to describe how the person will describe himself, you would probably predict a low rating of intelligence. But if you were asked to describe what the person is like, you would give a high rating of intelligence. The same kind of complication could arise in the other direction. An individual who believes that he or she is not seen accurately by others—that "everybody is always picking on me"—should provide very different answers to the question "How will others describe you?" compared with "What are you like?"

There is a different way to ask the question on which self-other agreement is compared. Instead of asking either party for their impressions of the other person's impressions, the researcher simply asks both parties for their judgment of what the target person is *really* like (e.g., Funder, 1980a; Funder & Colvin, 1988; Funder & Dobroth, 1987; Park & Judd, 1989). Self-other agreement in response to this question directly indicates how well two people agree about the target's actual personality. For a researcher with a realistic perspective, who is interested in the convergent validity of different judgments of a common target, this is the most appropriate way for the question to be asked.

Other-Other Agreement (Consensus)

Another kind of interjudge agreement has been studied less often over the years, although it has received renewed attention recently, particularly in the work of Kenny (1994). This kind of agreement arises between different observers of the same target, what has been called "other-other agreement" or "consensus." The subtle difference in wording discussed earlier in connection with self-other agreement has not arisen in this context, so far as I know. No researcher has asked subjects to estimate each others' judgments of a common target (though of course it would be possible). Instead, everybody is simply asked to judge someone they all know or have at least all seen, and an indication of accuracy is derived from the degree of agreement their judgments manifest.

The Calculation of Interjudge Agreement

Regardless of how the descriptive question is asked or whether self-other or other-other agreement is examined, the degree of agreement can be assessed in two fundamentally different ways. Agreement can be assessed in terms of mean differences or correlations. These two analyses are independent, and confusion has sometimes arisen in the literature when the difference between them was not sufficiently appreciated.

Mean Differences

The analysis of mean differences in personality judgment addresses the degree to which the *absolute level* of a trait rating agrees or differs across judges, different kinds of judge, or judgmental contexts. For example, do people generally give higher ratings on certain traits (such as desirable ones) to themselves than they do to other people? Do judges who are well acquainted with their targets give higher ratings than do strangers? Analyses of mean differences like these are often used in the pursuit of biases such as tendencies toward self-enhancement or acquaintance positivity (Funder, 1980a; Funder & Colvin, 1997; Brown, 1986; Kunda, 1987; Miller & Ross, 1975).

The differences between means examined in these analyses pertain to differences between groups of subjects rather than particular individuals. They can identify general tendencies for different kinds of judges to provide ratings that possibly are at different points on the rating scale employed. But they provide no information about the accuracy of judgments of particular individuals, nor do they address whether targets rated highly by one kind of judge on a given trait also tend to be rated highly by another kind of judge.

Correlations: Profile and Item-Level

To compare the covariance among different judgments of common targets, correlational analysis must be employed. Correlation coefficients may be calculated between self and others' or among different others' judgments, either holistically or one item at a time. These coefficients can reflect whether, for example, people who rate themselves relatively highly on sociability tend to receive relatively high sociability ratings from their acquaintances, compared to people who rate themselves lower on sociability. To the extent that this question can be answered in the affirmative, the ratings can collectively be said to have demonstrated a degree of self-other agreement and convergent validity.

TABLE 4-1

Judge		Profile Correlation Target = Jane			
	Item 1	Item 2		Item 100	
Jane (self)	X_{1j}	X_{2j}	....	X_{100j}	r_j = self-other agreement
Mary (other)	Y_{1j}	Y_{2j}	....	Y_{100j}	correlation for Jane

Target	Item Correlation Item #1 Score	
	Self-rating	Other-rating
Jane	X_{1j}	Y_{1j}
Carlos	X_{1c}	Y_{1c}
Philip	X_{1p}	Y_{1p}

$$r_1 =$$
self–other agreement correlation
for item 1

In most research, the correlations among judges' ratings can be computed either across personality profiles or on individual variables or items. The first method assesses the similarity between the complete set of personality judgments made by one judge and the complete set of personality judgments made by another (e.g., Andersen, 1984; Blackman & Funder, 1998). For this kind of correlation, the X variables are all the judgments by one judge, and the Y variables are all the judgments by another judge. Thus, the X variables might be the complete set of self-judgments of a given target, and the Y variables might be the complete set of judgments made by another person. This is "profile" agreement, and it is calculated for one target-judge or judge-judge pair at a time. It yields as many correlations as there are pairs of judges.

For example, consider the procedure depicted in the top half of Table 4-1. Self-other agreement is calculated for a target person: Jane. Jane herself and an acquaintance, Mary, both rate Jane on 100 personality traits (e.g., the 100 items of the California Q-sort; Block, 1978). Their "profile" self-other agreement is calculated as a correlation coefficient across the 100 pairs of ratings. This correlation refers only to agreement about Jane. For the next target in the sample, Carlos, the ratings of Carlos and his "other" judge would be compared in the same way, yielding a separate profile agreement score. This procedure is repeated for each *target person.*

The second method assesses congruence one variable at a time. Instead of comparing whole profiles, this methods correlates judges' ratings on a single personality item (e.g., Funder, 1980a; Funder & Colvin, 1988; Funder & Dobroth, 1987). The X variables in this analysis might be the self-judgments of all the subjects in the sample on this one item. The Y variables would be the corresponding judgments on this item offered by the subjects' acquaintances. Or the X and Y variables might refer to the ratings of the same item by two different judges.[4]

For example, consider the bottom half of Table 4-1. John, Carlos, Philip and other target persons are each rated by the self and by another. The "item" agreement in their ratings is calculated as a correlation coefficient across the pairs of ratings, of the first item only, for each target person. In this analysis, there are the same number of pairs as there are targets. The resulting correlation refers only to agreement on Item 1 (in the Q-sort, "Is critical, skeptical, not easily impressed"). For the next item, the ratings of all the judges of every target would be again compared in the same way, yielding a separate item agreement score. This procedure is repeated for *each item.*

The profile and variable or item methods each have advantages and disadvantages, as we shall see (see Bernieri, Zuckerman, Koestner, & Rosenthal, 1994, for a comparative analysis).

Profile Correlations and "Cronbach's Complaint"

The methodological critique by Cronbach (1955) that managed to shut down accuracy research for three decades was aimed precisely at profile correlations, the then-conventional method of calculating interjudge agreement.[5] Given this history, the issue probably deserves some extra care from accuracy researchers.

Cronbach's analysis showed how profile similarity scores had the potential to be influenced by several factors aside from the judge's ability to accurately discriminate properties of the target. Elevation, differential elevation, and stereotype accuracy refer to the effect of shared response styles between judges. Elevation refers to the possibility that, for example, a judge and a target, or two judges, might both prefer to give high rather than low ratings on all traits. Differential elevation refers to the possibility that judge and target, or two judges, might share tendencies to rate *certain* target persons as higher or lower than other persons, regardless of the trait being judged. Elevation, and differential elevation, can artificially enhance profile agree-

---

[4]In this case the designation of one judge as X and the other as Y is arbitrary, and so the intraclass correlation rather than usual Pearson r must be employed (Rosenthal & Rosnow, 1984). In practice, however, the two correlation statistics rarely differ by much.

[5]Other, related critiques were contributed by Hastorf and Bender (1952) and Gage & Cronbach, 1955.

ment scores that are based on the discrepancies between judgments (such as the inverse of the sum of the squared deviations).

Another Cronbachian confound is stereotype accuracy.[6] This is the component of interjudge agreement that arises from the "trait effect," the tendency of judges to rate some traits higher than others (e.g., most judges may rate "honesty" higher than "coldness" almost regardless of who is being described). To the degree this tendency matches across judges, or with the average tendency of the sample of targets, profile consensus or self–other agreement may arise that has nothing to do with the particular target being described. Consider again the case of self–other agreement. To the extent that the pattern of a judge's traits ratings of a *particular* target happens to resemble the average pattern of *all* targets, and simultaneously to the extent that the pattern of the target's self-ratings also matches this average, then the judge's rating may gain an illusory degree of apparent similarity with the target's self-rating. In other words, in some cases a judge can earn a fair amount of apparent accuracy, in terms of self–other agreement, simply by guessing on each trait the mean judgment of all targets, and ignoring the individual target of judgment altogether. This enhancement can affect both discrepancy and correlational measures of profile similarity.

As Douglas Jackson (1982) has noted, this is not the least bit illegitimate. Knowledge about people in general seems likely to be an important component of accuracy in judging particular people (Bronfenbrenner, Harding, & Galway, 1958; Hoch, 1987). Cronbach's point was that unless analytic care is taken, the sources of the accuracy—such as distinctive observations of a particular target versus knowledge about people in general—cannot be separately estimated.

With due analytic care, most of the potential artifacts identified by Cronbach are not difficult to eliminate. Those involving elevation, for example, can be removed by the use of correlations rather than discrepancy scores or by employing forced-choice rating techniques (e.g., a Q-sort) that constrain the ratings of all judges to have the same mean and variance across items. The matter of stereotype accuracy is more complex and can be dealt with in at least three different ways, depending on what the investigator regards as the most important aspect of the analysis.

Methods for Analyzing Interjudge Agreement

Several methods can be used to attempt to deal with the complications entailed in computing and interpreting interjudge agreement. Each has advantages and

---

[6]Cronbach's use of the term "stereotype" in this context was probably unfortunate. In context, the term refers only to the component of ratings that is consistent across targets, raters, or both. The component may or may not be inaccurate and may or may not be an actual "stereotype" of the sort addressed by the stereotypes literature. Psychology's use of the use of the term stereotype to refer to invidious portrayals of members of certain groups, along with its more technical meaning intended by Cronbach, has frequently led to confusion. "Stereotype" in Cronbach's meaning might have been better labeled "average," "baseline," "constant," or any number of other less pejorative terms. But the more familiar, albeit potentially confusing, term will be used in the present discussion.

disadvantages. The main methods are the social relations model, partial profile correlations, and item analyses.

The Social Relations Model

David Kenny's "social relations model" (SRM, e.g., Kenny, 1994) is designed to explicitly and precisely account for several components of agreement between judges' ratings. The SRM examines the agreement among judges' ratings of personality, one trait at a time. This focus on single traits, rather than profiles, bypasses the Cronbachian concern with stereotype accuracy. Indeed, Kenny points out that "Cronbach (1958) urged researchers not to measure accuracy across traits" (1994, p. 129). The SRM partitions the variance in trait ratings between the judge (or judges), the target, and their interaction.

This purpose requires a particular research design, a "round robin" in which all raters judge all targets, and vice versa.[7] The data are then entered into the model, which is based closely on the analysis of variance (and Cronbach's generalizability theory; Cronbach, Gleser, Nanda, & Rajaratman, 1972). Subsequent calculations provide estimates for the proportions of variance in ratings accounted for by the judge, the target, and the judge x target interaction.

Advantages of the Social Relations Model

The model is sophisticated and thorough. Components of judgmental agreement are not merely eliminated but instead are specifically estimated. Best of all, the method has yielded some interesting substantive findings that might not have become visible otherwise. For example, analyses using the social relations model have verified that individual judges tend to see the other people they judge as being somewhat similar to each other (Kenny, 1994). But at the same time, different judges of the same person tend to agree in their judgments, even after fairly brief acquaintance (Albright, Kenny, & Malloy, 1988). And two judges who rate each other generally do *not* describe each other as similar to themselves (Kenny, 1994).

One of Kenny's most important empirically based conclusions is that people agree with others about what they are like (self-other agreement) because both the target and the observer base their impressions on the same information, which is the target's behavior. That is, you see what I do, and I also see what I do, and this why we agree about what I generally do and therefore what I am like. This conclusion might seem obvious, and it indeed would be the most parsimonious explanation of self-other agreement even in the absence of any data. But it does directly

---

[7]One can also employ a "block" design, in which people are divided into two groups and each person interacts with all members of the other group, and a variant on the block called the "checkerboard" design, in which there are two people in each group and each person interacts with two other people (Kenny, Mohr, & Levesque, 1998). These designs have so far rarely been employed, however.

contradict the position of some theoretical perspectives in sociology, which maintain that our self-views are little more than "reflections" of the appraisals of others (see Mead, 1934; Shraugher & Schoeneman, 1979). Such theories claim, in effect, that I see myself the way I do *because* you see me that way. Kenny's conclusion is exactly the reverse.

Difficulties with the Social Relations Model

There is no perfect design for all research purposes. The right way to gather and interpret data can change depending on the phenomenon of interest. So it should be no surprise—nor be taken as unduly negative—to note that the social relations model is not perfect either. Its use entails several difficulties, which might or might not be important depending on the specific interests of the researcher.

The first problem is that full implementation of the social relations model requires a round-robin data-gathering design, in which all targets are evaluated by all judges (and generally vice versa; see also footnote 8). This procedure makes it difficult and perhaps impossible to study people who know each other well, because one's close acquaintances are seldom organized in a round-robin fashion (i.e., your friends do not all know each other as well as they know you). Furthermore, the procedure's requirements for subject recruitment and organization make it logistically difficult, time-consuming, and expensive.

This expense should not be an absolute bar, of course. But it should enter into a cost-benefit analysis for a potential researcher, who must calculate the expense of the procedure against its advantages for experimental control and data analysis. As will be discussed later, one of the main advantages of the procedure is that it controls for potential confounds such as "assumed similarity." This term refers to the possibility that close acquaintances might be similar to one another and that people might describe each other the way they see themselves. This *potential* confound is one that the round-robin design controls, but research by Funder, Kolar, and Blackman (1995) suggests its size under ordinary research circumstances may be vanishingly small (see also Stinson & Ickes, 1992). Of course, given unlimited time and resources one might wish to control for this possibility anyway. But a researcher considering the use of a round-robin design, or any other procedure, needs to consider carefully two issues: (a) Will the model allow the research questions of interest to be addressed? (b) Are the confounds for which a burdensome procedure controls of sufficient relevance or concern to justify the expense?

The social relations model also entails a couple of fairly technical difficulties that arise when one is trying to interpret its results as they are sometimes reported. First, the model does not yield measures of agreement, such as correlation coefficients, that are easily understood, nor individual accuracy scores for targets or judges. The model does a better job at comparing *relative* proportions of variance accounted for by various sources under specific circumstances than at reflecting in a more *absolute* sense how much congruence there is between ratings. Measures of interjudge agreement, such as the correlation coefficient, found in simpler analyses are easier to interpret and do provide an absolute as well as relative indication of effect size.[8]

A second complication of the social relations model is that its results are most cleanly interpretable when every judge and target has had exactly the same amount of contact with everybody else, which is difficult to ensure except under the most artificial circumstances. For example, a laboratory encounter could be set up within which people are constrained to interact with each other for exactly 5 minutes per person. However, such a context would be very artificial and I am not aware of any researcher who has attempted to do such a study. More often, researchers use class-room or living groups, which contain individuals who vary widely in how well they know each other. This variation in acquaintance is at least an important source of uncontrolled noise in the design. Occasionally, it has risen to the status of a confound, as in studies where conclusions were drawn about the development of mutual impressions in a living group, when some of the subjects had known each other for a year or more before the study even began!

A third complication is that the relative proportions of variance emphasized by the social relations model may not always be straightforwardly interpretable. Analyses using the model have occasionally yielded conclusions such as "in four . . . studies there is at least twice as much partner variance as actor variance" (Kenny & LaVoie, 1984, p. 154). Statements like this are of course accurate reports of the numbers obtained by particular studies. The problem arises with respect to their more general implications.

During the days of the person–situation debate, for a short time it was common practice to report analyses in which the proportion of behavioral variance accounted for by situations (experimental conditions) was compared to the proportion ac-counted for by persons (individual differences among subjects). An analysis by Ste-phen Golding (1975) halted these analyses in their tracks. Golding pointed out that there is a far leap from the *statistical* apportionment of variance in a particular study to the *conceptual* apportionment of variance in general.[9] To make a long story short, the basic problem is that the amount of variance contributed by any variable is critically dependent on its range (among other factors). If the range of the variable in a study is larger than its range in real life, its influence will tend to be overesti-mated. If it is smaller than in real life, its influence will tend to be underestimated. And if two variables are included in a study, one of which has a larger range of values than the other then, all other things being equal, that variable will tend to account for more overall variance and be seen as stronger. Some of the person–situation variance studies examined self-reported behavioral responses to a wide range of situations (riding a roller coaster, sitting by a lake) among people who were

---

[8]This is not to deny that the interpretation of correlation coefficients entails its own complications concerning scaling, variance, restriction of range, and other issues.

[9]Similar problems bedevil the apportionment of variance to genes versus environments in the study of behavioral genetics (Hirsch, 1986).

basically similar (college undergraduates). Not surprisingly, the usual finding in studies like this was that situations account for more variance than persons do, but the broader implications of this finding—if there are any—are far from obvious. As Golding pointed out, it would certainly be a mistake to conclude that situations matter more than persons, and it would probably be an even greater mistake to take the exact numbers yielded by these analyses terribly seriously.

A parallel concern arises in interpretations of relative proportions in the social relations model. A social relations study that uses targets who are relatively similar to each other will find less target variance than a study that uses targets who are relatively different from each other—the same goes for judges and "partner variance."[10] Even in a fully crossed design, in which every subject serves as a judge and target of all other subjects, actor variance will be restricted to the extent the sample is homogenous with respect to the properties that are judged. Partner variance will be restricted to the extent the sample is homogenous with respect to the properties that affect how one makes judgments. Very little is known about how these two kinds of properties might differ from each other, but they are not the same, and it may not be safe to assume they are equally variable. Yet this assumption is relevant to some interpretations of results from the social relations model, and it is critical to the extent that one takes seriously the exact numerical estimates that the model yields.

The SRM in Perspective

It should be made clear that in the broader context all of these comments are little more than quibbles. The social relations model prescribes both a research design and a data analytic method for estimating rather than merely attempting to eliminate or control several components of judgmental agreement. When the data or research questions match the prescriptions of this model, there is certainly no reason *not* to perform a social relations analysis. The point merely needs to be made that literal interpretations of numerical results from any quantitative analysis—not just the SRM—should *always* be looked at with a skeptical eye, and that in this as in all cases, the appropriate design and analysis depends on the research questions being asked.

Profile and Partial Correlations

A second method for assessing interjudge or self-other congruence is relatively simple and yields an agreement score for each interjudge or target-acquaintance pair. The method is to calculate either a correlation or a *partial* correlation across items between each pair of judgments. As mentioned earlier, this procedure yields

---

[10]Kenny and LaVoie (1984) have themselves noted this limitation; see also Kenny (1994).

as many correlations (or partial correlations) as there are pairs of judges in the sample.

What (if anything) the researcher should partial from these correlations, exactly, depends on the focus of the research. If the focus is on the sheer phenomenon of agreement, then no partialling at all should be performed, because to do so would distort and obscure the level of agreement that is actually observed. If, however, the focus is on *that proportion* of self-other agreement that is due to agreement about *distinctive* attributes of each target rather than about attributes all targets have in common, then one should partial out both the average self-description *and* the average description offered by all acquaintances of all targets. The prescription can be even more fine grained. If the research focus is on the ability of the judge to discriminate among different targets, then a semipartial correlation should be calculated that removes the average self-judgment of all targets. If the focus is on the ability of the target to discriminate how he or she is viewed from how others are viewed, then a semipartial correlation should be calculated that removes the average of the acquaintances' judgments.

In most (but not all) cases, the phenomenon of interest is each judge's ability to discriminate his or her target from other potential targets, so the appropriate semipartial is the one that corrects for the average self-judgment. However, three complications should be noted. The first is that in practice the average self-judgment and the average acquaintances' judgment, across targets, are highly correlated, so it actually matters little which partial or semipartial correlation is calculated. The correction is nearly the same, regardless. The case of interjudge (other-other) agreement is simpler because the only factor that is present for partialling is the average judgment across all judges and targets.

A second complication is more technical. It should be kept in mind that partial correlations are estimates based on additional variables measured with less than perfect reliability (always). As a result, partial correlations tend to be less reliable than nonadjusted correlations, and the more highly correlated either of the two variables being correlated is with the variable that is partialled, the less reliable the partial correlation will be. Sometimes, indeed, what remains after adjustment is a small and unreliable residual score that lacks the psychometric capability of correlating much with anything.

This fact is closely related to a third and very serious complication that arises from any use of partial correlations in any context: They often remove true score along with what might be considered error (Haig, 1992; Meehl, 1970). Although partial correlations are often characterized by virtuous language referring to the way they "control for," "hold constant," or even "correct" various influences, they can in fact distort as much as they clarify. It is in the very nature of a partial correlation that two (or more) variables that are nonorthogonal in nature are artificially orthogonalized. This can lead to strange "corrected" variables. For example, I have seen studies that "corrected" measures of psychopathology for social desirability! The effect of partialling is to produce a new variable that has taken on a different meaning from the original and, in some cases, may have lost its meaning altogether. For example, the meaning of a desirability-neutral pathology is obscure and perhaps absurd.

In the field of social judgment, the consequences can be nearly as bad. If one corrects for the average self-judgment as described earlier, then a rater is, in effect, penalized for knowing what people-in-general are like. For example, imagine that person A is a typical, average individual in all respects. Person B makes a personality judgment of person A, and describes A, accurately, as average. Then the average personality profile is partialled out of B's judgment. The correlation between A's personality and B's judgment will drop to 0, and B will be evaluated as having been inaccurate!

This is more than an obscure, technical problem. It is in the nature of averages that the scores of most people tend to be close to them. Agreement scores corrected for stereotype accuracy will distort estimates of overall accuracy, in a negative direction, the most for average targets who receive average ratings. To express this point another way, an accuracy score that has been corrected for stereotype accuracy will be high to the extent that the judge makes an unusual judgment of an unusual person. An average judgment of an average person will yield a lower corrected accuracy score and in an extreme case—when a perfectly average judgment is made of a perfectly average person—can yield an accuracy score of 0 even when there is a perfect match between judge and target.

The conclusion that should be drawn is this. Although it is sometimes useful to separate judges' distinctive knowledge of individuals from their knowledge of people in general, it is important to bear in mind that an adjusted score is far from easy to interpret. The worst interpretive mistake of all—and one that is occasionally seen—is to unthinkingly regard the adjusted score as virtuously improved, without considering closely what the adjustment may have done to either its psychometric properties or conceptual meaning.

Fortunately, for some purposes the correction for stereotype accuracy is unnecessary. For example, Blackman and Funder (1998) reported a study of self-other agreement that examined, in a between-groups experimental design, how such agreement increased across longer periods of behavioral observation. The agreement scores in this study were *not* adjusted or corrected in any way, because it was a true experiment. The judges were assigned randomly to different levels of information, so they could be assumed to hold equivalently accurate stereotypes, on average, across conditions. The potential confound in this case was controlled experimentally rather than statistically. To adjust the self-other agreement scores for stereotype accuracy would have served only to lower their reliability, without any corresponding gain by correcting for any artifact of possible relevance to the experimental results.

Whether a profile correlation is corrected or not, it can be a useful number. Its advantage is that it is a score that refers to each target-judge pair. This score can be correlated with other characteristics of the target to assess the nature of "judgability"

(Colvin, 1993a, 1993b). Or it can be correlated with other characteristics of the judge to assess the nature of judgmental ability (Colvin, 1993b). Or, as demonstrated by Blackman and Funder (1998), its mean level can be compared across experimental conditions to assess changes in agreement according to length of observation, context, or any other manipulated variable.

Item-Level Correlations

A final technique is to compute correlations separately for each personality item, across all judge-target or target-target pairs (e.g., Funder, 1980b; Funder & Dobroth, 1987; Funder & Colvin, 1988). Like the SRM, this technique has the advantage of obviating some of the concerns that arise with profile correlations, such as stereotype accuracy and the disadvantage of making certain phenomena—such as individual differences in judgmental ability—extremely cumbersome or even impossible to address. On the other hand, it enhances the ability to address other phenomena, such as the judgmental properties of different personality traits.

The method bypasses the issue of stereotype accuracy because it correlates single item ratings across targets rather than all items within targets. When a correlation is computed between acquaintances' and self-ratings on a single item across targets, the result is a number that is *not* enhanced by stereotype accuracy. In fact, any influence is in the reverse direction. If all subjects in a sample were simply to guess the mean "stereotype" for a given item, then this item would receive the same score from all judges or targets. Holding either variable in a correlation constant of course makes the calculation impossible (it entails a division by 0); as either variable *approaches* constancy the correlation will be attenuated and tend to approach 0. Thus, any tendency by raters to give the same, stereotypic ratings to all targets will attenuate rather than enhance item correlations.

Complications with Item Correlations

Item correlations still entail two complications. The first, as mentioned earlier, is that item correlations do not yield accuracy scores for individual targets or judges. This makes it difficult to analyze individual differences in judgability or judgmental ability. But it is not impossible. If, for example, a researcher were interested in a moderator variable hypothesized to affect judgmental ability, the researcher could divide the subject sample into two subsamples, of those subjects who scored above and below the median on that variable. If the "high" group yielded larger agreement correlations than the "low" group, then the hypothesis would be supported. However, this is a relatively crude analysis prey to all the shortcomings, including information loss, entailed by median split analysis.[11] Moderated multiple regression,

---

[11] Given a sufficient N the subject sample could of course be divided more finely (e.g., into thirds or quartiles) but the suboptimality of the analysis is in principle the same.

which allows the moderator variable to be treated as a continuous variable, uses more information but is also more difficult to interpret (see Bernieri, Zuckerman, Koestener, & Rosenthal, 1994, for a comparative use of these techniques). In a simpler case, if one has a genuine categorical variable—such as gender—hypothesized to affect judgmental ability, then the sample could be divided on this variable and the resulting analysis, calculating accuracy scores separately within each subsample, would be as good as any that is possible.

In general, item analyses are better suited for addressing other issues, such as differences between items. For example, Funder and Dobroth (1987) showed how more visible traits yielded better self-other and other-other agreement than did less visible traits (see also Funder, 1980a; Funder & Colvin, 1988). They did this by correlating self-other correlations, across items, with independent ratings of the items' visibility.

The second complication is potentially more vexing. The use of item correlations indeed escapes artifactual enhancement from stereotype accuracy of the sort Cronbach identified, the tendency that all judges might have to give the same description to all targets, regardless of any influence that might be particular to a given target (or judge). However, much of the research from our lab has recruited pairs (or larger numbers) of judges for *each* target person. We do this to obtain individuals who know each target well enough, in real life, to provide a good description of his or her personality. The potential disadvantage of this practice is that, to use the technical term, judges are now "nested" within targets. Each target has a unique set of judges.

Cronbach, who did not address the case where judges are nested within targets, did not consider this situation. However, it does raise a Cronbachian-type issue, which could be called "*differential* stereotype accuracy." This term refers to the possibility that judges each hold stereotypes of people in general that *differ* from those held by other judges. This possibility can become a potential confound if judges are nested within targets, and the differential stereotypes of judges are correlated with properties of their particular targets.

This is the situation that arises with regard to what Cronbach (1955) and others have called "assumed similarity." In the present context, the term refers to a special case of differential stereotype accuracy.[12] It refers to an interpretation of the acquaintance effect, the robust and repeated finding that self-other agreement is greater for target-acquaintance pairs that have known each other for longer periods of time. The simplest explanation of this effect, of course, is that all other things being equal, to know someone longer is to know them better. However, the concept of assumed similarity has been invoked to explain away the acquaintance effect as an artifact.

---

[12]Although Cronbach coined the term "assumed similarity" he did not discuss it as a basis for acquaintance effects or consider nested designs. The logic relating these concerns was outlined in detail by Kenny (1994 and elsewhere) and was also considered by Funder (1980a).

The explanation works like this. First, in the natural environment people detect which other people have personalities that are similar to their own. Second, they selectively form relationships with these people, rather than with those who are dissimilar. Third, when a researcher asks these people to describe someone they know, *they do not describe that target*. Rather, they describe themselves. As a result, their description will tend to resemble the self-description of their target, not because they have come to know the person better than a stranger would, but only because they happen to be similar to the target and "assume similarity" in their description of him or her.

This process has been touted by more than one psychologist as a reasonable explanation of the acquaintance effect. Indeed, some literature reviews have concluded that findings of an acquaintance effect in nested designs are illegitimate and uninformative. But before drawing that conclusion and deciding that nested designs must all be discarded in favor of crossed designs such as the round robin, one should consider some relevant theoretical and empirical considerations.

On a theoretical level, notice that the artifactual explanation of the acquaintance effect is complex, nonparsimonious, and even slightly self-contradictory. For it to be correct, people somehow must identify the *strangers* in their social environment who happen to have similar personalities. Then they must form relationships only with those people. Then they must, in effect, disregard a researcher's request to describe someone they know. They must, instead, describe themselves.

Perhaps each of these things does happen. Perhaps people are strangely sensitive to similar personalities in others, but if they do, this is an example of accurate personality judgment that the artifactual explanation seems otherwise at pains to deny occurs. Or perhaps people live in social groups that are homogenous with respect to personality but different enough from other social groups to allow accuracy correlations to occur across comparisons with members of other groups. And perhaps when asked to describe someone else the average subject is so mystified that he or she falls back on the only person he or she knows well enough to describe— the self.

None of these possibilities is simple, and it is easy to imagine research programs to verify the degree to which any of these happen. Such studies are rarely conducted, but one was reported by Funder, Kolar, and Blackman (1995). Their study looked at two aspects of the artifactual process described here. First, it asked, are natural acquaintances—the judges in a nested design—*actually* more similar to each other than to other people chosen at random? Second, when asked to describe an acquaintance, do judges provide descriptions that are distinctive to that individual, or do they merely offer descriptions of themselves? Perhaps surprisingly, the answer to both questions turned out to be no.

The study by Funder et al. was drawn from a data set in which the standard acquaintance effect was found. Target-selected acquaintances provided judgments that agreed better with targets' self-judgments than did randomly assigned strangers (who viewed them only for 5 minutes on a video). Out of 200 comparisons,[13] self-acquaintance agreement was higher than self-stranger agreement for 154. But the nesting of judges within targets raised the specter of assumed similarity.

Although the potential was there, the reality was quite different. Even though the acquaintanceship effect was strong, *no* tendency was evident for targets to be more similar to their acquaintances than to strangers. The average self-acquaintance similarity correlation across *the same items on which the acquaintanceship effect was found* was very near 0 ($r = .025$) and very close to the average self-stranger similarity correlation ($r = .015$; see Funder et al., 1995, Table 5; see also Stinson & Ickes, 1992). Moreover, assumed similarity was an important component of judgment *only for strangers,* exactly the reverse of the situation assumed by the assumed similarity hypothesis. For acquaintances, the contribution of their own distinctive description, over and above their own self-description, contributed significantly more to their accuracy than did their self-description alone. For strangers, the situation was reversed. The most important contribution to their accuracy was their own self-description; their distinctive description of the target added only a small amount to the validity of their judgments.

In a related vein, Baron, Albright and Malloy (1995) found that judges use stereotypes as an important basis for their judgment *only* when they have little information about the target. In this situation, it appears, judges fill in the missing information with general stereotypes or even, as we saw earlier, their own self-description (which itself is a sort of stereotype if applied to the judgment of others; Hoch, 1987). When you know someone well you can base your judgments on what you have seen. When you have little information, you fall back on stereotypes and self-knowledge.

Even this process seems to be selective. In a recent study, Vogt and Colvin (1998) found that the best judges of personality—"communal" individuals, according to their data—were those who knew when to use and not use assumed similarity ("projection") and stereotype information. They were most likely to use projection and stereotype information when judging targets similar to themselves and to the typical person, and they were less likely to utilize these processes when describing a target dissimilar to themselves or to the typical person. This variation in the use of stereotypes enhanced their judgmental accuracy (see also Hoch, 1987).

The assumed similarity hypothesis raises a legitimate possibility that deserved to be directly addressed. However, a close conceptual and empirical analysis indicates that it is extremely unlikely to provide a sufficient explanation of the acquaintance effect. The general lesson is this. When a researcher contemplates the use of a burdensome research design the main virtue of which is that it controls for unlikely artifacts, while raising the cost of research and making certain

---

[13] 100 Q-items were compared for two separate sets of pairings of acquaintances and strangers.

questions impossible to address, the benefits need to be carefully weighed against the costs.

BEHAVIORAL PREDICTION

Behavior is difficult to study, and it sometimes seems as if social and personality psychologists have therefore avoided it whenever they can. When trying to assess the accuracy of a personality judgment, it is much easier to calculate the degree to which it agrees with the target's self-judgment (despite the complications noted here) than it is to gather a reasonable sample of behaviors with which the judgment should be correlated if it is accurate. Nonetheless, behavioral prediction does offer attractive possibilities as a criterion for accuracy. If a personality judgment were to be accurate, it ought to be of some use in predicting the behavior of the person it describes. And, the criterion of behavioral prediction neatly gets around the kinds of measurement artifacts that plague the calculation and interpretation of interjudge agreement. For these reasons, several investigators have urged accuracy research to move beyond interjudge agreement to the examination of behavioral predictability (e.g., Funder, 1987, 1995a; Kenny, 1994).

Although behavioral criteria might seem to provide a gold standard for personality judgment, they are not without significant interpretational problems of their own. Most centrally, behavioral prediction has an asymmetric relationship with accuracy that is opposite to that described earlier with regard to interjudge agreement. As has been noted, accuracy implies agreement but agreement does not necessarily imply accuracy. In the case of behavioral prediction the situation is reversed. A judgment that can predict a behavior is accurate about something. But a judgment that cannot predict a particular behavior still might be "right" in the sense that it could be used to predict some other behavior.

For example, say a researcher is trying to evaluate the accuracy of the judgments of the "friendliness" of a group of target persons. The behavioral criterion chosen is how much the target persons are observed to smile. Say the researcher finds no correlation between friendliness ratings and smiling. Does this mean the friendliness ratings are wrong? Not necessarily, because the fault could just as well be in the criterion. Perhaps smiling is not actually a valid indicator of real friendliness. Perhaps if the researcher counted, instead, the number of conversations the target persons have per day, the friendliness rating might predict that (or some other criterion).

The point is that a failure of predictive validity is in principle equally likely to be the fault of choosing the wrong criterion as of the judgment itself being wrong. The researcher's difficult task is to match the *right*—not just any—behavior with a particular personality judgment, and this matching is always questionable, unless it works. This is why it is easier to use behavioral criteria to show that a judgment is right than it is to show that a judgment is wrong.

Choosing Situations and Behaviors

Beyond these interpretational conundrums, serious logistical and procedural difficulties are entailed in observing behaviors to be used as criteria for judgment. The researcher must set up a reasonable context for natural-enough behavior to occur, place a sufficient number of subjects in that context, and then code the right behaviors in a reliable and valid fashion. Each of these steps deserves comment.

Choosing Situations

It is no small matter to select and design a manageable set of experimental contexts in which subjects can be placed and in which some sort of reasonably meaningful behavior can then be expected to appear. As has frequently been noted, for all the sometime popularity of "situationism" in psychology, the field lacks an organized psychology of situations that would tell us what the important properties of situations are or how commonly they occur in real life (see Chapter 2). When trying to create a reasonable range of experimental situations, therefore, the researcher has only the loosest of intuitions to serve as a guide. Some of our own efforts to capture behavior "live," in reasonably realistic experimental contexts, will be described here. Our procedures, which place subjects into unscripted situations of various types where their behavior can be recorded on videotape, were originally inspired by William Ickes's pathbreaking work observing dyadic interaction in quasi-naturalistic settings (Ickes, 1983; Ickes, Bissonette, Garcia, & Stinson, 1990).

My research collaborators and I designed seven experimental situations for the Riverside Accuracy Project. We deemed this number the maximum feasible for our projected total of 160 target subjects. The situations varied along several explicit dimensions, according to the degree they (a) were unstructured, competitive, or cooperative, (b) involved interaction with a same-sex friend or opposite-sex stranger, and (c) involved a dyadic or a group interaction. The design thus includes two unstructured interactions, one with an opposite-sex, randomly assigned stranger and one with a same-sex, self-chosen acquaintance. The subjects also played a competitive game (Simon®) and completed a cooperative task (building a tinker-toy) with the same two individuals. The first two dimensions were crossed, and so that part of our procedure can be considered a 3 (structure) x 2 (partner) repeated measures design. Finally, the subjects engaged in a group discussion with four or five same-sex peers. As can be imagined, the logistical difficulties of setting up and running these seven procedures with a total of 160 subjects were formidable, and the task occupied several graduate students over a period of 3 years.

We believe the situations employed in our research varied along dimensions that are meaningful in real life, but other dimensions could have been chosen and perhaps would have been by other investigators. Moreover, even seven situations—more than in any previous research of which we are aware—is a paltry sample of the range of contexts that exist in real life. And compromises were necessary. For example, our stranger-acquaintance dimension was confounded with our same-sex opposite-sex dimension, a fact that we regret but were unable to overcome without either abandoning one of these dimensions or doubling the size of an already very expensive and time-consuming study.

A further source of difficulty with this kind of research is that the implications of its findings are limited, strictly speaking, to the specific contexts and behaviors that are employed, a fact sure to catch the notice of journal and grant reviewers. However, this limitation is no more or less true of this research than any other. Moreover, the inventory of psychological knowledge about the relationships between personality and directly observed behavior is embarrassingly thin, as was noted in Chapter 2. Despite the inherent difficulties, we hope the community of researchers manages to resist discouragement and persists with attempts to directly observe social behavior and assess its relations with personality.

Choosing Behaviors

A further issue is the choice of which behaviors to assess. The typical social psychological experiment includes one behavioral dependent variable. For a more thorough characterization of the subjects' behavior, we designed a technique to code 64 behaviors from each subject (the Behavioral Q-sort; Funder, Furr, & Colvin, 1998). These behaviors were chosen from a close study of the videotapes, along with an examination of the personality Q-sort and an attempt to write behavioral items that offered the possibility of being relevant to the personality items.

We might have coded behaviors in many different ways, of course, ranging from micro-measurements of movements of the facial musculature to quite general evaluations of the quality of social interaction. The trick for present purposes, as we saw it, was to capture behavior at a level of analysis that has most relevance to personality, to the general way a person is psychologically made up and lives his or her real life.

Some theories of interpersonal perception and personality are based on counts of "behaviors" or "acts" (e.g., Buss & Craik, 1983; Kenny, 1994). Unfortunately, no one has yet proposed a usable technique for counting behaviors or even identifying exactly what one behavior is. Consider the question of how many behaviors you, the reader, have performed so far today. How is such a number to be formulated? This is an issue that deserves more conceptual attention than it has so far received.

Assuming this issue can be avoided for now, another question arises. What level of analysis is the most appropriate for describing behavior? Some investigators are attracted to quite concrete, microlevel behaviors. For example, it has been suggested that friendliness should be indexed by smiling. But of course matters are not nearly so simple. People smile for many reasons, friendliness being only one of them. In our research, we have followed the principle that the level of analysis of what you are trying to predict should match the level of analysis of the predictor of interest

(Cairns & Green, 1979). If a researcher is interested in the accuracy of general personality judgments such as "is sociable," then the researcher needs to assess "sociable behavior" rather than smiles, words spoken, or other lower-level actions that might have many different meanings. This was the principle behind the development of the Riverside Behavioral Q-sort (RBQ), which attempts to measure behavior with adequate reliability through the use of multiple raters, while remaining at a level of analysis equivalent to the personality judgments to which we hope they are relevant (Funder, Furr & Colvin, 1998).

The putative advantage of coding more concrete, low-level behaviors is that such codings are seemingly more objective and reliable. However, that has not been our experience. Before the RBQ was developed, an early coding scheme in our research was designed to measure interpersonal distance, describe body posture, count the number of laughs and interruptions, and so forth. After being used for several months, the scheme was abandoned, for several reasons. First, it was extremely tedious and time-consuming. To code a single 5-minute segment required about 2 hours. Second, the reliabilities were not as high as one might have hoped (and no higher than those from the "less objective" RBQ developed later). Third, when all was done, it appeared that the essence of what had happened in the taped interaction had managed to escape the coding scheme. It was difficult to fit meaningful behaviors into such narrow categories, and so we ended up changing our entire approach, with some success (see Funder & Colvin, 1991).

The wisdom of using more general characterizations of phenomena rather than low-level and concrete operationalizations was eloquently described, in a different context, by the perceptual psychologist J. J. Gibson (1979, p. 100):

> Ecological events are various and difficult to formulate. But when we attempt to reduce them to elementary physical events, they become impossibly complex, and physical complexity then blinds us to ecological simplicity. . . . A too strict adherence to mechanics has thus hampered the study of terrestrial events.

The Procedural Burden

In our research, four independent coders, who were not allowed to view more than one segment for each target subject, viewed each videotaped behavioral segment. (The purpose was to keep estimates of cross-situational consistency uncontaminated.) This practice meant that an enormous number of coders had to be trained and supervised, and great efforts were made to ensure the quality control of the ongoing coding. The coding technique itself—the Riverside Behavioral Q-sort (Funder, Furr & Colvin, 1998)—was developed through several iterations over the course of more than 10 years. This kind of research is not easy.

These necessary complications and burdens should be borne strongly in mind by anyone who regards behavioral prediction as the gold standard for judging accuracy in personality judgment. The criterion is a reasonable one, and greater efforts should be put into it over the coming years. But nobody should be under any illusions that the right contexts or the right behaviors are easy or obvious to choose, or that the necessary procedures are more than rarely feasible within the resources available to the typical researcher.

Personality and Behavior

Even assuming all of these difficulties can be overcome, there still remains the critical issue of exactly how to use behavioral prediction as a criterion for accuracy in personality judgment. One problem is that a single behavior is not always or perhaps even usually very informative about personality (Epstein, 1979, 1980). Transient situational influences indeed affect what a person does at a given moment—Mischel (1968) was correct to this extent—and the influence of personality tends to emerge only over time and across situations. The limitations of behavioral research to date—even including the ambitious project described earlier—are quite severe in this respect. At best only a handful of situations are employed, making it difficult although not impossible for personality to emerge from the average of behaviors across them.

A second reason is that there is no reason to expect a one-to-one relationship between any personality trait and any behavior. A given behavior is due to a complex combination of personality and situational factors, and Ahadi and Diener (1989) demonstrated how a behavior influenced by as few as three traits would be extremely difficult to predict from any one. So we probably ought to be lenient when interpreting correlations between personality judgments and behavioral observations; sometimes I am astonished that not all of them are 0. More informative than the absolute level of predictability are the variables that moderate this level in a relative sense. For example, Kolar, Funder, and Colvin (1996) compared the ability of self-judgments versus peer judgments to predict behavior. Funder and Colvin (1991) compared the predictability of behaviors that differed along several dimensions.

The Meaning of Prediction

A technical consideration that arises in this context is the issue of what exactly is to be meant by behavioral prediction. In the accuracy literature, this term seldom if ever refers to an actual prediction that a judge makes in the form of "I predict Joe will speak first in the group interaction." Rather, the term prediction is employed in the sense of regression, in which the correlation between the personality judgment and the (hopefully) relevant behavioral criterion is an index of the predictive validity of the judgment.

This predictive correlation can be calculated in two ways. One way is to choose extremely broad behavioral criteria, such as aggregate factors derived from our Behavioral Q-sort items. The judges' ratings are similarly reduced to factors (usually five) and a multiple regression is calculated that reflects the capacity of these five factors in the judgments to predict each of the behavioral factors (e.g., Kolar et al., 1996). Another way to assess predictability is to select behaviors that one believes, on a priori grounds, to be relevant to certain personality characteristics. For example, 39 items in the Riverside Behavioral Q-sort were written to match items in the personality Q-set almost exactly. To name just one, RBQ item 8, "Exhibits social skills," was intended to provide an overt behavioral reflection of California Adult Q-sort (CAQ) item 92, "Has social poise and presence, appears to be socially at ease." The correlation between these two items, the first derived from a coding of a videotape and second derived from an observer's judgment, is treated as an index of the ability of the judgment to predict behavior (e.g., Funder & Colvin, 1991; Kolar, Funder, & Colvin, 1996).

GENERAL ISSUES OF DESIGN AND ANALYSIS

A final couple of issues are of general relevance to research in psychology but are particularly poignant with regard to research on the accuracy of personality judgment. These issues involve the distinction between experimental and correlational designs, and psychology's growing infatuation with analytic methods that are new, complex, and sometimes dangerous.

Experimental versus Correlational Designs

Experimental and correlational designs are not as fundamentally different as they are sometimes portrayed in textbooks. Both entail assessment of the relationship between an independent variable and a dependent variable. In experimental research, the independent variable is generally considered to be a *cause* of the dependent variable. For example, the content of the stimulus essay in the Jones-Harris (1967) study was varied across two conditions, and the difference in imputed attitudes was inferred to have been caused by this difference in content. In correlational research, the independent variable (traditionally labeled X) is viewed as a *predictor*— not necessarily a cause—of the dependent variable (traditionally labeled Y). For example, acquaintances' personality judgments in the Funder-Colvin (1991) study were found to be correlated with targets' behaviors in the laboratory. This relationship is not really causal; the inference is that the acquaintances' judgments and the targets' behaviors were both caused by the actual personalities of the targets.[14]

---

[14]Notice how the "third variable" in this case is *not* a confound but the underlying (latent) variable of interest.

Traditional social psychological research on person perception, and research on error in particular, typically employs experimental designs. Stimulus properties of *artificial* targets are experimentally manipulated, and the effects of these stimuli on judgment are the phenomena of interest. The use of artificial stimulus persons is concomitant with the use of experimental designs—only the properties of a hypothetical target can be experimentally manipulated.

Research on accuracy, by contrast, typically uses correlational designs. The study of accuracy requires the inclusion of stimulus persons who have real characteristics that a judge can be accurate about. In the paradigmatic case, a target's actual self-judgments are correlated with acquaintance's judgments of him or her, or judgments of a target's personality are correlated with direct measurements of his or her behavior.

Every methodological textbook I have ever seen touts the advantages of experimental over correlational designs. This may be one reason why accuracy research (along with personality research) still retains, in some circles, a slightly disreputable patina. The definitive advantage of an experimental design, it is said, is that it allows the imputation of causality. When some aspect of experimental procedure is varied across conditions, and the behavior of randomly assigned subjects varies across those conditions, one can say that the experimental variation caused the behavioral variation. Correlational designs, it is said, suffer from a "third variable" problem. Even if X is shown to be related to Y, it might not have caused Y. Both X and Y might be caused by some third variable (Z?). Some treatments of this topic go so far as to then claim that correlational designs are therefore inferior, and experimental designs should be used exclusively or at least whenever remotely possible.

The claims are wrong and the advice is bad. Experimental designs entail problems and correlational designs entail advantages that are not always appreciated. For example, because in experimental designs the values of the independent variable are selected and fixed, they can (and sometimes do) take on arbitrary values not found in nature. It is easy to have a difference in the independent variable across experimental conditions that is implausibly larger than any difference found in real life. This fact is sometimes touted as an advantage as well, because it allows for experimental designs to be more "sensitive." However, it also exaggerates the estimate of the size of the effect of the independent variable. Correlational designs, by contrast, use the range of the independent variable that is actually found in real life—more precisely, in a sample of actual subjects. The estimate of effect size from an experimental design, therefore, is likely to be uninformative and probably misleadingly large. The estimate of effect size from a correlational design, however, is more likely to be both informative and realistic.

Even more important is the fact that experimental designs also entail the third variable problem. The experimenter knows what affected subjects' behavior only at a superficial, operational level. That is, the experimenter knows how the experimental procedure varied across conditions. What the experimenter does *not* know is exactly which *psychological* aspect of the procedural variation was important. For example, the subjects in Jones-Harris might have been affected by the content of the essay, its mere provision, experimenter demand characteristics, or some combination of all of these. The way to get around this problem is through what Brunswik (1956) called *representative design*. A *series* of experiments must be performed, which uses a variety of procedures that samples from the many possible ways the *psychological* independent variable might be operationalized. If all of these experiments, each operationalizing the psychological independent variable in a different way, obtain the predicted results, then and only then can we begin to have confidence we know what the true causal factor is. However, representative design is almost never employed in social or in any other branch of experimental psychology.

The correction for the third variable problem in correlational designs is exactly analogous, and more often employed. First, of course, the third variable is not always a problem. As in the example of a judgment predicting a behavior, the latent third variable—the target's actual personality—is exactly what the research is trying to approach through both the judgment and the behavioral measurement.

When third variables are worrisome, however, the solution is the same as in the experimental case, to *also* include in the research as many of the plausible candidates as possible. Then one can check whether other variables besides the X variable of interest are associated with the Y or account for the relationship between X and Y. One never can include all possible third variables any more than representative design could check all possible experimental manipulations, but in both cases the wider the net that is cast, the more confidence one can have in the completeness of the catch.

Data Analysis

As we have seen, the analysis of accuracy in personality judgment entails the charting of complex webs of relationships between judgments of personality, indicators of personality, and personality itself. This enterprise is basically correlational in nature, which means that such research draws heavily on data analytic techniques based on a regression framework.

At its root, regression is simple and elegant. The general linear model ties a host of experimental and correlational analytic techniques to a common conceptual base. The Pearson *r*, the familiar correlation coefficient, is an ingenious invention that cleanly captures the covariation among variables while removing differences in their means and variances. Moreover, the *r* is easy to interpret, as long as one has the wisdom to avoid the traditional confusion entailed by squaring it to yield a "percentage of variance explained." The text by Jerry Wiggins (1973) and the article by Dan Ozer (1985) clearly explain a number of ways to interpret the *r*. Funder and Ozer (1983) provided some comparative benchmarks from the literature of experimental social psychology, and Rosenthal and Rubin's (1982) Binomial Effect Size Display allow quick translation from the r to actual outcomes of prediction.

Recent years have seen an explosion of new regression-based techniques, some of which are fearsomely complex. David Kenny's (1994) social relations model is essentially an extension of Cronbach's generalizability theory and involves complex partitionings of variance into orthogonalized sources. The techniques of structural equation modeling (SEM) such as LISREL (Joreskog & Sorbom, 1993) and EQS (Bentler, 1995) allow complex patterns of relationships—some perhaps causal—to be drawn between large numbers of variables simultaneously.

Judiciously employed, these can be useful techniques. But a couple of cautions are in order. First, they are easy to misapply. Structural equation modeling, in particular, is still characterized by a plethora of program limitations, analytic conventions, rules of thumb, fit indices, and so forth. Finding the "standard" way to do SEM analysis can be difficult and might not be possible because the right thing to do varies with the exact research circumstances (Hoyle, 1995; Williams, 1995). Few researchers, at present, are competent to make such decisions.

Competence aside, even experienced researchers face pitfalls with these techniques (Cliff, 1983; Freedman, 1991). The main pitfall is that the numbers yielded by such complex analyses are not easy to interpret in a psychological way. Exact proportions of variance are computed, or three different fit indexes are displayed to the fourth decimal point, but the meaning of these numbers—and the wisdom of pretending such precision—is often doubtful. One reason for this doubtfulness, as already discussed in the context of the social relations model, is that the numbers can move around considerably depending on such nonsubstantive factors as the range and reliability of the variables included and even the number of subjects recruited. Another reason is that all of the modern regression techniques rely heavily on the notion of the partial correlation.[15] The partial correlation is a tricky number to interpret because, as was discussed earlier in connection with profile correlations, a correlation between two variables with the influence of some other variable "partialled," "corrected," or "controlled" no longer reflects the actual relationship between those two variables in nature. Something that is a natural part of their relationship has been taken out. This removal may in some cases clarify interpretation of what remains. But it is as easy to remove true score as error and when considered closely partial correlations—and the resulting path coefficients in structural equation modeling—can turn out to be strange and distorted shadows of their former, uncorrected selves (Haig, 1992; Meehl, 1970).

For these reasons, I strongly urge the practice of examining data sets—especially complex data sets—as thoroughly as possible using the simplest possible methods. I sometimes tell my graduate students, not really facetiously, that they are forbidden to use anything more complicated than a *t*-test or zero-order (uncorrected) *r* until

---

[15]I have heard it said that structural equation modeling amounts to a complicated combination of partial correlations and the correction for attenuation. Or at another level, it is combination of path analysis and factor analysis. Either way, it inherits all of the complications and pitfalls of its component parts.

they are absolutely certain about what the data show. The more complex techniques are sometimes subsequently useful as a way of summarizing the complex patterns already understood. But they are extremely hazardous vehicles for the exploration of unknown terrain.

CONCLUSION

After surveying some of the factors that complicate the study of judgmental accuracy, Schneider et al. (1979) commented that the topic had "lost some of its intuitive charm" (p. 222). The updated survey in the present chapter may cause the reader to sympathize with Schneider's position. The topic is indeed fraught with difficulties ranging from complications in the exact calculation of the proper index of self-other agreement to philosophical conundrums concerning the ultimate knowability of reality.

Whatever damage these complications do to the topic's charm, however, they do not lessen its importance. As was argued in Chapter 1, the topic of accuracy in personality judgment contains both too much intrinsic interest and potential for application to be long ignored. Moreover, although the complications surveyed here and elsewhere are indeed serious, none of them makes accuracy research impossible. Indeed, at rock bottom I have my doubts it is really any more difficult than any other topic in psychology; it is just a field in which the difficulties have been made more explicit and therefore are better understood. I wonder how many other areas of research in psychology would benefit from the kind of close philosophical and methodological critique to which accuracy research has been subjected for more than four decades.

CHAPTER 5

The Process of Accurate Personality Judgment

Accurate personality judgment is the result of events that occur in the interpersonal world as well as within the mind of each judge. Therefore, the psychological process of accurate judgment is as much social as it is cognitive. The process begins with the person who is judged, who expresses or gives off information about his or her personality into the social environment. This information must then be picked up and used correctly by a social perceiver. If all goes well, the result is that the social perceiver is able to render a judgment of the target person's personality that matches one or more of his or her actual attributes.

THE REALISTIC ACCURACY MODEL

The theoretical analysis of the process of personality judgment to be presented here is called the Realistic Accuracy Model (or RAM[1]; Funder, 1995a). The most characteristic aspect of the model is its focus on *accurate* personality judgment. This focus

---

[1] I should apologize for this regrettable acronym, which not only sounds unduly aggressive but unfortunately rhymes with David Kenny's model, which he has dubbed "WAM" (Kenny, 1994).

on accuracy leads it to be unusual in two ways. First, the process of achieving accuracy encompasses the cognitive mechanisms of the judge, the actual attributes of the target, and the way information about the latter enters the former during transactions in the social environment. So the present model of accurate personality judgment stands in contrast to standard cognitive models of person perception, which typically contain all their action within the skull of the perceiver. Second, the model's focus on accuracy leads its overall orientation to be positive. RAM is not oriented toward searching for flaws in judgment that must be alleviated. Rather, it is oriented toward a search for capacities and possibilities for accurate judgment that might not always be fully utilized.

Basic Assumptions

The Realistic Accuracy Model begins with three assumptions. The first is that personality traits actually do, "realistically," exist. A reader who will not grant this assumption, at least for purposes of examining where it leads, might as well stop here. There is nothing further to talk about. If personality traits do not exist, then it makes no sense to study the processes by which they can be accurately judged.

To be sure, the long debate over the merits of personality trait concepts and the consistency of behavior, surveyed in Chapter 2, is likely to continue to simmer for decades more. And many psychologists, especially some who work outside the immediate area of personality, are still influenced by the dominant view of 20 years ago and regard personality traits as discredited concepts.

Still, it is worth considering what we might gain if, even for purposes of a temporary truce, we consider the issue settled in favor of the existence of personality. In this light, a range of issues concerning development, structure, and dynamics returns to the fore (Goldberg, 1993). It begins to make sense to consider how one person could ever make an accurate judgment of the personality traits of another.

RAM's second assumption is that people sometimes make judgments of the personality traits of others (and of themselves, see Chapter 7). As was discussed in Chapters 1 and 3, this assumption has been questioned by some Gibsonian theorists, who argue that we perceive use-values or "affordances" rather than abstract qualities such as traits. This argument stems from the Gibsonian dictum that "perception is for doing" (Zebrowitz & Collins, 1997).

Although this dictum is no doubt often correct, three responses can be made to it. First, it seems doubtful that *all* perception is for doing. At least some perception, it seems, is aimed at learning the structure of the physical and social world for its own sake.[2]1 Second, the distinction between perceiving a person as "somebody

---

[2]As was mentioned earlier, if it is claimed that perceivers learn about the nature of their world to stockpile knowledge that at some point might conceivably be useful, then the Gibsonian dictum loses much of its power and distinctiveness.

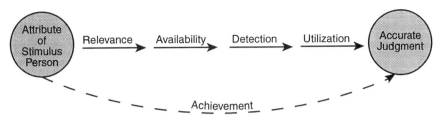

FIGURE 5-1   The realistic accuracy model. Adapted from Funder, D. C. (1995). On the accuracy of personality judgment: A realistic approach. *Psychological Review, 102,* 659, Figure 1. Copyright 1995 by the American Psychological Association. Adapted by permission of the publisher.

who will not rebuff me" (and so "affords" social interaction) and as "somebody who is friendly" (an abstract quality) is not completely clear. Many if not all trait terms seem to imply affordances almost directly, so the perception of an affordance often *is* tantamount to the perception of a trait, and vice versa. Third, even if the arguments just made are not accepted, the Realistic Accuracy Model really requires that the reader grant only this: that people make judgments of personality traits *sometimes.* This small concession is sufficient to bring us to the third assumption.

The third assumption is that these judgments of personality traits, that are made at least sometimes, are accurate at least sometimes. It is *not* necessary, for present purposes, to assume that the judgments are usually accurate, or even often accurate. All that is required is that the reader be willing to grant that lay perceivers have *ever,* even once, achieved accuracy in personality judgment.

Again, if this assumption is not granted then there is nothing more to talk about. But if it is, then an important question immediately arises: How? The purpose of the Realistic Accuracy Model is to explain how accurate personality judgment could ever be achieved.

How Accuracy Is Possible

If accurate personality judgment is to be achieved, four things must happen. First, the person being judged must do something—give off some kind of information— that is relevant to the aspect of personality to be judged. Second, this information must be in a form and a location where the judge can get it. Third, the information must register on his or her nervous system. Finally, the judge must interpret it correctly. If all four processes occur flawlessly, the resulting judgment of personality will be accurate. RAM's labels for these four steps of accurate judgment are, respectively, *relevance, availability, detection,* and *utilization.* These four steps comprise the core of the Realistic Accuracy Model (RAM; Funder, 1995a), portrayed in Figure 5-1.

Egon Brunswik (1956) conceptualized accuracy as the connection between the actual properties of a distal stimulus and a judgment of those properties (represented here as a dotted line at the bottom of Figure 5-1). He called the successful establishment of such a connection "achievement," and this term has been used here as well. The heart of the model, the description of the several steps between the distal stimulus and the accurate judgment of it, is also Brunswikian (Funder, in press). Brunswik spoke of the informational cues that are visible properties of objects, some of which are useful or have "ecological validity" with respect to the judgment being made. No cue has perfect validity; the relationship between cues and reality is always probabilistic (Brunswik's "probabilistic functionalism"). Moreover, only some of these cues, of varying validity, are likely to be actually used in any particular instance, depending on the perceiver's "cue utilization." RAM focuses on Brunswik's paths from the stimulus to the cue, and from the cue to judgment, breaking each of these paths, in turn, into two steps for a total of four.

Each of these four steps has important implications both for how personality can be known and how its judgment might be improved, as we shall see over the next four chapters. Chapter 6 will survey the major moderators of accuracy in personality judgment and attempt to account for each in terms of the Realistic Accuracy Model. Chapter 7 will begin to apply RAM to the problem of self-knowledge, and Chapter 8 will examine some prospects for improving accuracy. This chapter is concerned with the model itself: its structure, steps, and general implications.

THE STRUCTURE OF RAM

The assertion embodied in RAM is that for an accurate judgment of personality to ever occur, four things *must* happen. The range and sequence of these four events provides the basic structure of the model.

Basic Structure

First, the person in question must emit some kind of information that is *relevant* to the trait to be judged. Typically, this information takes the form of some kind of behavior. For example, if the trait to be judged is "courageousness," then the person must do something brave (leading to a high rating on this trait), cowardly (leading to a low rating), or in between (leading to a medium rating). If the person does not do something relevant, the process of accurate personality judgment can never get started because it has nothing to go on.[3] In some cases, however, the target of

---

[3]Of course, a perceiver might guess or invoke an invalid stereotype. The process of person perception can begin with anything. But the process of *accurate* personality judgment begins with relevant information.

judgment might more passively emit cues to personality such as aspects of physical appearance or grooming. Either way, the process of accurate judgment begins with the target and the relevant information that the target either provides or gives off.

Once this has happened, the relevant information must become *available* to a judge. For example, the judge must be present where and when the relevant behavior occurs. If somebody does something very brave but no one is there to see it, then the process of others accurately judging the person's courageousness will be stymied until and unless the person does something else relevant that does become available. Or if one judge is present and another is absent at the time, only the one who was present has the information available along with the opportunity for accurate judgment.

Third, the judge must *detect* the relevant, available information. The detection may not always be conscious or explicit, but obviously the informative stimulus must register in some way on the judge's nervous system. A judge who is inattentive, distracted, or otherwise imperceptive may fail to register any number of relevant, available actions, and thereby lose any chance of making an accurate judgment.

Fourth and finally, the judge must correctly *utilize* the relevant, available, and detected information. The judge must interpret the information correctly in terms of what it implies about the personality of the individual in question. This is not always—or maybe ever—easy.

Utilization is difficult because the implications of any behavior for personality judgment are ambiguous, for two reasons. First, the traits that are relevant to a behavior depend on the situational context. A hostile response to an attack on one's family has different implications for personality than a hostile response to a comment about the color of one's tie. Second, any given behavior may be, and probably is, affected by more than one trait at the same time (Ahadi & Diener, 1989; McCrae & Costa, 1995). Complications like these are the reason that multiple behaviors observed over time and across situations are more informative about personality than are single actions (Blackman & Funder, 1998; Epstein, 1979, 1980).

Even after this final utilization step is traversed, a further complication is introduced by the method through which the judgment is operationalized. The judge might be asked to report his or her judgment through a questionnaire, through a Q-sort, or in a free-response format. Each of these methods introduces possible opportunities for and obstacles to accuracy. More general influences on reporting of judgments, such as response sets, might also come into play. These influences on the reporting of judgments, however, as opposed to the making of judgments, lie outside the Realistic Accuracy Model at present.

A Cognitive and Social Process

As was mentioned at the beginning of this chapter, the model just outlined describes accurate personality judgment as the outcome of a process that is both cognitive *and* social. The model can be misunderstood because it trespasses across the traditionally separate domains of personality, social, and social-cognitive psychology. The *relevance* step is most clearly connected to personality psychology and its traditional concern with the connection between psychological characteristics and behavior (Wiggins, 1973). The *availability* step is relevant to this issue as well and additionally invokes the study of relationships and social interaction. Different behaviors become available to people who are in different relationships with a target person, because very different actions are manifested in the different contexts which they may share depending on whether they are lovers, coworkers, or casual acquaintances. The *detection* step is relevant to a few studies in the field of social cognition that address the circumstances under which people are sensitive to particular kinds of information. More often, however, the study of social cognition concentrates on the step that RAM calls *utilization*. Detection is removed as an issue in most social cognition research because the stimuli—usually artificial—are presented in a direct and even blatant fashion. This methodology shifts the emphasis to how such stimuli are processed and converted into final judgments.

This analysis shows how several traditionally isolated subdisciplines of psychology must come together for the study of accuracy in personality judgment, because each of them examines only a part of the whole puzzle. Personality psychology is relevant to the first step; social psychology is relevant to the second step; and social-cognitive psychology is potentially relevant to the third and fourth steps, but usually only examines the fourth. Such interdisciplinary work is not always an easy sell. Social cognitivists, for example, have more than once criticized accuracy research on the grounds that it pays attention to issues such as relevance and availability that have nothing to do with the cognitive processes of the perceiver. Personality psychologists have not always appreciated how traits are revealed only in particular circumstances under certain conditions. But a complete treatment of the process of accurate judgment must consider all of these issues.

Formulaic Representation

RAM can be alternatively represented in the shape of a formula (Funder, 1995a):

$$\text{Accuracy} =$$
$$[(\text{the relevance of behavioral cues to a personality trait}) \times$$
$$(\text{the extent to which these cues are available to observation})] \times$$
$$[(\text{the extent to which these cues are detected}) \times$$
$$(\text{the way in which these cues are used})]$$

In the traditional manner of quasi-mathematical theorizing in psychology, a Greek letter could be assigned to each term. Accuracy could be *omega*, relevance could be *rho*, availability could be *alpha*, detection could be *delta*, and utilization could be *upsilon*.

These conventions yield the formula:

$$\omega = (\rho \times \alpha) \times (\delta \times \upsilon)$$
$$(\text{omega} = \text{rho} \times \text{alpha} \times \text{delta} \times \text{upsilon})$$

Of course, as also seems traditional for quasi-mathematical models in psychology, there is no very good way to assign exact mathematical values to these terms (cf. Kenny, 1991, 1994). However, as Kenny and others have demonstrated, even though absolute or precise quantification of numbers like these are difficult to formulate or interpret, it can be useful to consider the causes and consequences of them taking on *higher* versus *lower* values. Thus, the present terms are probably best thought of quantitatively only to the following, limited extent.

Perfection in relevance, availability, detection, or utilization would equal 1. A behavior directly produced by a single trait and no other influence has a relevance value of 1. If that behavior occurs overtly in the presence of the judge, it has an availability value of 1. If it is detected, it gets a detection value of 1, and if it is correctly interpreted, it has a utilization value of 1. The resulting degree of accuracy would be $1 \times 1 \times 1 \times 1$, perfection. A behavior that is completely irrelevant, unavailable, undetected, or misutilized, on the other hand, would have an accuracy value of $0 \times 0 \times 0 \times 0$—none at all.

The interesting—and real—cases lie somewhere in between these two extremes. Intermediate values stem, for the most part, from the fact that in ordinary acquaintance personality judgment is something that occurs over time and across occasions. For example, a person who often expresses a trait through relevant behaviors would have a higher relevance score than someone who expresses the trait only seldom. A judge who spends much of each day with a target person will have more behaviors available to him or her than one who sees the target only occasionally. A perceptive judge might detect most of the cues that are available in the environment, and a less perceptive judge might miss many. Some judges might correctly interpret most of what they see, wheresa others correctly interpret less. The values of each variable might be affected by situational parameters as well. For example, some contexts might evoke more relevant behaviors than others; some kinds of information might be easier to detect than others.

It remains to be seen what gain might ultimately be entailed through further quantification of the Realistic Accuracy Model. But a few implications immediately emerge from thinking of it in the terms just described.

IMPLICATIONS OF THE REALISTIC ACCURACY MODEL

The first implication of the Realistic Accuracy Model, one which is particularly clear from the formulaic version, is that the accurate judgment of personality is difficult, more so than perhaps has sometimes been appreciated. The second implication is that if variables are found that make accurate personality judgment more or less likely, they must have their effect because of processes that occur at one or more steps of the model.

Accuracy Is Difficult

Before an actual attribute of a target person can enter the mind of a perceiver in the form of an accurate judgment, *all four* of the steps in the model comprise hurdles that must be traversed. If there is a failure at any of them, accuracy will not be achieved. In terms of the formula, if *any* of the terms ρ, α, δ, or υ is equal to 0, then ω, or accuracy, will also be 0. All the relevant cues in the world are no help if the judge does not perceive and use them; even the most astute judge is helpless in the face of a lack of relevant cues, and so forth.

A further implication of the formula is that accuracy is, at best, a probabilistic matter. Perfect accuracy is attained only when all terms in the equation equal 1, representing perfectly unambiguous and visible cues to the judgment together with optimal observation and integration of those cues. These kinds of perfection are theoretical limits rather than empirical possibilities; therefore, perfection of judgmental outcome represents such a limit as well.

Even the slightest imperfection at any step entails a heavy cost. If each of the terms in the RAM formula were to be regarded as nearly perfect, equal to .90, say, then overall accuracy works out to .66. If, perhaps more realistically, each term were to be regarded as about half as good as it might potentially be, or .50, overall accuracy drops to only .0625.

These calculations imply that only when all four links in the process of accurate judgment are strong can any substantial degree of accuracy be anticipated. This conclusion, in turn, leads to the perhaps surprising inference that in daily life these terms must take on higher values than might have been anticipated. Because in general ω, the accuracy of personality judgment, is pretty good (see Chapter 3), ρ, α, δ, and υ must all be fairly high under ordinary circumstances.

The Origins of Moderators

Either the verbal or schematic representation of RAM is sufficient to draw a further important implication. Any variable that is found to moderate the accuracy of personality judgment, to make it more or less likely, must arise because of something that happens at one or more of the four steps (see Chapter 6 for a detailed rendition of the connections between moderators of accuracy and the steps of RAM). Concomitantly, any efforts to improve accuracy, to be effective, must have an effect on relevance, availability, detection, or utilization. This observation leads us to consider even more closely the important events that happen at each step and the factors that can influence them.

THE FOUR STEPS TO ACCURATE PERSONALITY JUDGMENT

The process that connects a real attribute of personality to an eventual accurate judgment of it begins with the target person expressing some sort of informational cue—generally, a behavior—that is relevant to the trait being judged. The second step is for this information to become available to a judge. If all goes well, this is followed by detection and accurate utilization.

The Order of the First Two Steps

The very first, unpublished version of RAM had the first two steps in the opposite order, with availability preceding relevance. The idea was that people do many things, only some of which prove to be relevant. It fell to my Riverside colleague Dan Ozer to point out to me the that this ordering reflects a view of the process of judgment only from the judge's perspective. It is more faithful to the model's realistic assumption to think of the first part of the model from the perspective of the stimulus person who really has a certain trait. The idea, then, is that a person does certain things that are relevant to his or her personality, only some of which are available to a given judge. However, other relevant behaviors might become available to a different judge or to the same judge at another time. This is the sense in which relevance is prior to availability.

Relevance

Thus, the first stage of accurate personality judgment is relevance, wherein the target of judgment emits or gives off some kind of information that is potentially informative about his or her personality.

Personality and Behavior

As Jerry Wiggins (1973) pointed out in his definitive survey of the field, the first business of personality psychology is (or ought to be) the prediction of behavior. This is not because it is necessarily the ultimate goal of psychology to predict what people will do, but because the effect of personality on behavior offers the only route through which it can be known and, furthermore, is the reason it matters.

Personality is important *because* of the actions it affects, and we can only know about personality by *observing* what an individual does. The Realistic Accuracy Model begins with the latter point. A sociable person must do something sociable; a talkative person must talk; an assertive person must assert himself or herself; a dominant person must take command. Until and unless the person does one of these things, we have no way of knowing whether any of these traits are present.[4]

As was mentioned in Chapter 2, one might reasonably expect that personality psychology would by now have amassed a large catalog of the behaviors that are relevant to particular personality traits. Such an expectation, sadly, would be mistaken. Although our everyday, implicit knowledge of personality includes many beliefs about the connections between personality and behavior, personality researchers have not yet tested very many of them.

As more researchers take on the daunting task of observing directly what their subjects do, psychological knowledge about the connections between personality and behavior can be expected to slowly but surely grow. As an example, Funder and Sneed (1993) examined some of the behavioral cues that people believe are diagnostic, and that actually are diagnostic of each of the "big five" general traits of personality. Scherer (1978) has shown that the simple cue of speaking in a loud voice is a valid indicator of extraversion. Gifford and Hine (1994) have demonstrated links between extraversion and aloofness and observable, visible behaviors that perceivers in turn validly use to judge these traits. Gifford (1994) reported similar linkages with respect to nonverbal behavior, which can be highly relevant to personality (for more examples of personality-behavior linkages, see Chapter 8).

In many cases, relevance is not such a simple matter, of one behavior being directly relevant to one trait. Matters are complicated for several reasons. First, a given behavior can be influenced by more than one trait, making the connection between a trait and its underlying behavior difficult to discern (Ahadi & Diener, 1989; McCrae & Costa, 1995). Second, the trait to which a given behavior is relevant may in some cases only become apparent over time and repeated observations. For example, a gift might seem like an indicator of generosity; only after the whole pattern of an individual's actions over time is considered may it become apparent the gift really was part of a scheme of sneaky and manipulative behavior (Funder, 1991).

---

[4]On a metaphysical level, one could maintain that a person *does not have* a trait until and unless it is manifest in behavior. That is essentially the perspective of the Act Frequency Approach and other approaches that conceptualize behaviors as "samples" rather than "signs" of behavior (Buss & Craik, 1983; Wiggins, 1973). I prefer to think of traits as latent properties that a person could indeed have, just awaiting the moment of expression, as in the person who turns out, in a pinch, to be more courageous than anyone expected. But for present purposes this metaphysical issue can be avoided. Either way, personality judgment must begin with the target person emitting some sort of cue relevant to the trait that is judged.

A third complication with the relationship between behavior and personality is a bit different. The kinds of "behaviors" that are potentially relevant to personality span a range that sometimes strains at the very definition of the word behavior. For example, several aspects of physical appearance (e.g., wearing glasses, "baby-faced" features, attractiveness) and tone of voice are sufficiently relevant to personality to allow judges who view a target only briefly to render surprisingly accurate judgments (Ambady & Rosenthal, 1992; Berry, 1990, 1991; Berry & Brownlow, 1989; Borkenau, 1991, Bond, Berry & Omar, 1994). Such cues are behaviors in only the loosest sense, though typically they are affected by a person's behavioral styles (e.g., emotional expressiveness, grooming). But for purposes of the process of accurate personality judgment they reduce to the same essential thing, which is information given off by the target that is relevant to the judgment to be made.

A fourth and final complication is that relevance can be positive, negative, or neutral. A courageous act is relevant to courage, but so is a cowardly act (in a negative direction). Borkenau and Müller (1992) showed that people base trait ratings on acts that are negatively relevant, in that sense, as well as positively relevant. They reported further evidence indicating that even neutral acts can be informative, in that they add to the denominator in the relevant acts/total acts calculation. In other words, if a person does only a few things, nearly all of which are courageous, that will lead to a higher rating than if the person does many things, with the same number (and much smaller proportion) of acts being courageous.

Obstacles to Relevance

The notion of relevance can be clarified by considering some factors that might *prevent* the expression of personality-relevant information. An important factor in this regard is situational constraint. As was pointed out in an important article by Mark Snyder and William Ickes (1985), some situations are "weaker" and others are "stronger" than are others. A weak situation, in this sense, is one that does not channel everyone's behavior down the same narrow pathway but allows the relatively free expression of individual propensities. For example, an informal party is a context in which sociable people can chat, humorous people can tell jokes, and shy people can stand to one side. In a stronger situation, such as a church service, the rules for behavior are much tighter and fewer possibilities (although more than zero) exist for the expression of personality. At the extreme, imagine a person coming into a bank with an Uzi machine gun and shouting "hands up!" This is a strong situation. Everybody's hands will go up, and the behavior will be utterly uninformative about the distinctive nature of any individual's personality.

Different people live their lives within different situational contexts. Some allow more expression of personality than do others. For example, the job of a toll collector at the Golden Gate Bridge is not one that allows for the free expression of many behaviors during the workday. Relatively few personality-relevant behaviors will be displayed, and judging a toll collector's personality from what he or she does at work will be difficult. In contrast, the job of a psychology professor is one that allows for free expression of many aspects of personality.[5] His or her behavior during the workday will be much more relevant to the kind of person he or she is, and accurate judgment from observing that behavior will be easier. In his theoretical writing, Abraham Maslow (1987) argued that the best indications of what a person was really like would be found in his or her leisure time activities, not his or her behavior at work. Maslow's idea was that one's true personality only had a chance to emerge in the freer situations of life.

In traditional psychometric theory, it is a truism that more difficult items are more informative for distinguishing among individuals at high levels of a trait. One cannot compare the relative mathematical ability of a group of college math professors with a test of simple algebra; something more demanding will be needed to separate out those who are more and less skilled. This idea is just beginning to be applied to personality measurement (e.g., Waller & Reise, 1989). But in principle it works the same way. In an "easy" situation, nearly everybody might perform a certain behavior. In a more "difficult" situation, the behavior might become more rare and thereby more informative. This is why the behavior of charging into a burning building is more relevant to the judgment of bravery than is the behavior of managing to drive a car in heavy traffic. Although both behaviors might require a degree of bravery, most people can do the latter whereas fewer might do the former. Thus, behaviors most relevant to the accurate judgment that a person possesses an extremely high level of a trait are likely to occur in "difficult" situations in which such behaviors are rare.

The difference between situational contexts is qualitative as well as quantitative. They differ not just in how much expression they allow but in which attributes of personality they provide an opportunity to express (Kenrick, McCreath, Govern, King, & Bordin, 1990). For example, most situations do not evoke the trait of courage. But if someone is walking by a burning building from which cries for help can be heard, that individual suddenly is in a context that will allow the expression of whatever courage he or she might possess. But whatever the person does, that behavior is likely to be uninformative about his or her degree of sociability. The reverse could be said about the situation of the informal party. More consistent differences in context can influence large segments of individual's lives. The work context of a data entry clerk allows him or her to express whatever degree of conscientiousness he or she might possess, but not any artistic tendencies. The situation is reversed for the full-time artist.

Everything that has been said so far applies only to the target person. An individual could, in principle, perform actions fully relevant to a wide range of personality traits all day long, but that would be of no use for personality judgment unless a judge happened along to see them. So the time has come to add the judge to the equation.

---

[5] It is this opportunity for unusually free expression that attracts many people to the academic life.

Availability

Only some of the relevant behaviors performed by any given target person actually become available for use by any given judge. Behaviors can fail to become available for two reasons.

First, some behaviors are covert. If we include thoughts and feelings as "behaviors" that are relevant to traits—and I believe we should—then judgmental accuracy suffers from their typical unavailability. A nervous person might hold any number of alarming thoughts in his or her head but hold a smile on his or her face. An observer might never know of the behavior or the underlying trait. Or—and this is a stretch, but should be kept in mind as a hypothetical possibility—the "behavior" relevant to a trait might be a secretion of an internal gland, an acceleration of the pulse, or some other subtle physiological response. Such reactions might be relevant to personality, but will remain unavailable to observers except under the most unusual circumstances (such as when the observer is operating a polygraph).

The more ordinary limitations of availability occur due to the contextual dependence of behavior noted during the discussion of relevance. Across the situations of his or her life, the typical individual has an opportunity to express behaviors relevant to many—although perhaps not all—aspects of his or her personality. But in any given subset of situations, behaviors will be expressed that are relevant to only a subset of all possible traits. The perceiver who will judge a particular subset of traits accurately is the one who shares the relevant situations with the target person. Thus, a spouse has access to situations in which a person's degree of emotionality is displayed but might have no access to situations that reveal the person's occupational competence. The reverse could be true about the person's coworkers.

The more and more diverse contexts in which a perceiver is able to observe a target person's behavior, the more and more diversely relevant behaviors he or she will be likely to see. This is the reason, all other things (such as target's judgability and judge's perceptiveness) being equal, that a person who has known you longer would be expected to know you better. This expectation has been empirically verified in numerous studies (e.g., Blackman & Funder, 1998; Funder & Colvin, 1988; Funder, Kolar, & Blackman, 1995; see also Chapter 6).

Two other predictions emerge from this analysis that have yet to be subject to empirical test. First, a person who has known a target in contexts that allow freer expression of relevant behavior—"weak" situations in the phrase of Snyder and Ickes (1985)—should render more accurate judgments than a person who has known the target only in relatively "strong" situations. For example, an acquaintance who shares leisure time activities with a target person might judge him or her more accurately than would a coworker (Maslow, 1987). Second, a person who has known a target person in a *wider range* of contexts, holding number of contexts constant, is in a position to view a wider range of relevant behaviors and therefore would be predicted to render more accurate judgments of personality. For example, a person who has traveled around the world with a target person might judge him or her more accurately than someone who has been acquainted the same length of time, but in less diverse settings.

Detection

Assuming that one or more relevant behaviors of a target person have become available to a judge, the judge must still detect this information for it to do any good. Conceivably, this detection does not have to be conscious. Perhaps people can subliminally pick up stimuli that affect their judgments in ways that they fail to realize. But surely unless the information registers in some way on the judge's nervous system, his or her final judgment cannot be guided by it.

The detection step of accurate personality judgment is a particularly hazardous one, because many factors might interfere. The judge might be inattentive, unperceptive, or distracted. Or the behavior itself (e.g., a momentary facial expression), though available in principle, might be extremely difficult to see. The social environment and the behavior of others contain many, many pieces of information. Out of necessity, the typical perceiver picks up on only a small fraction of them.

The information that a perceiver is most likely to detect depends on several factors. Perhaps most obviously, some information is more obvious than other information. Events that are dramatic, vivid, or just loud are likely to be detected. Events that are routine, pallid, or quiet are less likely to be detected. To the extent the information most diagnostic of personality is also most salient in this way, judgmental accuracy will be improved. To the extent that the most meaningful information tends to be subtle, detection and subsequent accurate judgment will be handicapped.

Moreover, certain kinds of information tend to be detected and processed automatically, without requiring much or any conscious effort on the part of the perceiver. This information includes physical attractiveness (Locher, Unger, Sociedade, & Wahl, 1993), facial "babyishness" (Berry & McArthur, 1986), and the facial appearance of dominance (Keating, 1985). Perhaps other cues are picked up automatically as well; research on this topic is still in its early stages. To the extent this easily detected information is actually diagnostic of personality, the associated characteristics should be easier to judge accurately. The reverse is the case to the extent this information is misleading. As was mentioned earlier (see the discussion of relevance), in general this kind of information seems to have a small but real degree of validity for the purpose of personality judgment.

The detection of information more particularly depends on the nature and state of the perceiver. A person who is stressed, emotionally excited, or otherwise distracted can be expected to miss picking up information to which he or she might otherwise be sensitive. The cognitive effort entailed in managing the first impression one conveys to another can, under some circumstances, reduce the amount of information a perceiver picks up and remembers about his or her interaction partner (Patterson, Churchill, Farag, & Borden, 1991–1992).

In a related vein, James J. Gibson (1979) noted how a perceiver becomes sensitive to different information in the environment as his or her needs change. A person who is hungry will detect more subtle cues to the presence of food than someone who is sated. In a similar way, perhaps a person who is lonely will detect more subtle cues to the presence of friendliness than someone who already has more social life than he or she can handle.

Stable individual differences probably come into play here as well. Individuals whose self-concepts are organized around the concepts of honesty or intelligence are particularly attentive to information concerning the honesty or intelligence of others (Sedikides & Skowronski, 1993). More generally, individuals seem to be particularly prone to detect information that is "chronically accessible" within their cognitive systems or relevant to constructs contained within their "self-schemas" (Bargh & Pratto, 1986; Markus, Smith, & Moreland, 1985).

Utilization

The distinction between detection and the next step in accurate personality judgment, utilization, is the same as the distinction between perception and cognition, and it is just as blurry. Higher-order cognitive processes influence which stimuli a person perceives, and it is often a fine and difficult matter to determine whether a person has failed to actually perceive a stimulus, or whether the stimulus, while perceived, never progressed from the perceptual to the cognitive apparatus.

Nonetheless, the distinction is meaningful for analytic purposes. For example, the detection stage might be more important for understanding the judgment of strangers than of close acquaintances, for whom presumably everything potentially detectable eventually is detected. For close acquaintances, therefore, utilization is more likely to be important than detection (Vogt & Colvin, 1998). At a more general level, two observers who both detect the same relevant and available behaviors might still draw different conclusions about the person who performed them.

Cognitive Load

It is not difficult to think of reasons why utilization would fail to be ideal in many cases. Biases and the holding of fallacious stereotypes can mislead the way information is used in personality judgment, especially when the cognitive system is already overloaded (Bodenhausen, 1993; Fiske & Von Hendy, 1992). On the other hand, not all stereotypes are completely wrong, and when they include valid information their use—even their automatic use—will improve accuracy (Brodt & Ross, 1998; Funder, 1995a; Jussim, Lee & McCauley, 1995).

Research indicates that personality judgment is a process that is partially over-learned or automaticized and partially one that requires higher-order cognitive processing. Distraction or cognitive load interferes only with the second part of personality judgment. So, for example, the relatively automatic categorization of a behavior (e.g., as friendly) is followed by an almost-as-automatic correspondent inference (e.g., the person is friendly). This inference is modified in a third stage, *if* there is some reason to question the initial inference (e.g., the person is a car salesman) *and* sufficient cognitive resources are available (Trope, 1986).

Research by Dan Gilbert and his colleagues has further explored the effects of "cognitive business" on person perception. If a perceiver starts with an initial perception or "default option" that a behavior is caused by an attribute of the stimulus person's personality, this relatively automatic inference will be less changed by subsequent contradictory information to the extent the perceiver is otherwise mentally occupied (Gilbert, Pelham, & Krull, 1988). By the same token, if the default option is a situational attribution (i.e., the perceiver begins with the presumption that the situation caused the stimulus person's behavior), subsequent contradictory information will in this case also fail to correct the initial judgment to the degree the perceiver is busy (Krull, 1993).

In general, personality judgment is a demanding cognitive task, and interference from other tasks can be expected to degrade its quality (Patterson et al., 1991– 1992). All the other factors that undermine thinking in general, such as emotional upset, fatigue, and distraction, are likely to undermine the ability to fully process personality-relevant information as well. Even the act of worrying too much about whether you are reasoning correctly can function as a distraction that lessens the quality of judgment (Wilson & Schooler, 1991).

Error and Utilization

One particular subset of research on person perception/social cognition has had explicit ambitions to address judgmental quality. This is the literature on error (often going by the term "attribution error"), discussed in Chapter 3. Without rehashing that entire discussion, it should be noted here, yet again, that such research employs what Hammond (1996) has called "coherence" criteria for judgmental quality. Judgments are dubbed as erroneous to the extent that they do not derive from the proximal stimuli in the manner described by a normative model, such as Kelleyan attribution theory or Bayesian statistics. They are *not* evaluated in terms of their correspondence with the actual properties of the person being judged (Hammond's "correspondence" criterion), because typically no such real person exists.

This research has yielded a large amount of knowledge concerning the degree to which subjects' utilization of behavioral information is processed according the prescriptions of normative models. But because judgments derived from normative models are not always correct, it has yielded rather less knowledge concerning the cognitive processes that are associated with judgmental accuracy. This issue provides an important direction for future research.

Cue Utilization

A good deal of research in social cognition has focused on abstract, content-free aspects of judgmental *process,* such as how people retrieve and combine information (e.g., Srull & Wyer, 1989; Wyer & Srull, 1986). But accuracy is likely to have just as much or more to do with *content.* How do people interpret hostile facial expressions, friendly waves, and nosy questions? This is the question of what Brunswik (1956) called *cue utilization.*

The relatively small amount of research on cue utilization in personality judgment suggests that people are fairly good at it. Funder and Sneed (1993) showed that the behavioral cues people believed were associated with the "big five" personality traits[6] actually were, in four out of five cases (the exception being openness, a trait that laypersons apparently find difficult to understand). In this study, videotaped behaviors, coded using the Behavioral Q-sort (BQ), were correlated both with the five traits (as measured by the NEO Personality Inventory) in the target subjects, and with the judgments of the five traits rendered by observers of the videos. Correlations between behavioral cues and traits reflect what Brunswik called "ecological validity." Correlations between behavioral cues and judgments reflect cue utilization. Funder and Sneed found that the correlations between ecological validity and cue utilization by strangers for the five traits were .93 for extraversion, .61 for neuroticism, .73 for conscientious, .86 for agreeableness and .44 for openness.

Borkenau and Liebler (1992b) reported essentially similar findings. They found, for example, that the degree to which a target person dresses fashionably and has a stylish haircut leads lay perceivers to infer that the person is extraverted. Perhaps surprisingly, for the most part cues like these are valid, leading the lay perceivers to make mostly correct judgments.

Utilization is a difficult step toward accurate personality judgment. It is easy to misinterpret relevant, available, and detected behavioral information because the meaning of a behavior changes according to the context in which it occurs and because any given behavior may be influenced by more than one trait. The message conveyed by research on error often is that people are poor at this step. Research such as that just summarized, however, suggests that under the difficult circumstances, it is remarkable that lay perceivers do as well as they do.

Variations in utilization no doubt have an important affect on judgmental accuracy. Some people are probably better at interpreting the meaning of behaviors than others (though this has been surprisingly difficult to demonstrate empirically; see Chapter 6). And if the accuracy of personality judgment is ever to be improved, one

---

[6]Extraversion, neuroticism, conscientiousness, agreeableness, and openness.

possible method would be to improve the way people utilize the behavioral information that is relevant, available, and detected (see Chapter 8).

MULTIPLE CUES AND MULTIPLE TRAITS

As has been seen, the implications of RAM's description of the process of accurate personality judgment are by no means simple. Even so, RAM offers a description of the way accurate personality judgment could occur in real life that is both schematic and greatly simplified. The model essentially describes a one-trait one-cue process in which a single trait produces a relevant behavior, which then is available to and then detected and utilized by a judge, resulting in an accurate judgment of that trait. Social reality is, of course, more complicated than that. In a more realistic case, it seems likely that people simultaneously, or nearly simultaneously, detect and use numerous cues toward the judgment of numerous traits (Funder & Sneed, 1993) and that the final judgment comes from an integration of these cues extended over time.

This complexity probably has some important implications. It seems highly possible that the interactions among nearly simultaneous judgments of different traits would affect how each trait is judged (Patterson, 1995). An environment that contains multiple cues will yield judgments affected by interactions among those cues as well as by each cue considered alone (Borkenau and Liebler, 1992b). In addition, many different cues might be diagnostic of the same trait, whereas the same cues might be simultaneously diagnostic of different traits (Buss & Craik, 1983; Funder, 1991).

Perhaps most important, accurate personality judgment will seldom be based on just one behavior. Personality is something that emerges over time and across multiple situations and multiple behaviors. The right way to look at the Realistic Accuracy Model, therefore, is as a representation of the essential, core component of this process—the correct interpretation of a relevant, available bit of information. It is the accumulation of information as this process is repeated over time and across situations that truly allows for the possibility of accuracy (Blackman & Funder, 1998; Epstein, 1979, 1980; McCrae & Costa, 1995).

To acknowledge this point, it is necessary to broaden the interpretation of the Realistic Accuracy Model. The cues represented in Figure 5-1 are actually multiple, as are the traits judged, and these cues and judgments interact as well as flow from one to another. Accordingly, Figure 5-1 could be redrawn, with numerous lines, instead of a single one, running from left to right and numerous two-headed arrows interconnecting all of the lines. When the redrawing was finished, it would look much like a plate of black spaghetti.

Such a re-representation of RAM would more properly acknowledge the complexity of the phenomenon it seeks to model and would even be rather humbling, to be sure. But I believe the creation of such a messy diagram would accomplish little else at this time. To understand how cues and judgments interact will require much more than acknowledging that they probably do. It will require research, in which simultaneous cues are measured and simultaneous judgments are detected, to describe what specific cues or judgments interact with what other specific cues or judgments, and how and why.

RAM offers an initial, prototypic model of the core of this complex process that, as we shall see in Chapter 6, is sufficient to account for much of what is now known about accurate personality judgment and to organize research that is likely to be conducted in the near future. An appropriate task for the next generation of research will be to go further and to track down and empirically demonstrate specific inter-actions among cues and judgments and their effects on accuracy.

THE GOALS OF RAM

One goal of the Realistic Accuracy Model is to provide some order to the field of research on judgmental accuracy by providing a relatively simple process model that can organize and account for the many different variables that have been shown to affect accuracy. A further goal is to suggest new moderator variables that have not yet been tested and thereby to provide a framework for the next generation of research (see Chapter 6). Moreover, the Realistic Accuracy Model implies that if accuracy is ever to be improved, this improvement must occur through an interven-tion that affects one or more of the four steps of accurate judgment (see Chapter 8). Relevance, availability, detection, and utilization are variables that have higher values and lead to more accurate judgments in real life than might have been expected given the difficulty of the overall process. But there is room for improvement in each, and such improvement provides a prospect for the future that is at once daunting and promising.

As we have seen, from the perspective of the error paradigm, a judgment is accurate if it re-represents stimulus information according to the prescriptions of a normative model. From the perspective of pragmatic approaches to accuracy, a judgment is accurate if it proves useful to the judge. From the perspective of con-structivist approaches, a judgment of personality is accurate to the degree a com-munity of judges agrees that it is. But from the perspective of RAM, none of these criteria is enough. Its realistic approach demands that the same amount of effort go into gathering and synthesizing diverse information about what the target is actually like, as goes into examining what goes on inside the head of each judge (see DePaulo & Friedman, 1998).

A final purpose of RAM, therefore, is to direct a bit of research attention back to the properties of the individual—the stimulus person—that personality judg-ment is supposed to be all about. A personality trait is something that is real, interesting, important, and sometimes hidden. Its judgment, and the evaluation of that judgment, can only be attained through the most circuitous and difficult of routes. A realistic approach to the study of accuracy in personality judgment implies that personality and social psychology need someday to set aside their differences and begin to explore this route together, because each of them owns only part of the map.

CHAPTER 6

Moderators of Accuracy

During the two decades that the person–situation debate dominated the personality literature while the error paradigm dominated the study of person perception, much ink was spilled over the issue of whether personality judgments were characteristically inaccurate or generally accurate. With hindsight, it is easy to see that both positions were misguided—and may have been proposed as much for rhetorical as for as scientific purposes in any case. As was noted in Chapter 3, personality judgments are sometimes wrong and sometimes right, so a much better question for the study of personality judgment is not *whether* personality judgments are accurate, but *when*. This question leads to the study of moderator variables, the factors that make the accurate judgment of personality more and less likely.

In the several years of renewed research on accuracy that preceded the development of the Realistic Accuracy Model (RAM), an increasing number of studies identified numerous variables that affected the level of accuracy as assessed by various criteria. These variables can be organized into four classes. Accuracy was shown to be moderated by properties of the judge, the target, the trait that is judged, and the information on which the judgment is based. Because my more particular interest was in the variables that made personality judgment *more* likely to be accurate, several years ago I optimistically dubbed these moderators "good judge," "good target," "good trait," and "good information" (e.g., Funder, 1993a).

TABLE 6-1   Aspects of Judgmental Process Associated with Moderators of Accuracy

Moderator	Specific characteristic	Relevant RAM process variables
Good judge	Perceptiveness	Detection
	Judgmental ability	Utilization
	(Non)defensiveness	Detection, utilization
Good target	Activity level	Availability
	Consistency, scalability	Relevance
	Ingenuousness	Availability, relevance
Good trait	Visibility, frequency	Availability
	Operant/respondent	Relevance
	(Non)evaluativeness	Availability, relevance
Good information	Quantity (e.g., acquaintance)	Availability
	Quality (e.g., relationship)	Relevance

Note. These are representative examples of the process variables that RAM proposes underlie various specific moderators of accuracy, organized by four broad categories. RAM = Realistic Accuracy Model.
From Funder, 1995a, Table 1. © 1995 by the American Psychological Association. Reprinted by permission of the publisher.

Later, when I developed the Realistic Accuracy Model, my specific intent was to provide a theoretical explanation of accurate judgment that was general enough to account for research findings concerning all four of these moderators and to suggest where further moderators might be found. RAM's framework allows moderators to be presented not just as a laundry list of variables that affect accuracy but in a theoretical context that attempts to explain why and how each functions. Some of the links that can be hypothesized between moderators of accuracy and stages of the Realistic Accuracy Model are listed in Table 6-1, and these links and others are discussed below.

THE GOOD JUDGE

The oldest concern in the history of research on accuracy is the search for the good judge of personality, the kind of individual who truly understands his or her fellow humans. It is not entirely clear whether such a person exists (Schneider, Hastorf & Ellsworth, 1979); evidence of consistent individual differences in accuracy has been surprisingly difficult to find over the years. Perhaps some of the difficulty stems from the fact that most people are good judges, a "restriction of range" problem (DePaulo & Friedman, 1998). The basic tasks of person perception are so important that nearly everybody can do most of them, and individual differences in accuracy may tend to be found only when circumstances are exceptionally difficult. The

Realistic Accuracy Model leads to several expectations concerning the characteristics and background of people who might judge personality better than others, when the going gets tough, and the relatively thin base of relevant empirical research seems generally supportive of these expectations.

Theoretical Considerations

According to RAM, differences between judges of personality who vary in their accuracy must be a product of differences in how they detect or utilize available, relevant cues. The "good judge" therefore appears in the right half, and latter two terms, of the model (see Figure 5-1). The capacity to detect and to utilize available cues correctly can be divided into three components: knowledge, ability, and motivation.

Knowledge

The first component is knowledge about personality and how it is revealed in behavior.

Explicit Knowledge

Sometimes this knowledge might be verbally describable and be used consciously and deliberately. For example, a judge might be certain (rightly or wrongly) that a person who will not look you in the eye is dishonest, or that someone who has a weak handshake is unassertive. Putative knowledge like this is didactically teachable; one could read a book or listen to a lecture on the essential indicators of personality and remember to look for them.

The problems with this possibility, however, are several. First, under ordinary circumstances people do not typically seem able to describe exactly how they make their judgments. The judgments happen too fast and too automatically for the judge to be able to tell you exactly what he or she is doing. A second, related problem is that personality judgment is much more complex than one cue-one inference, despite the prevalence of clichés such as those referred to in the preceding paragraph. Personality judgment is produced by rich configurations of cues that include multiple behaviors along with information about the contexts in which the behaviors occur (Brunswik, 1956; Funder, 1991; McCrae & Costa, 1995). Such judgmental situations elicit "intuitive" more than "analytic" cognition (see Hammond, 1996, and Chapter 8). Intuitive cognition is configural, automatic, and not really verbalizable. Moreover, it is not didactically teachable; to the extent that personality judgment is based on intuitive cognition, a lecture on "how to judge personality accurately" would be of little use.

Implicit Knowledge

On the other hand, a judge who has amassed a store of *implicit* knowledge about the indicators of personality might be able to use it rapidly, effortlessly, and to good effect. How would one go about obtaining such knowledge? According to Hammond (1996), the route is through *practice* and *feedback* (see also Funder, 1997a, chap. 18). Therefore, experience in dealing with diverse persons in diverse contexts seems like a promising way to develop the ability to detect and appreciate behavioral cues others could miss.

The first expectation derived from RAM, therefore, is that the good judge of personality should be interpersonally experienced in contexts that allow useful feedback. In New Zealand, a standard practice for young people of college age is to get a year or two of overseas experience (OE), working their way across Europe or the United States before returning home to settle down. Another standard practice is for schoolchildren to regularly go off to camps with their schoolmates in order to gain social experience with each other outside of the school context. I know of no evidence that these practices lead "Kiwis" to be better judges of personality than anybody else, but from the viewpoint of the Realistic Accuracy Model they seem like good ideas. Certainly many people feel that experiences while travelling or serving in the military have been important steps in clarifying their views of the interpersonal world.

From this perspective (as well as others), shy people and introverts are at a severe disadvantage. A person sitting alone in his or her room or otherwise avoiding interactions with others is denying himself or herself the chance to obtain the experience that could develop interpersonal knowledge. This observation is consistent with the results of a study by Akert and Panter (1988), who concluded that "because extraverts have more experience in social settings than introverts" (p. 965) they are better at decoding nonverbal cues in social interaction. This advantage of social experience may be surprisingly wide-ranging; extraverts also seem to be better than introverts at distinguishing real from simulated suicide notes (Lester, 1991).

It is worth noting that it is important to obtain practice *and* feedback. Sometimes this is not a problem; the people we encounter may let us know fairly quickly when we have misjudged them. But it is not uncommon for feedback to be ambiguous or delayed, which makes learning from experience much more difficult (Hammond, 1996). Politeness norms can further interfere with the feedback process.

Consider the especially difficult situation of someone who grows up in privileged circumstances, such as a member of royalty or the very powerful. No matter what the princess does, every member of her court responds with an approving smile. No matter what the president of the company says, every member of his staff says "what a brilliant idea!" Although such responses may be pleasant in the short term, the obvious danger is that they deny these individuals the possibility of obtaining useful feedback, regardless of how broad her or his social experience might be otherwise. Such an individual is likely to turn out to be a poor judge of personality indeed, according to RAM.

Ability

The second component of the tendency to accurately perceive and utilize behavioral cues is sheer perceptual or cognitive ability. Obvious perceptual handicaps such as blindness and deafness may have interpersonal consequences that are not so obvious. Someone who cannot see, or cannot see well, is cut off from a whole rich channel of nonverbal facial expressions and body language that conveys important information about personality. Someone who cannot hear, or cannot hear well, is cut off not just from the words people use in conversation but subtleties of tone, emphasis, or accent that are potentially just as informative. Research has identified these kinds of sensory losses as important causes of distortions of social perception and social isolation in the elderly (Resnick, Fries & Verbrugee, 1997; Stein & Bienenfeld, 1992).

Perceptual handicaps aside, some people do seem to be more socially perceptive than others are. For example, some people listen closely to their conversational partners; other people are too busy planning their next monologue to be really aware of what anybody else is saying. Some people are acutely sensitive to the small mannerisms or body motions that can convey much; others are relatively oblivious (Rosenthal, Hall, DiMatteo, Rogers & Archer, 1979). Some people are very much a part of their social environment and keenly attuned to it, whereas others are distracted, lost in their own thoughts, or otherwise directing their attention elsewhere besides the other people who are present. In particular, some individuals are so busy at trying to manage the impression they convey to others that their ability to perceive others and judge them accurately is impaired (Patterson, 1994a, 1994b).

Individual differences in cognitive ability are probably even more pronounced than individual differences in perceptiveness. Perhaps the most venerable finding in differential psychology is the "positive manifold" exhibited by almost all measures of all kinds of ability, which seem to be positively correlated to some degree (Brody, 1996; Thurstone, 1935). People good at one thing tend to be good at most other things. So it is to be expected that IQ as well as more specific cognitive abilities will be associated with accurate personality judgment. At least two studies have found that judges with higher measured intelligence more accurately rated the performance and emotions of others (Havenstein & Alexander, 1991; Westbrook, 1974).

Motivation

The third component of the tendency to judge personality accurately concerns motivation, in two senses. First, situational circumstances and aspects of the judge's own personality can affect the degree to which the judge cares about the judgment he or she is making and whether it is accurate. Flink and Park (1991) found that subjects achieved greater consensus in their judgments of personality when they believed that important social outcomes depended on their judgments being accurate. In a similar vein, Neuberg and Fiske (1987) reported that subjects appeared to process information about other people more carefully when they expected to interact with them in the future. Further research showed that this effect might be limited to circumstances that judges otherwise find uninvolving and undemanding (Neuberg, 1989). Research aside, it seems obvious that a judgment that one does not care to make in the first place can scarcely be accurate.

Motivational factors that affect the content of judgment might also be relevant to accuracy. For example, defensiveness or other motivated styles of information processing could be expected to distort one's perception and judgment. An individual whose perception and thinking is motivated by the intense need to believe himself always to be in the right cannot be expected to achieve a high degree of accuracy when judging the actions and personalities of other people. Defensiveness and lack of humor about one's own shortcomings seem particularly likely to be associated with low accuracy, as should a narcissistic view of the self (John & Robins, 1994) or generally hostile or uniformly benign attitudes about others.

The Realistic Accuracy Model implies that all of the attributes discussed in this section—and probably others—should be associated with individual differences in judgmental accuracy. But RAM does not imply that self-assessments of ability will necessarily predict accuracy. By its nature, the relationship between self-assessment and ability is likely to be one sided. A good judge is likely to know that he or she is good, but there is nothing to stop a poor judge from also believing himself or herself to be a good judge. His or her very lack of insight can create an assessment conundrum, making it difficult to detect variations in judgmental ability through self-report. Thus, it is not surprising that self-assessments of judgmental ability are seldom found to be correlated with actual judgmental success (e.g., Fletcher, 1993; Ickes, 1993; Marangoni, Garcia, Ickes, & Teng, 1995, Swann & Gill, 1997; Vogt & Colvin, 1998).

Empirical Considerations

Although individual differences in judgmental accuracy are difficult to investigate properly, the existing literature does point to a few characteristics that seem to be associated with the ability to judge others.

Research Difficulties

The search for the good judge of personality is the oldest pursuit in the accuracy literature and was nearly its sole concern during the earlier incarnation from the 1930s to the early 1950s (Schneider, Hastorf, & Ellsworth, 1979). The prey proved to be unexpectedly elusive. Despite the research attention it has received, the good judge is the potential moderator concerning which the accuracy literature has the sparsest data and fewest firm findings to report. Perhaps this really is because there is no important variation in ability across judges of personality. But that seems unlikely despite the discouraging research. Moreover, research to date on the good judge has been plagued by several shortcomings.

First, most research has been rather atheoretical. Beyond vague (and nearly circular) notions that good judges of personality should be "sensitive" or "empathic," research has taken a shotgun approach correlating whatever individual difference variables were handy with one or another criteria for accuracy, usually self-other agreement (Taft, 1955). Without guiding hypotheses, a researcher must possess a good deal of luck to happen upon the variables that are truly important. Seekers of the good judge have not been notably lucky.

Second, most research on the good judge has been methodologically deficient in either or both of two respects. The earlier generation of research on accuracy fell victim to the problems pointed out by Cronbach (1955; see Chapter 4). The usual criterion for accuracy was self-other agreement (Taft, 1955), and these agreement scores were typically computed without heed to the complicating influences of stereotype accuracy, elevation, and so forth. These influences did not make such scores completely meaningless, as is sometimes believed. But it did make them multifaceted, unreliable, and difficult to interpret. The difficulties were perhaps greatest when an attempt was made to correlate these scores with characteristics of the judges. When complex, multiply determined criterion scores are correlated with simple measures of personality and ability, the researcher must be very fortunate indeed to find anything strong or meaningful and, as has already been noted, early accuracy researchers did not enjoy a surfeit of luck.

Although its first victim was research on the good judge, the Cronbachian critique raised issues relevant to all research on accuracy. A further methodological difficulty is more particular to the search for the good judge. To have any realistic chance of detecting individual differences in judgmental ability, each judge of personality must judge more than one target and preferably should judge many different targets. If each judge rates a different target (the problem of "nesting"), any variation in accuracy that is found is equally likely to be due to properties of the *target* as to properties of the judge. This fact creates, at best, a huge source of noise and, at worst, a serious interpretational confound for any attempt to detect properties of judges that are associated with their accuracy (Hammond, 1996; Kenny, 1994).

Ideally, what is needed is a study in which each judge rates several targets, and a large amount of criterion information (e.g., self-judgments, behavioral observations) is obtained about each of the targets. Such a study would be difficult and expensive but is not in principle impossible. Vogt and Colvin (1998) have reported an important, recent step in that direction. In this study, 102 judges watched each of *four* different stimulus persons in 12-minute videotaped, dyadic interactions and then attempted to describe his or her personality. The judges' own personalities were described on a wide range of self-report questionnaires and by their parents. The results are summarized in the next section. For now, it can be noted that this important study, as the first and best of its type in the modern era, points the way toward even more comprehensive investigations of the good judge in the years to come.

Research Findings

Reviews of the early literature on accuracy concluded that the search for the good judge had not been very successful. Findings did not seem to replicate across studies, and it appeared possible that judgmental ability might be so context-specific that general correlates of accuracy would never be found (Schneider et al., 1979; Taft, 1955). Some investigators concluded that what little generality was found across contexts was due to the stability of response biases such as leniency and restriction of range, rather than actual judgmental ability (Cline & Richards, 1960; Crow & Hammond, 1957; Gage & Cronbach, 1955). However, the theoretical and methodological shortcomings of this work should probably make us skeptical not just of its purported findings but also of this pessimistic conclusion. The good judge had not really had a fair chance to emerge.

Even the older literature did yield a few consistent conclusions. Taft (1955), for example, in the midst of a fairly pessimistic review allowed that overall, the best judge of personality tended to be intelligent, socially skilled, and psychologically well adjusted. These correlates, while perhaps unsurprising, are also sensible and largely consistent with research that has come later. Some hints do exist in the more recent literature to suggest the good judge might yet be found. For example, research in Paul Ekman's laboratory suggests that individuals who can detect deception in one context tend to be good at detecting deception in other contexts as well (Frank & Ekman, 1997). The industrial psychologist Walter Borman has found a moderate degree of individual consistency in the accuracy with which college students can judge effective job performance from observing videotapes (Borman, 1977, 1979b). From his own research and reading of the results of others, Borman concluded:

> Individual differences probably play a significant role in determining a person's accuracy in evaluating others' performance . . . the accurate perceiver of performance is generally even-tempered, outgoing, patient, affiliative, but socially ascendant. (1979b, p. 113)

Borman's subjects judged job performance rather than general attributes of personality, but it is somewhat heartening to see how his findings are parallel to expectations generated from the Realistic Accuracy Model in the discussion offered earlier, and even with the conclusion drawn from the older empirical literature by Taft (1955). His good perceivers are socially active and nonneurotic.

Over several decades, Robert Rosenthal and his colleagues have studied "nonverbal sensitivity," the ability to translate the meanings of facial expressions and body language. Their Profile of Nonverbal Sensitivity (PONS) test measures this ability by showing subjects a stimulus person on film, and research indicates that scores on the PONS have meaningful associations with other measures of social acuity (Funder & Harris, 1986). Bernieri, Gillis, Davis, and Grahe (1996) reported several studies that found accuracy in judging the rapport between two other people to be general across targets.

Two other recent studies also provide encouragement for the possibility that the good judge of personality might be found. Marangoni, Garcia, Ickes, and Teng (1995) reported appreciable consistency of judges' "empathic accuracy"—the ability to detect an individual's thoughts and feelings—across different targets. The accuracy with which a rater judged one target correlated an average of .60 with the accuracy with which he or she judged other targets. And Geoff Thomas (1998), in an extremely ambitious and wide-ranging study, also found that people who demonstrated empathic accuracy with respect to one stimulus person also tended to be accurate with respect to others.

None of the studies just listed directly addresses individual differences in the ability to judge *personality*. One study that did address this issue was David Kolar's doctoral dissertation (Kolar, 1995). This study used data from the Riverside Accuracy Project to examine individual differences in judging the personalities of same-sex acquaintances. The study employed two criteria for accuracy, self-other agreement (as corrected for stereotype accuracy) and behavioral prediction (profile correlations between personality ratings and relevant behavioral observations coded from videotapes). These two criteria were significantly correlated, $r = .41$ among males and $r = .39$ among females. Accordingly, they were combined into a composite accuracy score.

Judgmental accuracy scores were correlated with personality ratings obtained using both self-report scales and ratings from peers. Although the sexes were not found to differ in overall judgmental accuracy, different personality variables were associated with accuracy among male and female subjects. The male good judge of personality described himself as extraverted, likable, and well organized, and was not insecure, anxious, or oversensitive. Similarly, peers described the male good judge as extraverted, interesting, and reassuring, and as neither condescending nor overly prone to worry. These are strikingly reminiscent to the correlates reported by Borman and by Taft (both summarized earlier) and anticipated by the Realistic Accuracy Model.

For female judges, the correlates of judgmental ability were somewhat different. The female good judge of personality described herself as socially perceptive, having wide interests, concerned with philosophical problems, and neither conservative nor conventional. Unlike for males, this self-description did not much resemble descriptions offered by peers, to whom very few distinctive attributes of the female good judge of personality seemed to be visible.

Probably the most important finding from Kolar's study was the generality of accuracy across the two very different criteria. This methodological advance may compensate, to some degree, for the fact that each judge rated a different target. To my knowledge, this is the only study to compare the use of self-other agreement and behavioral prediction as criteria, and to find them correlated to an impressively high degree. This correlation suggests that the search for the good judge is more than a snipe hunt; a real creature seems to be out there somewhere.

The specific correlates would seem to be on somewhat shakier ground. A quick gloss of the findings suggests that the ability to judge personality might have a somewhat different basis among males than among females. For males, judgmental ability seems to be part of a pattern of extraversion and psychological stability. According to RAM, social experience and nondefensiveness ought to be concomitants of good interpersonal judgment, and that seems to be the pattern for males. For females, the basis of judgmental ability seems somewhat different and involves a pattern of interpersonal sensitivity and interest that is less tied to extraversion and overt social activity, and therefore is less visible to their peers.

The results of Vogt and Colvin (1998) were similar in most respects. They also found wide individual differences in judgmental accuracy and, further, that women were generally more accurate than men. Although this sex difference was not found in the study by Kolar et al., the correlates of accuracy seemed basically similar. Judgmental accuracy was associated with what Vogt and Colvin characterize as "interpersonal orientation" and "psychological communion." (The latter finding is consistent with the report by Bernieri & Gillis, 1995, that accuracy in judging rapport is correlated with psychological "femininity.") They interpret these results as implying that a motivation to interact with and understand others is associated with accuracy. However, they point out, this does not imply that individual differences in accuracy are simply a matter of motivation. Rather, it could well be that interpersonally oriented people interact more with others throughout their lives, and improve their judgmental ability on the basis of that experience. The ability to judge people, therefore, is likely to stem from both motivational and cognitive factors, and these two factors probably interact.

This complex and intriguing pattern of results deserves to be followed up in future research that employs both multiple targets per rater, like the study by Vogt and Colvin, and multiple criteria for accuracy including behavioral prediction, like the study by Kolar.

THE GOOD TARGET

The second potential moderator of accuracy is the flip side of the good judge—the good target. The idea here is that some people are easier to figure out than others are. The personality and general behavioral patterns of some individuals can be judged correctly from relatively few observations of their behavior, whereas others remain enigmatic even after prolonged acquaintance. Allport's (1937) poignant question in this context was "Who are these people?" (p. 443).

According to the Realistic Accuracy Model, individual differences in the tendency to be judged accurately are a matter of cue relevance and availability. People whose behaviors comprise numerous and informative (e.g., relevant, nonmisleading) clues to their personalities should be the easiest to judge.

This simple principle leads to a number of expectations, some of which were mentioned in Chapter 5, in the context of the discussion of relevance and availability. For example, some people simply perform more behaviors than do others, as a function of their general activity level. Others, those who are relatively inert, do less. RAM predicts that, all other things being equal, people with a high level of behavioral activity should be easier to judge than those who are less active, because more active people give the judge more to go on. Because they emit more behaviors, they concomitantly emit more relevant behaviors, and more relevant behaviors are therefore, on probabilistic grounds, more likely to become *available.*

This principle applies with particular force to social behaviors. A shy person who hangs back from social interaction and gives other people few clues by which to know him or her is likely to be relatively difficult to judge according to RAM. Socially active extraverts, by contrast, should make for much easier targets. By the same token, people who express their emotions readily should be easier to judge than those who hold their feelings hidden inside (Ambady, Hallahan, & Rosenthal, 1995). For example, several studies have indicated that women are more likely to be judged more accurately than men, apparently because they are more nonverbally expressive, including using a wider range of facial expressions and hand gestures (Buck, 1984; Buck, Miller, & Caul, 1974; DePaulo, 1992; Hall, 1990; Knapp & Hall, 1992).

Gaps in the Link from Personality and Behavior

The relevance stage of RAM reminds us that it is not enough for targets to emit *many* behaviors. They must also emit *informative* ones. The behavior that a person performs might fail to be relevant to and informative about his or personality for any of several reasons.

Situational Pressures

First, the behavior might be the result of situational pressures that are so strong as to wipe out any expression of individual differences. As Snyder and Ickes (1985) pointed out, "weak" situations yield behaviors that are more informative about behavior than do "strong" ones. But this is a matter of degree rather than an absolute. I have already used (in Chapter 5) the obvious example of a holdup man entering a bank with a gun and yelling "hands up!" The behavior of hand raising is not informative about the bank patrons' personalities. However, if one were to look closely at their behavior one might see more subtle individual variations in the manner or speed with which they raise their hands. In general, the stronger are the situational pressures to perform a behavior, the subtler and more difficult to see will be the individual variation.

Some people live much of their lives in situational contexts that restrict individual differences in behavior. I mentioned the difference in behavioral latitude— notice this includes even style of dress—between bridge toll collectors and college professors. Professors' personalities can be judged to some extent from what they wear, what they say, and how they spend their days. These factors are much more restricted for toll collectors, which is not to say individual differences in their behavior do not exist. But they must be looked for much more closely.

During our visit to New Zealand, my children attended public schools that required them to wear uniforms. One of their teachers offered a very interesting justification for this practice. "When all the children are dressed the same," she said, "they have to prove who they are through what they do, not what they look like." This is not only an excellent justification for uniforms, but also a valuable psychological observation. When individual variation on one or more means of self-expression is restricted, the means that remain will become increasingly important both for perceivers and for actors.

Deception

A second circumstance that would make behavior irrelevant to personality arises when a target of judgment is deliberately deceptive. For example, a person might say, "I love your tie" when he or she really hates it, or engage in other, more consequentially deceptive actions. Any behavior of the sort commonly dubbed "insincere" is, by definition, relatively uninformative about the personality of the person who performs it.

Snyder's (1987) construct of "self-monitoring" refers not so much to deceptiveness per se but rather to the possibility that some individuals adjust their behavior with great sensitivity to even subtle changes in the surrounding environment.[1] These individuals, called *high self-monitors,* should be more difficult to judge accurately than *low self-monitors,* who are theorized to more likely be themselves and to act consistently across situations. Low self-monitors should be easier to judge because, in terms of RAM, more of their behavior is relevant.

But even here the matter is one of degree. If one were to attend closely to the complex *pattern* of behaviors of a deceptive person or of a high self-monitor, or to subtle nonverbal signs of deception (Ekman, 1991), relevant information might still be found to be present. Indeed, a trait like "deceptiveness," "insincerity," or even "high self-monitoring" might itself be manifest through a variety of clues. But its

---

[1]Thus, deliberately deceptive behavior could be regarded as a special and extreme case of high self-monitoring.

configuration is much more complex, and therefore while technically *available,* to use RAM's terms, it is much less likely to be *detected.*

Incoherence

A third possible break in the link of relevance between personality and behavior appears in the case of the person who has an inconsistent, disorganized personality. In a classic article, Bem and Allen (1974) considered differences between people who were and were not consistent in their behavior across situations and found that those people who described themselves as consistent on a given trait were judged on that trait with better agreement by others. Other investigators have not always replicated this effect (Chaplin & Goldberg, 1984). However, an extensive meta-analysis of the literature concluded that the central claim, that individual differences in predictability can be identified, has held up reasonably well (Zuckerman, Bernieri, Koestner & Rosenthal, 1989).

The seminal insights of Bem and Allen have evolved over the years as other investigators have pursued the issue. Roy Baumeister and Dianne Tice proposed the notion of the "metatrait," which they define as the trait of having a trait. The idea of a metatrait is that people vary in the degree to which their behavior is consistent along a given trait dimension (see also Tellegen, 1988). This idea harkens back to Bem and Allen's classic demonstration of the way more and less predictable people could be distinguished from each other simply by asking them, "How consistent are you?"

A more subtle idea included in Bem and Allen's article, and pursued further by Kevin Lanning (1988), is the notion of *scalability.* Scalability refers to the possibility that the behavior of some individuals is not patterned in the way that ordinary trait constructs are supposed to be. In psychometric terms, these are the rare but interesting individuals who pass the hard items but flunk the easy items. Bem and Allen pointed out that most people find it easier to be relaxed and friendly one on one than in front of a group of 400 observers (such as a class full of students), and this difference in item difficulty is part of the typical structure of the sociability construct. But some individuals—such as Daryl Bem himself—find it easier to behave in a warm, friendly manner on a public stage than in a private setting and therefore are not scalable in the ordinary way. In RAM's term, this lack of scalability changes the *relevance* value of the behaviors, making the individual more difficult (though not, in principle, impossible) to judge.

The notion of scalability is a part of Item Response Theory (IRT), a branch of psychometrics that has been almost exclusively developed within and applied to the assessment of abilities (Drasgow & Hulin, 1990). Steven Reise and Neils Waller (1993) have pioneered the transfer of this technology to the practice of personality assessment. These investigators have developed the measurement of scalability to assess differences between individuals who are and are not scalable on particular traits as well as in general. The expectation derived from RAM is that people should be particularly difficult to judge along the dimensions for which they are "un-traited" or unscalable.

Tying It All Together: Judgability

Randy Colvin's (1993a, 1993b) conception of the *judgable person* attempts to inte-grate differences of the sort just discussed.

Judgable People

Some individuals, according to Colvin's analysis, are both more consistent in their behavior across experimental and real-life situations and more likely to agree about by diverse informants. This is not because their judgability is a trait in itself. Rather, judgability is, in part, an entailed manifestation of a coherent personality.

People with a coherent personality are those who, in the vernacular, "have their act together." They have worked out a style of life that serves them across the diverse situations they encounter, and as a result portray a strikingly similar image to each of the people they know. This kind of consistency leads them to be more judgable almost by definition. A word can be used to predict a deed, a deed to predict a thought, and an action at one time to predict an action at another time all because the behavior of this person is coherently organized.

The available evidence indicates that judgability is a fairly stable attribute. In an analysis of longitudinal data, Colvin (1993b) reported that the rank-order stability of judgability was maintained over a period of 5 years (from ages 18 to 23). More-over, judgability is associated with "ego resiliency," a construct closely akin to psy-chological adjustment. Similar results were reported by Asendorpf & van Aken (1991), who found that children who were higher in ego resiliency were those whose personalities were the most consistent over time. Moreover, the most "con-sistent children were characterized by socially desirable traits, and inconsistent chil-dren by undesirable traits" (p. 689). Over all, the available data suggest that consistency, and concomitant judgability, are attributes of those who enjoy stable, healthy personalities.

Unjudgable People

By contrast, some individuals have not yet worked out an approach to life that serves them well across the situations they encounter, and some of those never will. These individuals say one thing but often do another, and their behavior is so erratic that it is difficult to predict what they will do next, even if you know what they have done in the past. Adolescents are typically described in this way. They are still in the process of forming an adult identity as childhood gives way to a surge of hormones and societal pressures. They try out new identities, seeming to be one person at one moment and another person the next, only later settling on one as their own. During this period of transition, adolescents can be expected to be low on judgability. In RAM's terms, their behaviors are not as relevant to their personalities at this stage as they might have been when they were younger, nor as they might be again when they are older. This kind of temporary nonjudgability might characterize other people going through major life transitions as they try on new identities and experiment to find the behavioral patterns that are effective in their new situation. These could include the newly married (or newly divorced) people who have suddenly risen or fallen in social class (e.g., through winning the lottery or being laid off, respectively), or even students leaving home for the first time to attend college.

Other nonjudgable people might be lifelong neurotics whose anxiety or impulsiveness causes their behavior to be erratic and unpredictable. As Donahue, Robins, Roberts, and John (1993) reported from their data, being behaviorally inconsistent or "seeing oneself as having different personality characteristics in different social roles . . . is a sign of fragmentation of the self" (p. 834). In a similar vein, Reise and Waller (1993) reported that being less scalable in general, across traits, is associated with lesser well-being, less adaptive reactions to stress, greater alienation, more aggression, and less self-control.

Other kinds of personality disorders might also be relevant to judgability. Narcissists characteristically try to present inflated views of themselves, which might be difficult for some observers to penetrate (John & Robins, 1994; Raskin, Novacek, & Hogan, 1991). Technically, the difficulty in judging a narcissist occurs at the utilization stage. Narcissists indeed emit relevant and available behaviors that may not be particularly difficult to detect. The problem lies in whether the judge "sees through" the self-aggrandizing act being performed.

Finally, a nonjudgable person might simply be deceitful. For example, people with dishonest or otherwise socially undesirable tendencies will generally seek to conceal them, leading them to be difficult to judge accurately on the basis of their overt social behavior (Aronson & Mettee, 1968; Kuiken, 1981). The crooked car dealer and the heartless romantic manipulator will both approach you with a charming smile; it may be a difficult task to decode exactly to which trait this seeming sign of sociability is actually relevant. Individuals without this kind of hidden agenda, and those who otherwise have more socially desirable personality characteristics, have no reason to conceal them and so are more likely to display behaviors indicative of their true selves.

The Advantages of Judgability

These final considerations might suggest that there is something morally virtuous about judgability. Be that as it may, recent research does suggest judgability might be good for you, a finding consistent with long-held theories that the most psychologically healthful lifestyle is to conceal very little from those around you or to exhibit what is sometimes called a "transparent self" (Jourard, 1971). To the extent that you exhibit any kind of psychological façade and that large discrepancies arise between the person who lives inside and the person you display outside, according to these theories, you are likely to experience both anxiety and excessive isolation from the people around you. This isolation can lead to unhappiness, hostility, and depression.

Recent research seems to support this idea. James Pennebaker and his colleagues have shown that inhibiting the expression of emotion—especially negative emotions—can be harmful to one's physical health (Berry & Pennebaker, 1993; Pennebaker, 1997). Other recent research suggests that the roots of judgability reach into early childhood and that the association between judgability and psychological adjustment is particularly strong among males (Colvin, 1993b).

THE GOOD TRAIT

Judgability can be a property of traits as well as of individuals: Some are easier to judge than others. From the perspective of the Realistic Accuracy Model, the difference between traits that are more and less easy to judge derives from the existence of cues to their judgment that are *relevant* and *available*.

Visibility

In many cases, these two influences work together. For example, a trait like sociability, which is revealed by frequent and positive social interaction, is easy to judge because directly *relevant* behavior is, almost by definition, so often *available* to others. By contrast, a trait like "ruminates and daydreams" must be inferred from verbal statements ("I seem to daydream a lot"), which may not be uttered very often or even be always accurate. Even more ambiguously, the trait may have to be inferred from dreamy looks, distracted responses, and the like. Ambiguity is a problem here because any of these indicators may have other meanings as well or instead.

Research indicates that the differences between traits that are more and less visible, in this way, are not difficult to detect. Funder and Dobroth (1987) found that the independently rated visibility of traits was correlated highly ($r = .42$, $p < .001$) with interjudge (self-other and other-other) agreement. Self-ratings and other-ratings agreed with each other better to the extent the trait being rated was visible (see also Funder & Colvin, 1988). Findings consistent with these have also been reported by Bernieri et al. (1994), Borkenau and Liebler (1992b, 1995), Kenny, Albright, Malloy, & Kashy (1994), Kenny, Horner, Kashy, and Chu (1992), Kenrick and Stringfield (1980), Levesque and Kenny (1993), McCrae (1982), Park and Judd (1989), Watson (1989), and others. The most visible traits tend to be those associated with extraversion (e.g., Borkenau and Liebler, 1995) and social skill (Gifford, Ng, & Wilkinson, 1985); the least visible traits are associated with such non-visible attributes as "motivation to work" (Gifford, et al., 1985).

The effect of visibility on interjudge agreement might seem obvious. Indeed, it almost seems to reduce to the truism that more visible traits are easier to see. However, the finding does have at least one important implication. Some psychologists, reluctant to concede that lay judgments of personality might have any validity, have proposed that interjudge agreement is a result of conversations judges have had with one another, or with the subjects. Thus, these psychologists conclude, peer judgments are based not on the subjects' personalities, but only on their socially constructed reputations (Kenny, 1991; McClelland, 1972). This point of view is congruent with postmodern and deconstructionist viewpoints, which maintain there is no independent reality underneath individuals' perceptions of it.

This idea might seem plausible, but it is seriously undermined by the findings concerning trait visibility. If peers were to base their personality judgments only on arbitrary, socially constructed reputations, then there would be no reason why observable traits should yield any better interjudge agreement than unobservable ones. Other people can manufacture a reputation about your ruminativeness just as well as they can about your talkativeness. But while all traits are equally susceptible to being talked about, certain traits are much more difficult to observe. Therefore, the finding that more-observable traits yield better interjudge agreement implies that peer judgment is based more on direct behavioral observation than on arbitrary processes of social construction (Clark & Paivio, 1989).

Issues of Availability and Relevance

Availability and relevance are ordinarily tied closely together, but the Realistic Accuracy Model suggests some ways in which they might operate independently or even at cross-purposes. Talkativeness is a highly visible and available behavioral cue but its relevance can be problematic because it might be an indicator of sociability, nervousness, dominance, or a complicated combination of many traits. Other acts might be highly visible and so become available whenever they occur, but be seldom performed because the evoking situations are so rare. The act of saving a family from a burning building would be a highly visible (and easy to detect and utilize) indicator of courage. But the circumstances in which courage is so directly relevant to behavior are rare, so the chances for such diagnostic acts to occur are slim.[2] In a slightly different vein, the act of stealing might be unambiguously *relevant* to the trait of dishonesty but is not ordinarily *available* because the thief typically conceals the act as well as possible (Rothbart & Park, 1986).

---

[2]A researcher might seek to overcome this shortcoming by arranging a situation to evoke the otherwise-rare relevant behavior. For example, "bystander intervention" studies expose subjects to confederates apparently in distress to see what their reactions will be.

Different contexts and different kinds of behaviors contain information concerning different kinds of traits, with important consequences for relevance and availability. As we saw earlier, traits like extraversion and agreeableness are the ones most likely to become visible in overt social behavior (Funder & Dobroth, 1987; Kenny, 1994). But another place to look for signs of personality is in the "residue" of a person's life, such as the contents and condition of his or her bedroom, even when the person is not actually present. Such residue might contain important information because the state of one's living quarters is the accumulated result of the activities the person has performed there. Pryor, Chuang, Craik, and Gosling (1998) pursued this intriguing idea in an innovative study. They found that conscientiousness (indicated by tidy bedrooms) and openness to experience (indicated by the presence of a variety of books and magazines) were the two traits that were easiest to judge accurately from the appearance of one's bedroom. These results suggest that the visibility of a trait may vary according to the lens through which the trait is viewed.

Evaluative Properties

The dishonesty-and-stealing example is an illustration of a more general point. Traits differ from one another in their evaluative or connotative meaning. Some traits are those all people would wish to possess and display (such as courage and intelligence); other traits were those that people might prefer to avoid broadly displaying (such as dishonesty or certain sexual tendencies). The motivations for self-presentation that naturally result from this difference can be expected to make some traits less often or less directly displayed—or exaggerated—in overt behavior, leading to distortions in their availability and relevance.

In support of this hypothesis, Oliver John and Richard Robins (1993) reported that extremely desirable or undesirable traits tend to yield lower self-other agreement in their ratings, compared with more neutral traits. Consistent with the logic just outlined, John and Robins inferred that judgments of evaluatively loaded traits are particularly prone to being distorted by self-protective and self-enhancing motivational processes.

Adaptive Importance

Evolutionary biology has some interesting implications when applied to person perception. It implies, for instance, that if the perception of certain traits in others has historically been important for survival, the currently living members of the human species should be the descendants of those individuals who were particularly good at perceiving those traits. Unfortunately, the derivation of hypotheses from this principle is not so simple as it might seem. The problem is that the same traits that are adaptive to *perceive* are often the same ones that are adaptive to *conceal*. Our ancestors who successfully detected dishonesty might have had a greater probability of survival, but the same can be said about our ancestors who successfully deceived their fellows. The result of countervailing tendencies like these can be a sort of evolutionary "arms race" in which succeeding generations become better both at deception and at detecting deception, but with the result being no net change in the probability that a given deceptive act will be detected.

An exception to this trade-off could occur concerning traits that are adaptive both to detect and to display. One of these might be "sociosexuality," the willingness to engage in sexual relations with minimal acquaintanceship with or commitment to and from one's partner (Gangestad, Simpson, DiGeronimo, & Biek, 1992). It seems that certain advantages for reproductive success could result both from successfully detecting and displaying this trait, to the extent one possessed it. Consistent with this hypothesis, Gangestad et al. found that individual differences in this trait, as measured by self-report, were more accurately detected by observers than were traits such as social potency and social closeness. In an interesting further wrinkle, although this finding held true regardless of the sexes of the perceiver and the person perceived, females judging the sociosexuality of males were especially accurate, and males judging the sociosexuality of other males were even more accurate! But males, probably to their eternal regret, were not particularly good at judging the sociosexuality of females.

GOOD INFORMATION

The final moderator of accuracy in personality judgment concerns the information on which the judgment is based. For personality judgment, information consists of anything the person who is judged says or does that might be relevant to the kind of person he or she is. "Good information"— the kind of information that promotes accuracy—has two facets, quantity and quality.

Quantity

A simple but important consideration is whether the judge has observed the target person enough to enjoy the reasonable possibility of making an accurate judgment. Some recent research suggests that surprisingly little information is necessary for judges to begin to have a degree of accuracy. A number of investigators, using a variety of experimental procedures, have consistently found that encountering the target briefly without exchanging any words is enough to raise accuracy above the zero level. It is even somewhat informative to see only a brief, "thin slice" of his or her behavior or the room in which or she lives, without meeting the target at all (e.g., Ambady & Rosenthal, 1992; Albright, Kenny & Malloy, 1988; Pryor et al., 1998; Watson, 1989).

The Acquaintanceship Effect

However, more information appears to be better. The impact of increased chances for behavioral observation on judgmental accuracy is called the *acquaintanceship effect* (e.g., Funder & Colvin, 1988). Funder and Colvin reported that acquaintances who have known their targets for about year provide personality judgments that agree better with each other, and much better with the targets' own self-descriptions, than do judgments provided by relative strangers, who have viewed the targets for only 5 minutes on videotape. Many other investigators have reported essentially similar findings (e.g., Bernieri, Zuckerman, Koestner, & Rosenthal, 1994; Blackman & Funder, 1998; Cloyd, 1977; Colvin & Funder, 1991; Funder, Kolar, & Blackman, 1995; Jackson, Neill, & Bevan, 1969; Norman & Goldberg, 1966; Paulhus & Bruce, 1992; Paunonen, 1989; Taft, 1966; Watson & Clark, 1991).

The simplest, most parsimonious explanation for this consistent result can be framed in terms of the Realistic Accuracy Model: more information is *available* to acquaintances than to strangers, making their judgments more accurate (Stinson & Ickes, 1992). Years ago, Egon Brunswik made a related point:

> The general pattern of the mediational [judgment] strategy of the organism is predicated upon the limited ecological validity or trustworthiness of cues . . . this forces a probabilistic strategy upon the organism. To improve its bet it must accumulate and combine cues. (1956, p. 20)

As was discussed in Chapter 4, some investigators have questioned the seemingly straightforward assertion that more information improves chances for accuracy. Over the years, a study by Passini and Norman (1966) has been cited many times in this context. The study found that personality ratings of target persons provided by acquaintances and by strangers yielded similar factor structures (patterns of correlations among ratings). As Colvin et al. (1997, p. 172) point out, "This finding led many writers to conclude—quite incorrectly—that acquaintanceship and accuracy are unrelated (e.g., Berman & Kenny, 1976; Schneider et al., 1979)." The conclusion was incorrect because factor structure is orthogonal to accuracy, and also because later research in the same program found that acquaintances' judgments agreed better with self-judgments than did judgments by strangers (Norman & Goldberg, 1966).

Skeptics continue raise the possibility that demonstrations of the acquaintance effect such as listed earlier might have been plagued by one or more artifacts (e.g., Kenny, 1994; Park, Kraus, & Ryan, 1997). The most important of these is assumed similarity, the possibility that well-acquainted judges resemble their targets, project their own personalities onto them, and therefore achieve better self-other agreement on that basis alone.

As was described in Chapter 4, Funder, Kolar, and Blackman (1995) empirically tested this theoretical possibility. They examined a data set within which acquaintances provided judgments of target subjects that agreed much better with the targets' self-descriptions than did descriptions by strangers. But the acquaintances in fact *did not resemble* the targets any more than the strangers did, and they did not base the descriptions of their well-acquainted targets on their own self-images in any event. Therefore, neither actual nor assumed similarity is a necessary condition for a robust acquaintanceship effect; the effect can be found even when both of these influences are near zero.

Blackman and Funder (1998) reported further evidence concerning the basis of the acquaintanceship effect. In this experimental study, different randomly assigned groups of perceiver-subjects watched from between 5 and 30 minutes of the videotaped behavior of one of six target subjects. Then they attempted to provide comprehensive descriptions of the target's personality (using the Q-sort). The major finding was that descriptions offered after 30 minutes of observation agreed better with the targets' descriptions of themselves than those offered after only 5 minutes of observation. This is a direct, controlled, experimental demonstration of more information leading to more accuracy. Its results are consistent with those reported by Marangoni et al. (1995), who in another experimental study found that the longer one observed a target of judgment, the better one became at judging accurately his or her thoughts and feelings (see also Bernstein & Davis, 1982; Neimeyer, Neimeyer, & Landfield, 1983).

Information and Consensus

The findings of Funder, Kolar, and Blackman included a further interesting aspect. Although self-other agreement—accuracy in this context—improved with observation, other-other agreement or "consensus" did not. Consensus started high but went no higher after further observation. Accuracy started much lower but rose, over the course of the 30 minutes of observation, to a level equal to consensus.

What is going on here? This study's seemingly surprising findings were actually anticipated by the theorizing of David Kenny (1994). Kenny theorized that when judges share stereotypes (as members of a community are wont to do), they will achieve consensus in their personality judgments early on. Over time, these (presumably largely erroneous) stereotypic judgments will be replaced by judgments based on actual behavioral observation, but this process will change the content of the consensus rather than its level. Indeed, Funder and Blackman (1998) found that the average judgment of all judges—their consensus—better matched the subjects' self-judgments after 30 minutes of observation than they did after just 5 minutes. But the sheer amount of agreement—the level of consensus—did not change, just as Kenny's theory anticipated.

Perhaps an example can make this process more clear (taken from Blackman & Funder, 1998). Consider the plight of Sue and Sally. Co-owners of a garage that needs a new mechanic, they interview an applicant, Ed. Based on little more than his physical appearance, they agree that he seems conscientious, reliable, and intelligent. Ed is hired on the spot. Sadly, only two weeks later, Sue and Sally are forced to reconsider. It turns out that Ed has consistently left half the repairs on his work orders undone, forgotten to remove his tools from customers' cars, and repeatedly made foolish and expensive mistakes that Sue and Sally were forced to rectify. They now agree that Ed is incompetent, unreliable, and must go.

The point of this woeful tale is that that the level of agreement between Sue and Sally—their consensus—did not change between the beginning and end of Ed's brief career. They agreed at the beginning that he was a good mechanic and they were wrong; they agreed at the end that he was incompetent and they were right. But their agreement per se was unaltered. Accuracy and consensus can have different bases and can be affected differently by changes in the level of available information.

Consensus and Accuracy: A Longer View

The findings of the experiment by Blackman and Funder (1998) were that accuracy and consensus happened to become almost exactly equal after 30 minutes of observation. This appears to be an interesting coincidence. Of course, the study cannot address what would happen after still longer periods of observation. But psychometric considerations, one further analysis of Blackman and Funder's data, and a reading of the empirical literature lead to a couple of expectations.

First, it seems unlikely that adding more 5-minute segments of observation will increase accuracy or consensus much beyond what was found by Blackman and Funder after six segments (30 minutes in all). No trend was evidenced for consensus to increase between 5 and 30 minutes, and there is no reason to expect that it would suddenly increase between, say, 30 and 60 minutes. And accuracy cannot much exceed consensus, for the same basic psychometric reason that validity cannot exceed the square root of the reliability (Kenny, 1994). So the findings of Blackman and Funder probably fairly represent what would be found in other experiments of similar design, even those that employed somewhat larger ranges of information. On the other hand, if judges could observe a single, long interaction (say, an hour), more diagnostic information might emerge as the relationship among the participants develops and they begin to reveal new areas of themselves and others that go beyond "Hello, who are you?" This possibility deserves to be pursued in further research.

What about the much higher level of acquaintance and information that becomes available in close and long-lasting interpersonal relationships? In Blackman and Funder's data are Q-sort personality descriptions of the six target subjects rendered by acquaintances who knew them for an average period of 14 months. The average correlation between the descriptions offered by these close acquaintances, and the self-descriptions of these six targets, was $r = .46$, much higher than the maximum level of .26 achieved by the experimental judges who observed the targets for 25 to 30 minutes. Even more remarkably, the consensus among the close acquaintances was .40, again much higher than the consensus of .25 achieved by the experimental judges in the high information condition.

Some of the cross-sectional studies of acquaintanceship cited earlier—such as Funder and Colvin (1988)— that compared close acquaintances (known for a year or more) with relative strangers have also found an increase in consensus concomitant with an even stronger increase in accuracy. Longitudinal, experimental studies have not shown this effect (Kenny et al., 1994), but for understandable reasons none has lasted long enough to assess the effect of truly close acquaintanceship on consensus and accuracy.

At this point it is useful to recall the finding by Funder et al. (1995), that none of the artifacts sometimes used to explain away the acquaintance effect in cross-sectional designs in fact appear empirically to be necessary for the effect to be obtained. When this observation is combined with the findings summarized earlier, a reasonable inference is that at high levels of acquaintance—beyond those included in currently available experimental, longitudinal studies—increases in both accuracy and consensus can be expected. At some point, as it becomes high enough, accuracy will *require* consensus. Perfectly accurate judgments must agree, even though judgments that agree might not necessarily be accurate.

A final observation is that this effect should be particularly evident when detailed, subtle personality judgments are sought. As Paunonen (1989) showed, even less visible traits become more judgable when the judge and the target are closely acquainted. To know somebody longer is not necessarily to learn more and more about how extraverted they are. With longer acquaintance, more and more subtle aspects of personality slowly become visible.

Context and Acquaintance

The advantage of longer acquaintance, as strong as it seems to be, may not hold under all circumstances. In a study by Colvin and Funder (1991), the criterion for accuracy was behavioral prediction rather than self-other agreement. Under those circumstances, the results were interestingly different.

As in other research, judgments of personality were obtained from strangers who watched 5 minutes of videotaped interaction and from acquaintances who had never seen any videotapes but had known the target subjects for about a year or longer. These judgments were then used to predict (using multiple regression) the behaviors the targets exhibited in a further videotaped interaction. Under these circumstances, the advantage of acquaintances over strangers vanished. That is, personality judgments by acquaintances did no better than judgments by strangers when the criterion was the ability to predict behavior in a situation similar to one that the strangers have seen, but that the acquaintances have not.

As is so often the case, this complex finding might be best clarified with an example. During most academic quarters, I lecture before 150 or more undergraduates two or three times a week. As a result, there are many people who have seen me lecture but who have no way of knowing what kind of person I am in other, nonacademic settings. My wife, however, has known me well for more than a dozen years but has never seen me deliver a lecture (this seemingly strange situation is actually not rare among college professors and their spouses). If one of my students and my wife are both asked to predict how I will behave in lecture next week, whose predictions will be more accurate? If you take seriously the results by Colvin and Funder (1991), your answer is that the two predictions should be about equally valid. On the other hand, if you were to ask these two people to predict what I might do in any *other* context—such as asking them how I would describe myself— my wife would have a clear advantage.

In the 1991 article, Colvin and I interpreted this phenomenon as a "boundary" on the acquaintanceship effect, because we seemed to have found the one circumstance under which personality judgments by close acquaintances were no more accurate than judgments rendered by almost total strangers. In retrospect I think our interpretation should be reversed.

From a reversed perspective, an even more remarkable phenomenon becomes apparent. Even though a close acquaintance—such as a spouse—has never seen you in a particular situation, he or she will be able to generalize from observations of you in *other* situations with accuracy sufficient to predict your behavior in that situation as well as somebody who has actually seen you in it. From casual observation in daily life, for example, the acquaintances were able to extract information about the subjects' personalities that was just as useful in predicting how they would behave under the gaze of an experimenter's video camera as was the strangers' direct observation of behavior in a highly similar situation. This impressive ability of an acquaintance to make a judgment from one set of contexts, that has the ability to generalize to and predict behavior in a vastly different context that the acquaintance has never seen, may be the real news of this research.

Quantifying Acquaintanceship

Implicit in the notion of the acquaintanceship effect is the idea that acquaintanceship can be quantified. At a gross level, such quantification is not difficult. Funder and Colvin (1988) and Funder et al. (1997), for example, compared judgments from individuals who had known their targets for about a year to judgments from individuals who had viewed their target once for 5 minutes. The former individuals obviously have "more" acquaintanceship with their targets than the latter individuals. But if an attempt were made to define this variable more finely it is easy to see there would be problems. For example, it is not clear that you have more information about somebody you met a month ago, as opposed to a week ago. It depends on how much time you actually spent with that person. But estimating such time with any accuracy would be difficult.

Other investigators have attempted to finesse this issue by asking judges "how well do you know" the target person. This question is not only vague, it runs the risk of circularity if judges rate targets as well known only when they can judge them accurately. Other investigators have suggested that the appropriate quantitative variable is the "act." The more acts a judge has seen, in this view, the more information the judge has available. But attempts to examine accuracy as a function of the number of acts an observer has seen may not in the end lead research very far, for two reasons. First, the concept of the "act" and plausible ways to count acts are far from clearly established (see Block, 1989). Second, even if this difficulty could be overcome, it seems likely that behavioral observations differ radically in how informative they are and what they are informative about, depending on what behavior is observed and in what context. It may be time, therefore, to move from considering acquaintance as simply a quantitative variable, to appreciating it as a qualitative one.

Quality

Beyond the sheer amount of information available to a judge, quality also matters. In terms of the Realistic Accuracy Model, the quality of information pertains to *relevance*. Observations of certain kinds of behaviors, emitted in particular contexts, are informative about certain traits. Observations of other behaviors in other contexts may be less informative.

In a pioneering study of the quality parameter, Andersen (1984) demonstrated that listening to a person talk about his or her thoughts and feelings leads to more accurate personality judgment than does listening to the same person talk about his or her hobbies and activities. This experimental finding suggests that, in real life, knowing someone in a context in which you might have a chance to learn about his or her thoughts and feelings—as a close friend might, for example—is likely to lead to more accurate overall impressions of that individual's personality. By contrast, knowing someone in a context in which you see only what he or she does—as a coworker might, for example—the resulting impressions of personality might be less accurate. This conclusion seems plausible, but has never been empirically tested as far as I am aware.

As research attention turns to the effect of quality of information on accuracy in personality judgment, we can look forward to findings that are informative about the best places to look when we want to learn about personality. When trying to learn about someone's extraversion, what behaviors should we watch for, and in what circumstances? And when trying to learn about a person's emotional style, what should we watch for and where, instead? The answers to these two questions—and those involving many other different aspects of personality—are unlikely to be the same.

TABLE 6-2   Interactions among Moderators of Accuracy
in Personality Judgment

Moderator	Judge	Trait	Target	Information
Judge	—	Expertise	Relationship	Sensitivity
Trait	—	—	Palpability	Diagnosticity
Target	—	—	—	Divulgence
Information	—	—	—	—

From Funder, 1995a, Table 2. © 1995 by the American Psychological Association. Reprinted by permission of the publisher.

INTERACTIONS AMONG MODERATORS

The four general moderators of accuracy just outlined—good judge, good target, good trait, and good information—inevitably overlap and interact. For example, as we have seen, a good target is someone who emits good information, and certain traits may be more visible in some targets than in others. The four basic moderators of accuracy yield six unique interactions, which are shown in Table 6-2. The table also shows the term by which each is denoted in the Realistic Accuracy Model (Funder, 1995a). It should be noted that each of these terms has, in this context, a technical meaning that is related but not equivalent to their everyday meaning. It should also be noted that each of these terms is provisional; several have been changed already more than once and further development can be expected in the future.

Judge × Trait: Expertise

The research literature contains more than a few hints that the ability to judge personality may not be completely general. For example, some judges might be good at judging some traits, but poor at judging others. This difference could arise from variations in judges' knowledge across traits or differential ego involvement concerning various traits.

Differential knowledge across traits might arise from differential experience. A particular judge might have experience in one domain—say, observing how people perform under extreme pressure—that another judge does not. Or one judge might have received explicit teaching—perhaps in a clinical training program—that another judge has not. The resulting variation in knowledge could be associated with differences in the cognitive availability of certain traits that make information about them more likely to be perceived and used accurately. In this vein, Park and Judd (1989) showed that judges who had a greater cognitive readiness to judge others' intelligence, honesty, and conscientiousness also tended to judge these traits with greater consensus.

Motivation might be as important as cognition in this regard. A particular judge might be ego-involved or defensive with regard to a particular trait and may therefore judge it more poorly than a judge in whom the trait does not raise such reactions. For example, a person who has doubts about his or her own intellectual ability may be a poor judge of this attribute in others, because even thinking about it raises too much emotional energy and defensiveness. Research has shown that self-serving differences in judges' conceptions of traits can be an important source of interjudge disagreement and, presumably, of inaccuracy (Dunning, Perie & Story, 1991).

The interaction between a specific judge and his or her ability to judge accurately a specific trait, as opposed to traits in general (which is the main effect of judge), is called *expertise* within RAM. A particular judge's expertise consists of the traits he or she is particularly good at judging. The term refers not just to knowledge or skill but also to a judge's freedom from emotionally relevant or motivated distortions in processing information relevant to the trait in question. Therefore, RAM's technical usage of the term expertise does not exactly match its meaning in ordinary language. Expertise concerns the detection and, more particularly, the *utilization* stages of the Realistic Accuracy Model, in which information already relevant and available is or is not detected and evaluated in a manner that produces an accurate judgment.

Judge × Target: Relationship

Certain judges might be able to judge some targets more accurately than they can judge others, who might in turn be more accurately judged by still other judges. Such an interaction could arise for any of several reasons. A target's most central trait might happen to be those about which a particular judge has *expertise,* as just defined. Or the relationship between judge and target could be of a sort that enhances rather than interferes with accuracy (Buck, 1993).

For example, when a judge and target are competing with each other for a common goal, this might be expected to interfere with cue utilization and lessen judgmental accuracy. As a result, what a person says about a competitor is ordinarily not to be trusted, even though he or she might sincerely believe what he or she is saying. Under ordinary circumstances, judgments made of someone who is disliked tend to be relatively inaccurate (Skarzynska, 1982).[3] In a parallel vein, Sillars and Scott (1983) observed that although marriage and dating partners might be extremely knowledgeable about each other, the nature of their relationship and their interdependency can make objectivity in their mutual perceptions difficult to

---

[3]This finding was obtained when the context of observation was "neutral"; it was reversed in a "diagnostic" context, perhaps because people were interested in judging the personality pathology of their enemies (Skarzynska, 1982)!

achieve (Anderson, Ansfield, & DePaulo, in press; Gottman & Porterfield, 1981; Noller, 1981; Stiff, Kim, & Ramesch, 1992). For example, dating couples in insecure relationships may avoid detecting the degree to which their partner is attracted to another person (Simpson, Ickes, & Blackstone, 1995).[4]

Still another possible basis for this interaction is that a judge might evoke informative behaviors from a particular target, perhaps because of their mutual ego involvement, which would not be visible to another judge who lacked the same evocative effect. For example, colleagues, lovers, people who are attracted to each other, and people who loathe each other probably will all display behaviors in each others' presence that might not be displayed to other observers and therefore be able to judge each other on dimensions that others could not.[5] In RAM, this process occurs at the *relevance* stage, in which the presence of particular person evokes behaviors relevant to particular traits.

Target by judge interactions can arise for still other reasons. A judge will obtain different information during the course of acquaintanceship as a function of the setting and type of relationship. Coworkers will be exposed to different behaviors than siblings. Or as a judge's relationship develops from acquaintance to friend to lover (and, in some cases, perhaps to enemy), the judge moves into positions from which different kinds of behavior can be observed and therefore different kinds of inferences accurately made. Little research to date has examined the effects of evolving relationships on personality judgment, but this issue deserves to be addressed in more detail in the future.

A related prediction can be derived from the Realistic Accuracy Model concerning gender differences. Social psychologists have frequently observed that female friends spend much of their time discussing emotions and relationships, whereas male friends are more likely to engage in work or play activities or to discuss less personal matters such as sports or politics (Reisman, 1990; Sherrod, 1989). If this observation is combined with Andersen's (1984) findings, that conversations that reveal more personal information yield better information on which to base personality judgments, the following prediction can be derived: Well-acquainted women ought to judge each other with more accuracy than do well-acquainted men. Data relevant to this prediction are surprisingly rare, but a sex difference in the predicted direction has reported by Harackiewicz and DePaulo (1982) as well as in a recent study by Vogt and Colvin (1998). The general (albeit small) superiority of women over men in the detection of emotional states is a long-standing staple of the literature (Hall, 1990; Kirouac & Dore, 1985; but see Ambady & Rosenthal, 1992). Within this literature, it has been suggested that the sex difference arises because men are more often assigned leader roles, and followers tend to be more accurate

---

[4]If this is the only dimension on which inaccuracy is motivated, then technically this result would reflect a three-way judge x target x trait interaction.

[5]Again, to the extent this phenomenon is trait specific it would actually reflect a three-way interaction.

about the characteristics of leaders than vice versa (Snodgrass, 1985, 1992; Snodgrass, Hecht, & Ploutz-Snyder, 1998).

Notice how RAM's prediction concerning gender differences in accuracy is based on the information derived from the distinctive interactional styles of each gender and the information yielded therefrom. It does not stem from any intrinsic quality of men or women and none is assumed. RAM would also predict that a pair of male friends who did discuss emotional matters would be just as accurate as any women, and a pair of women friends who engaged solely in work or hobby pursuits together would be just as inaccurate as any men. In the same way, male subordinates would be expected to be as sensitive to female superiors as female subordinates are to male superiors when that relatively rare relationship structure is present. More generally, the basis of all of RAM's predictions concerning the effect of type of relationship on accuracy is the kind of information that is yielded by the behaviors that become visible within it.

Any interaction between two people constitutes a relationship. Therefore, the two-way interaction between judge and target that affects accuracy for any of the reasons just summarized is called the *relationship* variable within RAM.[6] The term is meant to capture any unique alignment between two individuals that has the effect of enhancing or lessening the accuracy of the judgments that one makes of the other. The term is not equivalent to its meaning in ordinary usage, which is broader and includes aspects of relationships that might have no effect on accuracy.

Judge × Information: Sensitivity

Judges might vary in the kinds of information they are liable to detect and correctly utilize. A judge might be acutely aware of anything that suggests competitiveness or dominance, for example, or might tend to emphasize any information that becomes available relevant to a target's religious or political leanings. Sedikides and Skowronski (1993) showed that when honesty or intelligence is an important part of a person's self-concept, he or she tends to be particularly attentive to information about the honesty or intelligence of others. Judges also vary in their ability to detect or recognize nonverbal behaviors that might be diagnostic of emotion or personality (Hall, 1990). This interaction between judge and information, which is characterized by the tendency of certain judges to detect and utilize certain information or to weigh certain information heavily, is called *sensitivity* within RAM.

This sensitivity is conceptualized as specific rather than general. A judge could be highly sensitive to one kind of information at the same time he or she is oblivious to another kind. Bargh and Pratto (1986) showed how some individuals are particularly affected by information relevant to constructs that are "chronically accessible"

---

[6]I thank William Ickes for suggesting this term to refer to this interaction.

within their cognitive systems. Similarly, Markus, Smith, and Moreland (1985) reported that the nature of information structures or "schemas" in the self-concept can affect how one perceives and interprets the behavior of others.

When the information to which a judge is particularly sensitive tends to be accurately diagnostic of a particular trait, this interaction becomes equivalent to the Judge x Target interaction described earlier. But notice how sensitivity is not necessarily expertise. If one were sensitive to information that turned out to be misleading, then such sensitivity would harm rather than enhance accuracy. As noted earlier, expertise is particularly relevant to the utilization stage within RAM. Sensitivity, by contrast, is relevant to the detection stage.

Trait × Target: Palpability

Certain traits might be easy to judge in some targets but not others, or certain targets might have traits that can be judged easily and others that cannot. As with all of these interactions, it is important to consider this interaction separately from the main effects of its two components. The interaction refers to traits that might stand out in certain targets, relative either to the same trait in other targets or other traits in the same target. For example, a particular person's deeply ruminative style might be the most salient and easily judged aspect of him or her, even though in general this is one of the least visible traits (Funder & Dobroth, 1987; Kenrick & Stringfield, 1980). Or a person's high degree of anxiety might be clearly visible even though his or her other traits are almost completely obscure.

Research on individual differences in behavioral consistency usually has focused on individual differences in the consistency of particular traits (e.g., Baumeister & Tice, 1988; Bem & Allen, 1974; Lanning, 1988; Reise & Waller, 1993). Bem and Allen examined differential consistency in the traits of friendliness and conscientiousness, and later work also has usually assessed traitedness or scalability one or two traits at a time (Koestner, Bernieri & Zuckerman, 1989). Therefore, it is more precise to characterize this research as addressed to this Trait x Target interaction rather than to the main effect of target discussed earlier.

Research has shown that traits that are central to a person's self-concept or are seen by the individual as "personally relevant" tend to be easier for others to detect, leading to greater interjudge agreement (Koestner, Bernieri, & Zuckerman, 1989, 1994). The reason seems to be that people are motivated to be seen by others in ways that verify their self-concepts, and certain central traits are not only important to the self-concept but serve to organize it (Sedikides, 1993; Swann, 1997). The Realistic Accuracy Model refers to the property of certain traits of being particularly judgable in certain persons by the term *palpability*. This term refers to the relative obviousness and detectability of certain traits in certain individuals. A trait that leads an individual to emit many relevant behaviors often enough to be available to many different observers would be relatively *palpable* within that individual.

Trait × Information: Diagnosticity

Some traits can be judged only on the basis of particular kinds of information, that becomes available in particular contexts (Zebrowitz & Collins, 1997). For example, Park and Judd (1989) found that extraversion was generally easier to judge than was conscientiousness, but this difference was reliably reduced when the context of observation was changed to focus on conscientiousness-related traits. In another example, Colvin and Funder (1991) showed that viewing a 5-minute videotape was a relatively poor (although far from useless) source of information for judgments of general aspects of personality. However, this same source of information was as good a source for predictions of the target's future performance in a specific, similar situation as was the information other observers derived from long acquaintanceship. In a related vein, Paunonen (1989) showed that whereas some traits can be judged accurately (by the criterion of self-other agreement) on the basis of quite minimal observation, others can be judged accurately only on the basis of extended acquaintanceship.

This last point deserves more attention than it has received so far in the literature. Research on the acquaintanceship effect, in particular, has tended to treat all judged traits alike. The effect of information on judgments of one of them is assumed, implicitly, to be equivalent for all of them. But it seems likely that the information-accuracy function is quite different for different traits. If one is judging someone's extraversion, for example, brief observation in one or two social contexts may be enough. Knowing this person for years longer may tell you little about his or her extraversion you did not know after the first 10 minutes. But if you wish to judge the degree to which someone has a consistent moral code assiduously adhered to, or deep-seated emotional problems, then more extended acquaintance across a wider variety of settings will almost certainly be necessary.

A prediction could be offered, therefore, that the information-accuracy curve would tend to be quite steep for highly visible traits. Ratings of extraversion will quickly attain a high level of accuracy and not get much better thereafter. But the function for less visible or subtler traits will have a shallower slope. Accuracy will be achieved only gradually and slowly over long acquaintanceship, and even after long acquaintanceship a judge might still be discovering something new.

The interactive relationship between the information that becomes available and the particular trait that is judged is called *diagnosticity* within RAM. The sense of the term is that certain kinds of information yield relatively directly and immediately to the accurate judgment or diagnosis of certain traits, whereas other information may be irrelevant, useless, misleading, or simply insufficient.

Target × Information: Divulgence

Certain kinds of information might tell a judge a great deal about one target but relatively little about another. A particular individual's impoverished upbringing, for example, might go a long way toward explaining a wide range of his or her actions or traits. The very same background in another individual might signify relatively little. Similarly, one individual's racial or ethnic identity might be a key to understanding his or her personality, whereas for another member of the same group his or her ethnicity might have little or nothing to do with the kind of person he or she has become (Azibo, 1991).

This interaction between particular kinds of information and the particular target to whom it refers is denoted in RAM by the term *divulgence*. The term refers to the way that all information about a given individual is not created equal and certain kinds might disclose and reveal (the dictionary definition of *divulge*) much about the personality of one individual, while revealing little about the personality of another.

CONCLUSION

The aim of this chapter was to show how each of the general moderators of accuracy that has been demonstrated empirically can be accounted for theoretically by the Realistic Accuracy Model. Historically, these moderator variables were identified before RAM was developed (e.g., Funder, 1987). But I think they are more usefully and comprehensibly presented in terms of an explanatory theoretical model, as this chapter has tried to do. The first-order interactions among these moderators were discussed. Some of the many possible higher-order interactions (e.g., Target x Trait x Information) were also mentioned as they became relevant.

A theoretical accounting for the demonstrated moderators of accuracy has the potential to do more than just provide order to an otherwise seemingly arbitrary list of variables. It should also identify gaps in the empirical research, point out possible new moderator variables, and provide a framework for future research. These are among the goals of the Realistic Accuracy Model.

CHAPTER 7

Self-Knowledge

*In certain quite important respects it is easier to find out what I want to know
about you than it is for me to find out the same sorts of things for myself.*

—Gilbert Ryle (1949, pp. 155–156)

Understanding one's own self is a task that turns out to be more difficult than it seems it should be. On the one hand, there is nobody each of us knows better; we are present to see how we behave in all the settings of our lives, and each of us has available a vast reservoir of private thoughts, inexpressible feelings, and just plain secrets that nobody else knows. On the other hand, both the importance and difficulty of self-knowledge are suggested by such maxims as the Socratic injunction to "know thyself" and Freud's insistence that a psychoanalyst's first patient should always be himself or herself.

Psychological research also suggests that a lack of accurate self-knowledge can create problems. These problems range from failing to accomplish all one could because one's self-efficacy is lower than one's abilities (Bandura, 1997), to developing an alienating style of social behavior because one's self-view is unrealistically inflated (Colvin, Block, & Funder, 1995; John & Robins, 1994).

SELF-PERCEPTION VERSUS OTHER-PERCEPTION

In its initial development, the Realistic Accuracy Model (RAM) was designed to address the process by which an observer might manage to make accurate judgments of the personality of *another* person. It said little that was explicitly relevant to the processes by which one might come to accurately know oneself. But perhaps the two processes—other knowledge and self knowledge—are not so different.

Self-Perception Theory

One of the best-known, classic theories in social psychology, Daryl Bem's (1972) self-perception theory, regards self-knowledge as a phenomenon that can be reduced to a special case of one's knowledge of people in general. "To the extent that internal cues [to the nature of the self] are weak, ambiguous, or uninterpretable," Bem maintained, people must judge themselves using the same data and judgmental processes they would use to judge anybody else (Bem, 1972, p. 2). And despite the caveat just quoted Bem made it clear in his writings that he regarded "internal cues" as *typically* weak and ambiguous. In the view of self-perception theory, one's self is just another person one happens to know.

Other people are judged primarily on the basis of what they do. Concomitantly, according to Bem, self-judgment is primarily based on observations of one's own behavior. For example, if one hears oneself espousing a point of view, one may come to believe this point of view must be one's own opinion. During much of the 1970s, Bem and other researchers amassed an impressive body of evidence, much of which demonstrated the seemingly paradoxical process just described.[1]

For example, many studies demonstrated the "forced compliance effect." This effect is manifested when subjects infer they actually hold beliefs they have been induced to espouse. Bem and others showed that this self-inference is most likely to occur under the same circumstances when they would make the same inference about another person, such as when external incentives for the espousal are small (Bem & McConnell, 1970; Funder, 1982). In general, this research showed that many of the same attributional principles social psychology had already demonstrated to be relevant to the perception of others also seemed to affect perceptions of the self (Bem, 1972).

In its heyday, the aspect of self-perception theory that seemed most remarkable was its startling assertion that you do not really know yourself much better than anyone else does. As far as I know, it was never interpreted to mean that self-knowledge is actually *more* difficult than other knowledge. But some indications suggest even that might sometimes be the case.

Difficulties of Self-Knowledge

Several considerations suggest that self-knowledge is difficult to achieve.

---

[1]Much of this research was performed in the context of a debate with cognitive dissonance theory (e.g., Festinger & Carlsmith, 1959) over which perspective provided a better account of several robust experimental phenomena.

Self-Enhancement (and Self-Diminishment) Biases

The putative tendency of people to see themselves through rose-colored glasses has received a great deal of attention from psychological research over the years. One wide-ranging review even suggested, influentially, that distorting the self-view in a positive direction—seeing yourself as better than you really are—is not only typical but is actually good for you (Taylor & Brown, 1988). This conclusion seems doubtful; the long-term costs of self-deception are likely eventually to more than balance what short-term gains might accrue (Colvin & Block, 1994).[2] What does not seem doubtful, however, is that people often have trouble seeing themselves objectively and in particular tend to exaggerate their contributions, accomplishments, and abilities (Brown, 1986; Kunda, 1987; Miller & Ross, 1975). In particular, self-enhancement has frequently been observed in perception (Erdelyi, 1974), memory (Greenwald & Pratkanis, 1984), and attributions of responsibility (Lerner, 1980; Tetlock & Levi, 1982). It has even been argued that there might be evolutionary advantages to considering members of one's in-group—including oneself of course—more favorably than other people (Krebs & Denton, 1997).

But the tendency is not universal. Two considerations suggest limits to the phenomenon of self-enhancement. One is technical. The assessment of self-enhancement requires that a comparison be made between an individual's self-perception of personality and some *independent* criterion for truth. Surprisingly little research includes such a criterion, making many putative studies of self-enhancement open to a variety of alternative explanations (Colvin & Block, 1994). For example, some studies compare self-enhancement scores with scores on various adjustment questionnaires, finding the two to be positively correlated. Such a correlation may be due to the effects of self-enhancement on both instruments, rather than showing that self-enhancement is good for you.

Another limit on self-enhancement is more substantive. Some kinds of people are more prone to this sort of exaggeration than are others. For example, consider the phenomenon of narcissism (John & Robins, 1994; Robins & John, 1997). Narcissists are individuals who have grandly inflated opinions of themselves. Such people have been shown to be particularly likely to render inaccurate assessments of their contributions to a group discussion, believing their contributions to have been better and greater than is judged by other participants as well as by neutral observers. On the other hand, any sizable group also contains some self-diminishers, who view their contributions as less valuable than they appear to others. In one study, approximately 35% of subjects showed clear self-enhancement bias, 15% showed self-diminishment bias, and 50% were fairly accurate (John & Robins, 1994). A member of either of the first two groups—a narcissist or a self-diminisher—is prone

---

[2]This debate is reminiscent of an argument a decade earlier concerning the reverse point: whether depressed persons are "sadder but wiser" and actually hold a more realistic view of the world than the nondepressed (Alloy & Abramson, 1979). Subsequent research failed to support this hypothesis as well (e.g., Campbell & Fehr, 1990; Dunning & Story, 1991).

to render inaccurate judgments in the sense that their self-views will fail to match the views others have of them.

Self-Deception

When people present grandiosely inflated views of themselves it is often not clear exactly who is the true target of deception—those to whom the view is presented or the presenter him or herself. In the case of narcissism, it seems apparent that the most important audience for narcissistic self-presentation is the self, whose esteem sorely needs bolstering (Raskin, Novacek & Hogan, 1991). More generally, the habitual deception of others can become self-fulfilling, either by causing a person to believe his or her own act or even by causing the person to change.

In his novel *Mother Night*, Kurt Vonnegut wrote "We are what we pretend to be, so we must be careful about what we pretend to be" (Vonnegut, 1966, p. v). Vonnegut's point was a moral one and is also true in many other domains because our self-view so often comes through feedback concerning our own behavior. Even the wearing of a happy or sad facial expression can affect the emotions that one experiences through a process that appears to be biologically rooted (Ekman & O'Sullivan, 1991). As the song says, when you whistle a happy tune you not only fool others into thinking that you are not afraid, you fool yourself as well.

Which raises an interesting point. If the expression of a behavior or emotion changes the actual underlying disposition or emotion, then a behavior that started out deceptive might, in the end, become not deceptive at all. In Vonnegut's novel, the protagonist was an Allied spy who pretended to be an ardent Nazi propaganda broadcaster. He was so good at this act that it became unclear which of his roles was more effective, the spy or the propagandist. This uncertainty made ambiguous whether, in the end, he was "really" on the side of the Allies or the Nazis. The deception of others can create a self-deception that causes itself to become *true,* in a way perhaps more powerful than the effects of self-fulfilling prophecies inflicted by others have turned out to be in most circumstances (Swann & Ely, 1984).

The Fish-and-Water Effect

At a very basic level, there is a particularly powerful reason to expect one's own personality to be particularly difficult to see: It is always there. Kolar, Funder, and Colvin (1996) dubbed this the "fish and water effect," after the cliché that fish do not know that they are wet because they are always surrounded by water. In a similar fashion, the same personality traits that are most obvious to others might become nearly invisible to ourselves, except under the most unusual circumstances. The reader will probably have no difficulty thinking of examples, among his or her personal acquaintances, of individuals who seem to be the only people around who do not understand certain obvious aspects of their own character. For just one example, some people are so habitually penurious that the associated behaviors have become automatic and invisible. However, their behavior of hiding from the dinner check when it arrives or never being the one to bring the bottle of wine to a social function might be one of the first things a new acquaintance notices.

In their experimental study, Kolar et al. obtained personality judgments from subjects' close acquaintances as well as from the subjects themselves. In nearly every comparison, the acquaintances' judgments manifested better predictive validity than did the self-judgments. For example, acquaintances' judgments of assertiveness correlated more highly with assertive behavior measured later in the laboratory than did self-judgments of assertiveness. Although the differences were sometimes quite small, the same finding appeared for talkativeness, initiation of humor, physical attractiveness, feelings of being cheated and victimized by life, and several other traits of personality and behavior. A further study by Spain (1994) showed that the degree of difference in accuracy between the self and others depends on the criterion used. When the criterion for accuracy was the ability to predict overt, social behavior, this latter study found, self-judgments held no advantage over judgments by others (no advantage for the others was found in this study). But when the criterion was on-line reports of emotional experience, self-judgments of personality afforded better predictions than did peers' judgments.

The bottom line seems to be this: Notwithstanding the obvious advantages of self-observation, in some ways it may be surprisingly difficult. But this depends on the aspects of the self that are in question. Other people have a view of your social behavior that is as good as and sometimes even superior to the view you have of yourself. In the domain of private experience, the self is still the king and most valid observer. As will be discussed later in this chapter, however, the self may not be infallible even there.

The Obscured Vantage Point of the Self

The perspective that the self has on one's own social behavior has several other potential disadvantages besides the fish-and-water effect. One appears to be a matter of observational perspective, both literally and metaphorically. Most people have had the experience of viewing a photograph or videotape of themselves, or listening to an audiotape of their own voice, and responding "That *cannot* be me!" Our impressions of our own voice, appearance, and behavioral style often seem stunningly at odds with how we sound and look from the perspective of another. It can be even more disconcerting to realize that although photographs of one's self seldom seem accurate, photographs of other people generally seem to do rather well at catching them as they really are.

Our literal observational perspective makes it difficult to attain an accurate view of our appearance and social behavior. We cannot see our own face or even most of our own body without some kind of outside assistance from a mirror or camera. We hear our own voice as it resonates through the bones of the skull, making it sound deeper and smoother than it really does. Perhaps most tellingly of all, we see our own behaviors through the prism of what we thought we intended to do at the time, rather than in terms of the effects they actually had. This may be an important basis of one of the most robust and extensively researched phenomena in social psychology, the *actor-observer effect*.

The Actor–Observer Effect

With a few exceptions, research has found that the "actor" who performs a given behavior will typically self-report that it was determined by situational factors. An observer, by contrast, will be more likely to conclude the behavior was determined by "dispositional" personality attributes possessed by the actor (Jones & Nisbett, 1971). At a more general level, when presented a list of trait terms to check off with the option "depends on the situation" offered next to each term, people will check the "depends" box more often when describing themselves than when describing friends or acquaintances (Nisbett, Caputo, Legant, & Marecek, 1973). In this way, it sometimes seems as if personality is something only *other* people have.

The conventional wisdom in social psychology, firmly established over the years, is that this discrepancy arises because the actor is right and the observer is wrong (Jones, 1979; Monson & Snyder, 1977). It has been pointed out that the actor has a number of advantages over the observer in understanding his or her own behavior,and that the observer is prone to commit the "fundamental attribution error" (Ross, 1977; see Chapter 3).

A conclusion of the present analysis is the reverse of the conventional wisdom. A variety of considerations suggests that an important basis of the actor-observer difference is that one's own personality, and its effects on one's own behavior, is extraordinarily difficult to perceive. Observational perspective has already been mentioned. Individuals may be in a poor position to see their own behavioral consistencies, both because of the literal angle from which they view themselves and the circumstances under which they do the viewing.

In addition to the considerations already discussed, it has been pointed out by Jones and Nisbett (1971) and others (e.g., Storms, 1973) that the observational perspective of the actor is onto the surrounding environment. But from the perspective of an observer, the actor is located in a perceptual field alongside other actors with whom the individual is then naturally compared (Heider, 1958). Several studies have manipulated this aspect of observational perspective, while holding constant other aspects (e.g., information about the actor's behavior in other situations). Their consistent finding is that subjects who take the observer's perspective make attributions for behavior that are more dispositional, and less situational, than subjects who take the actor's perspective.

For example, when actors watch themselves from the observer's perspective by viewing a videotape, they come to make attributions for their own behavior that are equivalently dispositional as those offered by observers (Storms, 1973). Similar findings are obtained when perspective is altered using mirrors (Duval & Wicklund,

1973), explicit instructions to take the observers' perspective (Frank & Gilovich, 1989), and the sheer passage of time (McKay, O'Farrell, Maisto, Connors, & Funder, 1989; Moore, Sherrod, Liu, & Underwood, 1979; Peterson, 1980). Frank and Gilovich (1989) summarized the literature in this way:

> All of these manipulations serve to make actors more aware of themselves and their actions and thus also lead them to attribute their behavior more dispositionally. (p. 402)

This comment implies that the influence of personality on behavior is easier to see from the outside than from the inside. Research on the topic of "objective self awareness" supports this implication. Judgments of personality made from an external vantage point—that arises either because an individual is dispositionally "self aware" or simply is watching himself or herself in a mirror—tend to be more accurate than those made from an internal vantage point. Even completing a self-report personality inventory in the presence of a mirror can enhance the validity of the resulting scores for predicting future behavior (Scheier, Buss, & Buss, 1976). On the other hand, moving to an external perspective is no help for narcissists. According to Robins and John (1997), viewing themselves from an external perspective (via videotape) only exacerbates narcissists' tendencies toward self-enhancement.

For present purposes, the point is not that observers are better than actors at judging behavior, though some researchers have suggested this possibility (Hofstee, 1994, Kenny, 1994, p. 194). Rather, the point is that under ordinary circumstances, self-awareness is far from privileged. It is at least as problematical as is the perception of others, especially when one wants or needs to accurately perceive the consistent attributes of one's own social behavior.

Observing versus Inhabiting Personality

A further difficulty for self-awareness is the fact that we must inhabit our personality at the same time we try to observe it. This makes the observation difficult to do.

Daily life is pretty demanding. It demands all the cognitive resources we can muster to simultaneously perceive our physical and social environment, respond emotionally, and act in an appropriate manner. Indeed, this is the challenge of being alive and awake: to constantly respond to the environment in the best possible way under constantly changing circumstances. Our personality consists to a large extent of the characteristic strategies each of us has developed for simplifying this task. We have basic categories and ways of perceiving situations; we have characteristic ways we respond to certain kinds of situations (and these are often different from the characteristic responses of others, which is what makes each of us unique and the topic of personality interesting).

In one of Gordon Allport's most trenchant phrases, personality has the capacity "to render many stimuli functionally equivalent" (1937, p. 295). The tendency to view different situations as similar causes a person to respond to them in a like manner, and the patterns of behavior that result are the overt manifestations of traits.

The interpretation of a trait as a subjective, situational-equivalence class offers an idea about phenomenology—about what it feels like to have a trait, to the person who has it (Funder, 1991). The answer is that ordinarily it doesn't really feel like anything. The only subjective manifestation of a trait *within* a person will be his or her tendency to react and feel similarly across the situations to which the trait is relevant. As Allport wrote:

> For some the world is a hostile place where men are evil and dangerous; for others it is a stage for fun and frolic. It may appear as a place to do one's duty grimly; or a pasture for cultivating friendship and love. (1961, p. 266)

It is these differences in perception that create differences in behavior. A sociable person does not ordinarily say to him- or herself, "I am a sociable person; therefore, I shall now act in a sociable fashion." Rather, he or she responds positively to the presence of others in a natural, automatic, unselfconscious way. An unsociable person, who perceives the presence of others differently, accordingly also responds differently. And a highly emotional person is too busy experiencing strong emotions to notice that his or her very emotional responsiveness may be one of his or her strongest, most characteristic and (to others) most obvious personality traits.

But access to one's own traits is not completely impossible. On reflection one can indeed begin to come to opinions about one's own traits (Bem, 1972; Thorne, 1989). For example, although it seems nearly impossible to analyze all the determinants of one's own emotional reaction while one is still having it, such an analysis might be possible later. As the philosopher Gilbert Ryle observed, "States of mind such as these more or less violent agitations can be examined only in retrospect" (1967, p. 160). For example, alcoholics asked to relate the causes of a drinking relapse near the time it occurred attributed it to stress and other situational factors. Only after the passage of time could they acknowledge that not everybody reacts to stress by getting drunk and that an important cause of their binge was their own dispositional alcoholism (McKay et al., 1989).[3]

The kind of retrospective analysis that makes the consistent attributes of one's own personality more clear to oneself can happen late at night, lying in bed and staring at the ceiling, musing about the events of the day. That is the time when you are in the best position to realize, "I always react that way (darn it)," or "I guess I could have done that differently." Such reflection is also sometimes induced in conversations with a trusted friend, or on a therapist's couch. In psychotherapy the client typically is encouraged to relate past experiences, and the client and therapist

---

[3] The viewpoint of the alcoholic also reflects the difference in perspective noted by Heider. From an internal perspective, the alcoholic is correct in attributing his or her drinking to stress, if he or she doesn't get drunk unless under stress. The comparison is within subject, between the times the alcoholic does and does not drink. From an external perspective, however, one can note that different people respond to stress in different ways, and not all of them get drunk. This is why the alcoholic gives a situational attribution, an outside observer (such as a wife or husband) offers a dispositional one, and both are, in separate senses, correct.

together come up with interpretations. Whether labeled in this manner or not, these interpretations often involve a mutual discovery of the client's situational equivalence classes, or traits. Certain profound life experiences might also stimulate this kind of otherwise rare conscious retrospection.

APPLICATION OF RAM TO SELF-JUDGMENT

Beyond the general observations discussed so far, the Realistic Accuracy Model offers a new, alternative, and somewhat more structured way to examine self-knowledge. An important part of the agenda for future theoretical development is to extend RAM to cover some aspects of the process by which one might come to an accurate understanding of one's own personality.

At first glance, some of the four stages of RAM might not seem to pertain to self-judgment. In particular, availability and detection might have less application to self-judgment than does relevance or utilization. However, on close examination I believe each of the stages of RAM identifies at least a few issues that might otherwise be missed, and illuminates others, already identified, in a somewhat new and different light. Perhaps most importantly, RAM may have the potential to organize many of the diverse influences on the accuracy of self-knowledge into a single, relatively simple framework shared with the analysis of the accuracy of the knowledge of others.

Relevance

As was related in Chapter 5, relevance concerns the connection between personality and behavior. If a target person never emits a behavior relevant to a given trait, then it is difficult to see how that trait could ever be accurately judged. In the same way, it will be difficult and perhaps impossible to know something about one of your own personality traits if you have never performed a behavior relevant to it (Bem, 1972).

Situational Constraints and Opportunities

Behavior is relevant to personality when the individual's own propensities have a chance to affect what he or she does. Behavior is not relevant to personality when it is stimulus driven, when the situation or the stimuli the situation contains are so powerful as to wipe out individual differences and the expression of the unique aspects of the self. This limitation on behavioral relevance can affect self-knowledge as well as the knowledge of others.

Consider an individual who lives in a behaviorally restrictive culture. His or her behavior may be driven almost entirely by social norms. In some cultures, one's occupation, one's leisure-time activities, and even one's spouse may be chosen by others. Such "collectivist" cultures, as they are called (see Triandis, 1994), may promote social harmony and a sense of belonging (Markus & Kitayama, 1991). But they are not exactly rife with opportunities for self-knowledge. When so much of one's behavior and life choices are determined by important other people or by the community at large, what chance does one have to find out where one's own talents, interests, and inclinations lie? In this light, it perhaps should not be surprising that members of collectivist cultures have a lesser sense of possessing a unique self than do members of individualistic cultures that allow more range for behavioral expression (Shweder & Bourne, 1982). It might *not* be the case that, as is sometimes argued, people in such cultures literally do not have an individual self. Rather, they may enjoy few circumstances under which they have a chance to learn what it contains.

The same comment probably applies to persons within individualistic cultures who inhabit family or occupational contexts that restrict some or many aspects of behavioral self-expression. If the family or social environment rigidly suppresses one's sexual impulses, for example, then it is only to be expected that one will experience some confusion about what they really are. If you spend years in an educational system that discourages the expression of your own opinions, you may cease having any original ideas. Likewise, if your occupational choice is guided by family history or a mindless search for whatever kind of job seems to offering the largest starting salary this year, you may never have a chance to discover what you are really good at.

On the other hand, a family and cultural environment that encourages self-expression, an educational environment that encourages independent thought, and an occupational choice guided by one's talents rather than by the expectations of others will yield very different results. Situations like these can be expected to yield individuals who enjoy a frank, honest, and accurate knowledge of their own capacities, limitations, and propensities.

Intentional Manipulations of Relevance

It is possible to do things that either restrict or enhance the relevance of one's own behaviors to one's personality.

Restricting Self-Relevance

Strange as it may seem, people sometimes seem to deliberately cut themselves off from opportunities to learn about themselves. Perhaps the best researched of these tactics is "self-handicapping" (Baumgardner & Brownlee, 1987; Berglas & Jones, 1978). This is the perverse strategy for protecting self-esteem by throwing obstacles in the way of one's own performance. For example, a student who does not begin studying for an important test until the night before has a ready-made excuse for his or her failure. The poor test performance the next morning does not have to be seen as a result of inability, but rather can be safely attributed to lack of preparation and lack of sleep. If I *had* started studying earlier, the student can still believe, I would have been at the top of the class.

In terms of the Realistic Accuracy Model, self-handicapping comprises a deliberate short-circuiting of the relevance stage.[4] By creating so many situational obstacles to performance, the individual ensures that his performance remains uninformative about—*irrelevant* to—his or her dispositional ability. The same thing can happen in the social domain. Some shy people withdraw from opportunities for social activity in order to avoid the possibility of learning things about their social selves they might rather not know (see Snyder, Smith, Augelli, & Ingram, 1985). The diagnostically relevant behaviors never have a chance to appear, and self-knowledge has no way to develop.

On a more general level, an important attraction of the use of drugs and alcohol seems to be that it interferes with self-awareness and self-knowledge. Drugs do this in two ways. First, many drugs and particularly alcohol seem to have direct effects on the nervous system that lessen the degree of self-awareness (Hull, 1981). Second, a behavior performed under the influence of drugs or alcohol can be regarded as no longer relevant, in the sense the term is used by RAM. An aggressive punch, a lewd pass, or simply dancing on the table with a lampshade on the head can all be reinterpreted as not relevant to personality because "that wasn't really me." To the extent that a person is chronically using drugs or alcohol he or she is deliberately cutting himself or herself off from self-knowledge in both of these ways.

Enhancing Self-Relevance

On the brighter side, some individuals deliberately do give themselves extra chances to emit behaviors that might enhance self-knowledge. Some people "test themselves" by bungee-jumping, climbing Mt. Everest, or simply by taking on challenging tasks and performing them to the best of their abilities. The overseas experience (OE) that is traditional for many young New Zealanders is deliberately undertaken, by many, in order to confront novel people and situations and to thereby learn more about the self. This is consistent with what might be RAM's prescription for following the Socratic injunction to know yourself: Get out more (see also, Chapter 8).

Personality Coherence

In the discussion of the "good target" in Chapter 6, Colvin's (1993b) notion of the "judgable person" was summarized. Briefly, the idea is that some people have

---

[4]The use of the word *deliberate* is not meant to imply the use of self-handicapping is always conscious. The literature is unclear on this point. It does refer to the source of the obstacle to relevance being in the person's own behavior, as opposed to coming from without (as in the examples of restrictive environments discussed earlier).

coherent, well-organized personalities in which "what you see is what you get." Words match deeds, deeds at one time match deeds in another time and place, and the whole pattern of the person's behavior generally makes sense. Such people are relatively easy for others to judge accurately; the same should apply to self-judgment. Other people might have trouble figuring themselves out because their selves are truly confusing.

Sometimes the confusion is temporary. A war veteran returning to his bucolic hometown might find his battle-taught reactions, formerly essential to his survival, suddenly out of place. Even a new college student leaving home for the first time will take some time to evolve a new, consistent style of social behavior that works in this unfamiliar setting. And Chapter 6 already considered the plight of the adolescent in transition, who is probably as confusing to him- or herself as he or she is to everybody else.

But sometimes the confusion is more permanent. People with schizoid or borderline personalities might find their erratic behavioral styles difficult to assimilate and are unlikely to understand themselves much better than anyone else does. People whose behavior is affected by hormonal imbalances, neurological disturbances, or drugs also may find their own behavior confusing, because it really is erratic and therefore irrelevant to personality in any broader sense.

Any sound judgment of personality must occur on the basis of behaviors that are relevant to the traits being judged. Even for the self, such relevant behaviors might be more rare than could be wished.

Availability

The availability stage of RAM raises different issues. Assuming that the person has indeed emitted one or more behaviors that are relevant to an attribute of personality, under what circumstances will this behavior become available? At first glance it might appear that surely everything a person does is available at least to himself or herself. It probably is also true that a larger proportion of relevant acts is in fact available to the self than to anybody else. Still, at least a couple of circumstances can be identified that might limit the availability of relevant behaviors to the self.

Subtle Physiological Cues

Not everything that one's own body is doing is immediately obvious, even if it is important. Your heartbeat might accelerate at the sight of certain kinds of people, or your blood pressure rise when certain things are said to you, and these reactions—which are essentially behavioral—might be highly relevant to one or more important aspects of your personality. But they might not be available to you without special equipment or training.

That is the purpose of some species of biofeedback (Blanchard & Epstein, 1978). Through the use of physiological monitoring equipment, it appears that people can learn to identify the presence of physiological events within the body that otherwise might be undetectable. People do seem to use these cues when they are able to perceive them. In a classic study, Valins (1966) showed that men reported being more attracted to women whose photographs were displayed at the same time that the men were led to believe their heart rates had increased. (The same effect seems to work for women viewing pictures of men; Woll & McFall, 1979). Although some researchers are skeptical about how often this happens in real life (Parkinson, 1985), it still seems well established that people at least sometimes base conclusions about themselves—such as their own reactions and preferences—on seemingly relevant physiological cues that happen to become available.

Feedback from Others

Another limitation in the availability of relevant information to the self comes from without. An important source of information about our behaviors and their impli-cations for personality is the way our actions affect others. Indeed, many personality traits only take their meaning through interactions with others (Mead, 1934). Con-sider dominance, social skill, or charm. If you lived alone on a desert island, how could you possibly form an opinion as to whether any of these traits characterized you? Social traits like these are bona fide aspects of personality, and we can learn about them only to the extent that the effects of our relevant behaviors become available to us through social interaction.

These effects, in fact, are not always available, even when other people are pres-ent. Often, the problem is politeness. Questions ranging from "What do you think of my new haircut?" to "Do you think she liked me?" are not particularly likely to be answered truthfully. People instinctively and automatically strive to save each other's face and not hurt anybody's feelings. They will therefore cut people off from feedback that their assertive behavior is really rude, their jokes are offensive, and their very best conversational openers are impossibly trite and boring. Research has shown, for example, that people with negative self-views do things that elicit unfa-vorable reactions from others but fail to appreciate this fact because their interaction partners "[conceal] their aversion behind a façade of kind words" (Swann, Stein-Seroussi, & McNulty, 1992, p. 618). As a result, they live in social worlds that deprive them of corrective feedback that might allow self-improvement.

If this situation persists long enough, it can create a real social dilemma. Examples include the aunt who must always sing at family gatherings because everyone has always told her she has a beautiful voice, the colleague who dominates departmental discussions because nobody has told him that he rarely makes sense, and the person who continues to make ever-accelerating demands on the time and resources of others because nobody has had the courage to tell her no. These are all people who badly need a dose of accurate self-knowledge, but to achieve that, the relevant social effects of their behaviors need to be made available to them. In some cases, that may never happen. The danger is particularly acute if the individual is of high status or power, which might inhibit frank feedback from others, or if the person reacts with hostility to anyone who dares to tell him or her about the real social effects of his or her behavior.

Politeness is not the only danger here. If one is surrounded by people determined (or merely inclined) to damage one's self-esteem, one may be cut of from the availability of positive aspects of one's behavior. Another New Zealand cultural practice I first heard of while writing this book is something called the "great Kiwi battering machine." This term refers to the practice of trying to tear down those who seem in danger of achieving too much. The intention, apparently, is to avoid having anyone believe he is any better than his fellows. This may be a laudable egalitarian goal, but it probably cuts some individuals off from achieving to their potential or learning about how talented they really are.

In any culture, it is highly possible that nobody will ever tell you have talent, make sense, or deserve to be put in charge, even if you do. If they never do tell you, it is not clear how you can ever know.

Detection

Relevant information about your personality might be available right there in front of you, but you still might fail to register it. The various kinds of blindness (and perceptiveness) that arise in self-observation are all relevant to the *detection* stage of the Realistic Accuracy Model. The term is probably most usefully reserved for the situation where relevant information is present and available to a self-perceiver, who then does or does not attend to it.

Detection, and the failure of detection, has two parts. The first part is to look at the available information. If a perceiver is looking (or listening) elsewhere or chooses not to look at what is otherwise right in front of him or her, then this information will never register. The other part is to see what one is looking at.

Looking at or Looking away

Several factors can influence whether a person will detect information about the self that is otherwise relevant and available.

Intentionally Looking the Other Way

The reader may recall the conclusion of the film *The Paper Chase*. The main character, a law student, is anxiously awaiting the outcomes of his final examinations. When the dreaded envelope finally arrives, he pauses, then instead of opening it he tears it up! RAM (still 20 years in the future when this film was made) would describe this as a (deliberate) failure at the detection stage. The information was surely relevant, and unquestionably available, but because the character never looked at it, the information never got a chance to register on his nervous system.

The film character was of course fictitious, but the example is worth bearing in mind if we want to analyze the effects of the detection stage on self-knowledge. When do people, metaphorically speaking, "tear up the envelope" that contains potentially important information about themselves? The answer is not obvious, but probably includes those occasions when we avoid overhearing the conversation we do not want to hear, or distract ourselves from attending to social situations that might otherwise be unpleasant. Some people cut themselves off from otherwise informative social feedback fairly effectively by immersing themselves in books, by surfing the Internet for hours on end, or by never taking off the headphones to their Walkman. Others do the same thing in a more metaphoric way.

Self-Consciousness

According to analyses by Creed and Funder (1998), some people are more self aware than others are, being attentive to and conscious of the indicators that are informative about the state of one's own mind. This kind of positive self-consciousness can be expected to be associated with enhanced performance at the detection stage. Research that experimentally provides opportunities for subjects to reflect on themselves also has shown that such opportunities lead to self-insight according to a variety of criteria, including enhanced agreement with others in their self-judgments of personality (Hixon & Swann, 1993).

But there is another kind of self-consciousness, the kind that gives being "self-conscious" a bad name. People who ruminate excessively about their own states of mind and personalities appear to generate cognitions that have the net effect of interfering with rather than enhancing self-insight (Anderson, Bohon, & Berrigan, 1996; Lyubomirksy & Nolen-Hoeksema, 1993). They may obsessively search for negative information or dwell on unpleasant facts to the exclusion of balancing information on the positive side. This kind of self-consciousness should not be confused with self-awareness, which is characterized by an interest in and attention to the self that is more line with Socratic idea of knowing oneself (see also Sartre, 1965).

In terms of the Realistic Accuracy Model, the wrong kind of self-consciousness interferes with detection, as we have just seen. It also interferes with relevance. Behavior that is overly "self-conscious" is not true to the self, because it is thought about too much. The right kind of self-consciousness enhances detection.

Task Complexity

Life often makes heavy demands on the cognitive resources that an individual has available to deal with it. At any given moment a person might be under threat, hard at work, or engaged in a complicated set of social negotiations. Even the simplest social interaction requires a fair amount of effort to coordinate one's behavior with the behavior of the other person, attending to self-presentation and the maintenance of one's self-image all the while. Self-awareness must come from whatever attention is left over to attend to one's own actions.

Chronic Distraction

Other people may fail to attend to self-relevant information because their attention is characteristically focused elsewhere. A paranoid individual, for example, may be so occupied with searching for and detecting slights and threats that he or she fails to notice the most rudimentary facts about his or her own behavior (including aspects of his or her own actions that may be the root cause of the slights and threats, to the extent they actually exist). A hypochondriac may be so occupied with searching for and over-interpreting new physical symptoms that he or she has little attention to spare for anything else. Or, less pathologically, a person may just be extremely busy. A single parent of small children or a business executive with similarly complex and relentless responsibilities may have little attention to spare for anything else. To attain self-knowledge individuals like these may need, first and above all else, a vacation.

Looking and (Not) Seeing

Even if one is actually looking at a piece of information, the information still will not necessarily be seen. An example of this is the fish-and-water effect discussed earlier. An aspect of one's own behavior and personality can be so constantly present that it becomes, in effect, invisible. This is not really a problem of attention on the part of the self-perceiver, but of habituation—the gradual retreat of information into invisibility with repetition.

The psychoanalytic process of repression may have a similar effect. Although the research on this process has been controversial over the years, on balance sufficient evidence seems to indicate that people often manifest a tendency to avoid the perception of stimuli that are potentially disturbing (Erdelyi, 1974; Westen, 1998). Of course, the information that has the potential to be the most disturbing is information about the self, and so such processes could be expected to be particularly important influences on the detection stage of otherwise accurate self-judgment.

Some people seem to be able to keep problematical information out of awareness better than others can. Davidson (1993) found that the same people who were best able to suppress unwanted thoughts tended to be those who did not share the opinions of their peers about how hostile they were.

Further research suggests that people do not work just to maintain positive views of themselves. They seem to become attached to *any* opinion they develop about themselves, positive or negative. The strategies people use for "self-verification" span several the stages of self-judgment suggested by RAM. According to research by Swann (1997), people with negative self-views seek relationship partners who view them negatively (relevance), elicit negative evaluations from partners (availability), and "see" more negativity in the reactions of others than is actually there (detection and utilization).

On a more positive note, some individuals are surely more sensitive than others to information about themselves. These are the lucky people who manage to always look at themselves with fresh eyes and who do not seem to need to cut off or distort the information they see. Like all experts, they make it look easy, and the magnitude of their accomplishment may therefore not always be appreciated. It is much easier to think of people who manifest one or more of the failures of self-observation that have just been discussed.

Utilization

As was discussed in Chapter 5, RAM's distinction between detection and utilization is neither hard-and-fast nor always easy to establish. What one perceives depends on what one knows, and vice versa. There can be a fine line, if any, between a failure to perceive something and a failure to think about it. In other words, the distinction between detection and utilization is no more clear than another useful distinction in psychology, that between perception and cognition.

When applied to self-knowledge, the utilization stage of accurate personality judgment is largely equivalent to the cognitive processes already discussed in relation to this stage in Chapter 5. All of the same issues apply concerning general and domain-specific knowledge, memory organization and retrieval, and other processes of social cognition. Indeed, an impressive series of studies by Stan Klein and Judith Loftus (Klein & Loftus, 1988; Klein, Loftus, & Burton, 1989) has convincingly established that cognitions about the self are not as distinctive as is sometimes assumed. In structure and relevant process, they resemble cognitions about other people, just as Bem's (1972) self-perception theory anticipated years earlier.

Aspects that concern motivation and emotion seem more likely to be distinctive about self-cognition or, in RAM's terms, the utilization stage applied to the self. Some people are motivated to take on the effort—and the risk—of thinking hard and clearly about themselves. Indeed, for some philosophers this hard work at illusion-free self-knowledge is an existential imperative, regardless of where it may lead (Sartre, 1965; see also Funder, 1997a, Chapter 14).

Trying Not to Think about It

Like failures of detection, failures of utilization are probably more obvious than successes. One of those, which every reader surely has observed, is the phenomenon of the person who "just doesn't want to think about it." *It*, in this phrase, may refer to some particular self-relevant issue or in some cases to anything concerning the self at all. People who say—or act according to—this cliché are seldom those renowned for their self-insight.

Ironically, Dan Wegner has amassed evidence suggesting that trying deliberately not to think about something is one of the surest ways of causing it to come repeatedly to mind (in fact, he calls this an "ironic process," Wegner, 1994). The classic demonstration is the effect of telling a subject not think about a white bear. As long as the subject continues to try to push the image from mind, he or she will actually think of little else. On the other hand, distraction works fairly well. Rather than not think of something, it works better to simply think of something different, preferably something interesting. If the new topic garners more attention than the old topic, then the old topic has been successfully driven out of mind.

A person who finds something more interesting to think about, therefore, may successfully avoid self-confrontation. More typically, however, a person who is trying hard not to think about something self-relevant ends up obsessing about it. This kind of obsessive thought rarely leads to self-insight. Instead, it consists of ruminatively repeating the same negative thoughts over and over to oneself, with little progress being made toward understanding (Lyubomirksy & Nolen-Hoeksema, 1993).

Distortion

As has been discussed already, a complex debate has arisen in the psychological literature concerning whether people in fact distort information in their favor, and whether it is adaptive for them to do so (Colvin & Block, 1994; Taylor & Brown, 1988). The Realistic Accuracy Model does not imply a position on this issue but does separate out the different parts of the process of self-enhancement to the degree it occurs. At the detection stage, a self-enhancing person either fails to notice unfavorable information that is present and available to be noticed or distorts that information in a favorable direction.

CONCLUSION

It is not always clear whether a failure to achieve knowledge about oneself is due to shortcomings of relevance, availability, detection, or utilization, or a complex combination of all four. But the Realistic Accuracy Model does remind us that failures of self-insight come in several varieties. It also reminds us that to the extent we might wish to improve our yield of knowledge about ourselves, there are several promising locations in which we could begin prospecting. We could seek out contexts where we will perform self-relevant behaviors, seek candid feedback from others about our performance, look at ourselves frankly from a fresh, outside perspective, and put some effort into the difficult cognitive task of making sense of it all. Nobody ever said the path to self-knowledge was easy (Sartre, 1965).

CHAPTER 8

Prospects for Improving Accuracy

I can say with confidence that something ought to be done to improve the manner in which we human beings decide what to do.

—Kenneth Hammond (1996, p. 6)

It is truth that makes you free. Although psychologists and others occasionally propound the virtues of seeing the world as better, or at least different, than it really is, surely the benefits of illusion are short term at best (Colvin & Block, 1994; Colvin, Block, & Funder, 1995). Only an accurate understanding of yourself and your fellows can put you in a position to choose clearly what, by your own lights, is the right thing to do, both pragmatically and morally. How could an inaccurate view of the social world allow such a choice?

The Realistic Accuracy Model (RAM) implies that possibilities for the improvement of accuracy in personality judgment arise at four points. To enhance the *relevance* stage of accurate personality judgment, information must be obtained or produced that is more informative about the trait to be judged. To enhance the *availability* stage, the judge must obtain more information (e.g., with longer acquaintance), across a broader range of contexts, to increase the probability that whatever relevant information exists will become available to him or her. To enhance the *detection* stage, the judge's powers of attention and observation must be improved. Finally, to enhance the *utilization* stage, the judge must think better. His or her explicit and implicit knowledge needs to be improved and brought to bear on the relevant and available information that he or she has managed to detect so that a more accurate judgment of personality can be the result.

187

RELEVANCE

The possibility of an accurate personality judgment does not begin until and unless the person being judged emits some kind of information—does something—that is relevant to the judgment. As we have seen in previous chapters, relevant behaviors are sometimes suppressed or simply never arise because strong situations constrain behavior or because the person never experiences a context that elicits a relevant behavior. For example, a person in a restrictive family or cultural environment may exhibit behavior that is determined more by the mores of others than by his or her own personality. A courageous person may never find himself or herself in a dangerous situation or have such situations arise so seldom few judges ever have a chance to observe his or her behavior in them.

Improving Relevance in Real Life

The improvement of relevance can be attempted in two ways.

Observation

First, the judge can take care to observe the person being judged in the contexts that are most informative for the trait in question (Zebrowitz & Collins, 1997). To judge social traits, one must observe the target person's behavior in interpersonal situations. To judge occupational competencies, one must observe the target person's job behavior. This seemingly obvious point is often neglected. People too often infer traits from the observation of behavior in contexts where no relevant information could be expected to occur. People are hired because they are likable in social settings; they are befriended because they make good colleagues; sometimes these inferential leaps across context are made successfully but when they are, it is a matter of luck rather than of logic.

Contrivance

A second way to improve relevance is to do something to *create* the appropriate observational context. Some kind of stimulus might be created that will lead the target person to emit a behavior that is relevant to the behavior that the judge wants or needs to evaluate. This is not as unusual a tactic as might first appear.

The simple act of asking someone a question is an example. When you ask a question, you present the person with a stimulus and await his or her response. Surprisingly often, the purpose of conversational questions is diagnostic in this sense. A potential employer might ask you, "Why did you leave your last job?" A potential date might ask you, "What is your mother like?" In both cases, and many others, the purpose of the question is to elicit personality-relevant information from the person being asked, as much as it is to obtain the information literally being requested. People who are better judges of personality might, to an important degree, be those who know how to ask better questions. A good question, in this sense, is one that elicits relevant data about personality, an informative answer.

Occasionally people even set up little situations to test the behavior—not just the words—of the person of interest. An employer might ask someone being considered for promotion to "take charge for a week while I'm away." A parent might ask a child to perform some task alone, while watching surreptitiously both to make sure the task is done safely and to assess the child's degree of maturity. Even more elaborate and sometimes deceptive behavioral tests are occasionally deployed, such as when police—or even spouses—set up a "sting" to gauge someone's honesty or faithfulness.

It is also possible to set up social contexts in which more informative behaviors are likely to appear. If a situation is relaxed and informal, for example, people are more likely to be their real selves (Funder & Colvin, 1991). A supervisor who wants to know what his or her employees are really like might do well to bear this principle in mind. Another approach is to create environments that restrict irrelevant behavior. As my daughter's teacher in New Zealand observed, when all children wear the same school uniforms then they are no longer judged by teachers or fellow students by the way they dress. Instead, their relevant behaviors become the focus.[1]

Improving Relevance in the Laboratory

A couple of methods are also available to a researcher who would gather more relevant behavioral information. To improve relevance, psychologists often use methods parallel to those real life-life tactics just described.

Observation

Occasionally, observational methods are used to try to find out, unobtrusively, what a target person does in one or more informative contexts. For example, students in a classroom might be observed surreptitiously while their degree of dependence on teacher, aggression toward classmates, helpful actions, or play behavior is observed and measured.

Contrivance

Much more typically, the psychologist administers some sort of stimulus that, it is hoped, will elicit a relevant response. The classic and most frequently used example

---

[1] Technically, in terms of RAM, the restriction of behaviors that would be irrelevant (clothing choice) is a manipulation of relevance. The resultant change of focus onto behaviors that are relevant is a manipulation of detection.

of this approach is the ubiquitous psychological questionnaire. Every question is a stimulus in search of a response, and the questions asked by psychologists on printed forms are no exception. The trick, as every psychologist who has ever worked in questionnaire development knows, is to ask good questions. Elaborate methods are used to develop and test the "validity"—the relevance, in RAM's terms—of questionnaire measures of personality (Wiggins, 1973). But the basic principle is very simple: Ask the right question, and the answer that is given will be *relevant* to some aspect of personality. This principle holds equally no matter which method of questionnaire development is used: rational, empirical, or factor-analytic (Funder, 1997a).

A more elaborate technique—which is nonetheless in principle the same—is the "assessment center" (see, e.g., Wiggins, 1973). The purpose of an assessment center, such as those conducted over the years by the Institute of Personality Assessment (IPAR) at Berkeley, is to set up a range of situations over a weekend or longer period of time in which subjects can be observed to perform behaviors that—it is hoped—are relevant to important aspects of their personalities. Subjects might play charades, engage in a leaderless group discussion, or even be induced to get drunk, all in the service of eliciting relevant behavioral information.

A final example of this genre is the psychological experiment. Again, every experimental situation is set up in the hope of creating a context in which subjects will perform behavior that is relevant to the psychological attribute or process of interest. For example, in our own "accuracy projects" we have had subjects engage in unstructured dyadic conversations, build tinker-toys, play Simon®, and so forth. The intention—if not always the accomplishment—of these and all such experimenter-imposed settings is to create a context in which *relevant* behaviors will occur. Much of the art of research and experimentation lies in the clever design of such contexts (Aronson, Brewer, & Carlsmith, 1985).

AVAILABILITY

The improvement of availability, as this stage is defined by RAM, is in principle (perhaps not in practice) simpler. Where relevance is a complex matter of quality of information, availability is typically a matter of quantity. The relationship between the two is that of the relevant information emitted by a target, only a fraction is available to any given judge. But the odds of seeing something relevant improve as more information becomes available. These odds improve still further if information is obtained across a variety of contexts, to which different aspects of personality will be relevant.

The improvement of availability, therefore, requires the judge to observe more behaviors in a wider variety of contexts. The first of these considerations, the quantitative variable, is sometimes considered to be a matter of "acquaintance" (e.g., Blackman & Funder, 1998; Funder, & Colvin, 1988; Kenny, 1994). The longer a judge has known the target, the more information becomes available and the better the chances that the judge has learned something relevant to the judgment he or she must make.

The more neglected, second consideration, is that knowing somebody better is not just a matter of knowing somebody longer. The wider range of situations, and more informative situations, in which a judge has observed a target, the more accurate that judge has a chance to become. For example, a judge who knows someone both at work and at home—where behaviors relevant to different aspects of personality are displayed—could be expected to be more accurate, overall, than a judge who has observed the same target for a similar period of time but only in one of these settings.

Moreover, some settings may be more informative than others. Andersen (1984) demonstrated that watching someone talk about thoughts and feelings yielded more accurate judgments of his or her personality than did watching this person talk about hobbies and activities. The larger implication—still to be pursued systematically by research—is that some settings yield particularly informative behaviors. Anecdotally, many people are convinced that they have learned an exceptional amount about others by observing them in combat, or under stress, or simply by the way they interact with children. It has not yet been proven that any of these settings in fact are especially informative, but the possibility deserves to be investigated.

The astute reader has noticed that this discussion has drifted back to issues that might more precisely be said to pertain to relevance, which illustrates how closely connected these two stages are. The point being made specifically about availability is this: Because behavioral information varies both in how informative it is and what it is informative about, the more and wider range of such information is available to the judge, the more chances he or she has of finding out what he or she needs to know.

DETECTION

The detection stage of accurate personality judgment is where the relevant, available information first registers on the nervous system of the judge. To some degree such detection may not be conscious and so remains beyond the judge's control. But there are at least a couple of things that a judge can do to improve detection.

First, the judge can simply watch closely. By attending carefully to the behavior of the person in question, the judge improves his or her chances of detecting whatever relevant information is available (Ickes, Stinson, Bissonnette, & Garcia, 1990). This does not come without cost, however, so it should be done judiciously. A judge who concentrates closely on the actions of a particular individual cannot attend so closely to the actions of other individuals, nor to other events in the physical and social environment, nor to planning his or her own actions. So advice to "watch everybody closely all the time" would be foolish. Focusing hard on the actions of a particular individual is an activity that is best to do only when for some reason you must.

In a similar vein, a distracted judge will garner less information about another person. If the judge is preoccupied with worries of his or her own, or by extremely salient events in the environment, then relevant and available information about a target person that might otherwise have been detected may instead pass him or her by.

Perhaps the most important thing a judge can do to improve the detection stage is to learn what is important to detect. As has been mentioned in earlier chapters, detection and utilization, within RAM, have roughly the same fuzzy relationship to each other that perception and cognition have within cognitive psychology. There is a two-way influence between them; one's perception affects one's knowledge and vice versa. In the case of personality judgment, some judges have learned to attend to certain cues that others might entirely ignore.

For example, Ekman (1991) has shown that movements of the body are better clues to deception than are facial expressions. So somebody trying to catch a liar is better served to look at the potential liar's body language than at his or her face. Some perceivers (such as those who have read Ekman's work) know this and therefore are more likely to detect this class of cues than those who do not enjoy this knowledge. By the same token, deceivers who have read Ekman's work may put more effort into controlling the movements of their body while lying.

Unfortunately, our knowledge of the cues that are similarly informative about personality, though beginning to develop, is still far too thin. As was discussed in Chapter 2, until recently personality psychologists largely failed in their duty to accumulate facts about the visible behavioral indicators of personality. Helping to change this situation are researchers such as Peter Borkenau (e.g., 1991; Borkenau & Liebler, 1995), who with his colleagues has begun the painstaking enterprise of accumulating knowledge about the particular behavioral indicators of various personality traits. For example, styles of dress and of movement seem to be related to traits such as extraversion, openness, and even intelligence (Borkenau & Liebler, 1995). At a more molar level of analysis, our own laboratory has also accumulated some information about the behavioral items on the Riverside Behavioral Q-Sort (RBQ) that are associated with the "big five" personality traits of extraversion, neuroticism, agreeableness, conscientiousness, and openness to experience (Funder & Sneed, 1993). A few other studies that have found links between personality traits and visible aspects of appearance and behavior are summarized later in this chapter.

UTILIZATION

The utilization stage of accurate judgment involves thinking. The relevant and available information has been detected, and now the judge must do some interpretational work to figure out what it all means.

Social versus Solitary Thought

Research indicates that this work is best done alone. When people get together to talk about their judgments before rendering them, apparently factors of group dynamics rather than valid inferential reasoning take control of the judgmental output. People discussing their judgments become concerned about self-presentation, saving face, politeness, making friends, achieving dominance, and a host of other issues that are irrelevant to accuracy. As a result, personality judgments are more accurate when made by individuals working alone than by those who have discussed their judgments with others first (Borkenau & Liebler, 1994; Borman, 1982). To optimize accuracy, these independently formulated judgments can then be combined arithmetically into an average that is much more reliable than any one of them would be.

Analytic and Intuitive Cognition

A compelling analysis by Ken Hammond (1996) suggests that cognitive work at the individual level takes one of two forms, analytic or intuitive.[2] Each is important and both are typically used either together or in quick alternation, but the implications for improving the accuracy of each type of cognition are quite different.

The Combat between Analysis versus Intuition

The distinction between analytic and intuitive cognition has several sources. One is the distinction between statistical and clinical prediction (Meehl, 1954). Another, even older, is Freud's distinction between secondary process and primary process thinking. In both cases, the analytic kind of thinking (statistical, secondary) is traditionally seen as superior to the intuitive (clinical, primary) kind.

Clinical versus Statistical Prediction

Consider the literature on "clinical versus statistical prediction" (Grove & Meehl, 1996; Meehl, 1954). Vast numbers of studies have pitted clinical judges (in medicine or clinical psychology, for example) against algorithmic formulae, and they have typically found the clinical judges sorely wanting. In almost every case, the formula yields more accurate predictions of the outcome, whether the outcome is the presence of appendicitis, criminal recidivism, or just college grade point average (Grove & Meehl, 1996). The implication sometimes drawn from such results is that clinical judges—and "intuitive" judges in general—are rather pathetic creatures. As in the

---

[2] To be more precise, Hammond locates any given cognitive process as lying on a continuum between these two poles; the two kinds of cognition are typically mixed.

legend of John Henry, their proudly acquired skills are easily surpassed by a machine, no matter how hard they work.

This conclusion is inappropriate. One key to where it went wrong can be found in a famous observation of one of those who drew it, Paul Meehl. Meehl pointed out that when one goes to the grocery store, one does not point one's shopping basket and say to the clerk "that looks like about $27 worth." Instead, the total is added up. This is an informative example because it points us toward looking for real-life situations that are equivalent and those that are not. In Meehl's grocery store example, it is important to obtain a precise answer; the value of each of the components is known, as is the correct formula for combining them, and the domain of application is predefined and circumscribed. Under such circumstances one indeed should go for the adding machine.

In a similar way, when medical research has examined enough cases to determine the cues that are associated with the presence or absence of a heart attack, as well as the correct formula for combining those cues, and knowledge about heart attack is *all* one needs, then again a formula will outperform a clinical judge. But while many medical and nonmedical situations fit this model, many more do not. All too often in medicine and in life, one does not know what one is even looking for, and even when one does, there is often little or no base of prior knowledge on which to base an "optimal" calculation. Indeed, the choice of which variables to put into an optimal model cannot be made on the basis of an optimal model! Although human judges may be poor at integrating multiple and inconsistent predictors, they are good at—and essential for—determining which predictors should be paid attention to (Camerer, 1981).

Primary versus Secondary Process Thinking

Consider also Freud's assumption—surprisingly similar to Meehl's—that secondary "rational' thought is needed to overcome wrongheaded primary, intuitive processes. Freud saw secondary process thinking as rational, conscious, and controllable. Primary process thinking is more primitive, immediate, unconscious, and uncontrolled. And the goal of psychological adjustment, from a psychoanalytic perspective, is to bring the irrational under the control of the rational—for secondary process to take command of primary process.

While endorsing the distinction between two fundamentally different modes of thought, Seymour Epstein (1994) pointed out that from an evolutionary perspective it makes little sense for the most primitive, long-established one to be dysfunctional:

> [Primary process in Freud's view] is essentially a maladaptive system, capable, perhaps of generating dreams and psychotic abberations but not up to the task, for either human or nonhuman animals, of promoting adaptive behavior in the real world . . . [this] leaves unexplained the questions of how the maladaptive system evolved in the first place and how nonhuman animals are able to adapt to their environments at all without a secondary process. (Epstein, 1994, p. 709)

Intuitive versus Analytic Thinking

Epstein's solution to this dilemma is to suggest that intuitive, primary process thinking, a function of what he calls the "experiential system," in fact evolved as an efficient means for animals (including humans) to react quickly and adaptively to their environments. "At its lower levels of operation [such as found both in animals and humans], it is a crude system that automatically, rapidly, effortlessly, and efficiently processes information. At its higher reaches, and particularly in interaction with the rational [secondary] system, it is a source of intuitive wisdom and creativity" (Epstein, 1994, p. 715).

Egon Brunswik (1956) pointed out another advantage to intuitive thinking: it is more robust. Analytic thinking, when it fails, often fails drastically. This fact, he theorized, derives from the essentially binary nature of analytic logic:

> The entire pattern of . . . [analytic] reasoning . . . resembles the switching of trains at a multiple junction, with each of the possible courses being well organized and of machine-like precision yet leading to drastically different destinations only one of which is acceptable in light of the cognitive goal. This pattern is illustrative of the dangers inherent in explicit logical operations. (Brunswik, 1956, p. 91)

Analytic cognition is an excellent source for precisely correct answers in delimited contexts in which all the inputs are knowable, known, and unchanging. In dynamic environments in whch many different variables are operating, however, and in which many of them may not even be known, it can go drastically wrong. Intuitive cognition, by contrast, rarely yields the precisely correct answer (when there is one). However, because it utilizes so many different variables simultaneously, and is always open to the inclusion of new ones, it usually yields an answer that is at least close to being correct, and its errors are seldom catastrophic.

Seymour Epstein expressed the tradeoffs this way:

> The rational system . . . is a deliberative, effortful, abstract system that operates primarily in the medium of language and has a very brief evolutionary history. It is capable of very high levels of abstraction and long-term delay of gratification. However, it is a very inefficient system for responding to everyday events, and its long-term adaptability remains to be tested. (It may yet lead to the destruction of all life on our planet.). (Epstein, 1994, p. 715)

For all these reasons, Hammond pointed out, it is extremely doubtful that one would want to utilize putatively optimal, analytic cognition all the time even if that were possible. Indeed, it is probably a foolish exercise to pit intuitive and analytic cognition against each other at all. Each is necessary, and sometimes you need to use both on the same problem. In real thought, rapid and frequent shifting back and forth between the two modes is necessary and typical. To pursue the implications of this insight, a better distinction between the two modes of cognition needs to be drawn, one that goes beyond simply categorizing one of them as mysterious—or foolish—and the other as mathematical—or perfect.

A proper appreciation of the relationship and mutual dependence between analytic and intuitive cognition must begin with a clear understanding of the nature of each. Most of the distinctions drawn in the literature are unsatisfactory, tending to contrast rationality with irrationality, or mathematical logic with intuitive illogic. Even champions of intuitive judgment have sometimes described it as something mysterious and ineffable, if not spiritual. Such a romantic notion may be attractive, but does not advance understanding very far. Ken Hammond's distinction between the two fundamental modes of cognition, however, is extremely helpful and is the principal basis of the discussion that follows (see also Epstein, 1994).

Analytic Cognition

Analytic cognition, like Freud's secondary process thinking, is what we ordinarily are referring to when we talk about "thinking." It is characteristically slow, explicit, and self-aware. It is the kind of thinking that can be put into words or expressed as a formula. It is logical and coherent. And it is most usefully applied to situations that are relatively simple.

For examples, consider legal reasoning and long division. The first is a specialized form of logical thinking in which each step is based on laws and precedents that can be specifically cited. Appeals to nonexplicit criteria, such as truth or even justice, are specifically *excluded*. The second is a mathematical procedure that is conducted in small, painstaking steps. Each step is simple, but a typical problem (e.g., 180,642 divided by 238) may require so many of them that memory is taxed. Most people can eventually reach the correct result (759) but only if they write down the result of each step.

Simple

Although they might seem complex, both of these situations are in fact simple as reasoning problems go. The steps in logic are finite and clearly defined and, perhaps even more important, the range of inputs that must be considered is known, limited, and narrow. Legal contexts specify quite exactly what facts are to be presumed, and legal analysts are careful to insist that nothing else but the facts as proven or stipulated are to be included in the analysis. Mathematical contexts are typically even simpler; long division requires as its inputs only the numerator and denominator. As a class, the problems best suited to analytic cognition are those in which the logical steps are finite and known and the inputs are limited. In other words, analytic cognition is best suited to closed systems.

Slow

A second important property of analytic cognition is that it takes time, and the situations best suited to it are those in which time is unlimited. A lawyer usually can take all the time in the world (and charge by the hour). Almost any person with a primary-school education can correctly complete a long-division problem if time is unlimited.

When time limits are imposed, however, errors immediately begin to arise, and the computation might not even have a chance to begin. Long division is bad enough. Imagine trying to perform the complex calculations of analytic geometry required to decide the moment it is safe to pull one's car into heavy traffic. The distance and speed of the oncoming traffic and knowledge about the acceleration capabilities of one's vehicle must be simultaneously considered. In principle a driver could pull out a calculator and do all the necessary calculations, but in practice the situation is impossible. There would never be enough time. By the time the result was ready, it would be too late (the traffic pattern would have changed), and the driver would have to start all over again. In general, analytic cognition requires too much time to be applicable to most of the problems of day to day living (Epstein, 1994).

Effortful

The slow, painstaking, step-by-step nature of analytic cognition is probably the reason it feels subjectively like work. A person sitting down to do some "hard thinking" is about to try to do some analytic cognition and afterward may feel tired, for good reason. Analytic cognition is something one must try to do, and to do it well requires a considerable amount of effort.

Explicit and Teachable

Analytic cognition is explicit in the sense that its steps can be exactly described and even verbalized on-line (as in "thinking out loud"). A lawyer can describe every step of his or her legal reasoning; a plot of the solution to a long-division problem (which teachers insist on when they tell pupils to "show your work") shows exactly how it was attained. When psychologists of decision making present the "optimal" decision-making formula, it typically takes the form of a multiple-regression equation in which each term and its weight is given a specific numerical value. There is no mystery to any of this; the practitioner of analytic cognition can tell you exactly what he or she is doing and why.

As a result, analytic cognition is didactically teachable. One can hear a lecture or read a book about the necessary steps and then do them. The best instruction is the most specific. For example, a good instruction manual included with a "some assembly required" toy describes every step in the process of putting it together. A poorer manual (such as the kind often first read on Christmas Eve) leaves too many steps to the reader's imagination. Similarly, the principles of legal reasoning and of long division can be written down, read, learned, and applied.

Coherent

Analytic cognition is evaluated according to what Hammond (1996) calls *coherence criteria*. When a judgment is internally coherent, when its steps follow the rules of logic or mathematics, then it is said to be good. When the logic is internally inconsistent, or follows no known rules of logic or math, then the cognition is said to be poor.

Although this practice certainly seems reasonable, it is important to notice how truth fails to enter in. An illogical, internally inconsistent, or mathematically erroneous judgmental result is flawed, according to coherence criteria, even if it reaches the right answer.[3] And a logical, internally consistent, and mathematically correct judgment is seen as perfect, even if it reaches the wrong answer. The latter case might seem particularly perverse. However, it often arises in the context of legal reasoning, in which decisions by appellate courts generally depend on the coherence of the reasoning by prior courts, *not* on the actual guilt or innocence of the accused or any other matter of factual truth or subjective justice (Funder, 1987).

Fragile

Analytic cognition is fragile in the sense that if any of the assumptions that it employs are incorrect, or if variables not included in the analysis turn out to be important, then its results can become drastically wrong (Brunswik, 1956). When an automated factory continues to turn out engines even after it has exhausted its supply of a crucial part, or when a taxpayer receives a government refund check made out for $1 billion (or one-billionth of a cent), something like this has happened. Within the closed universe of the factory's or tax collector's computer program, no doubt both the factory and the billing software were doing the right thing. It will require a nonoptimized human mind—open to variables not included in the programs—to fix the mistake.

Intuitive Cognition

Intuitive cognition is more difficult to describe and sometimes has been held out as something mysterious and unknowable. That is not a useful characterization. Intuitive cognition is best described in contrast to the properties of analytic cognition. Whereas analytic cognition is simple, slow, explicit, didactically teachable, and coherent, intuitive cognition is complex, fast, implicit, *not* didactically teachable, and correspondent rather than coherent.

---

[3] We saw in Chapter 3 how this criterion has been used by research within the "error paradigm" to evaluate various possibly useful practices of human judgment as fundamentally flawed.

Complex

Intuitive cognition is applied, out of necessity, to complex situations and open systems. When dozens or thousands of variables are all relevant at the same time, or when new inputs that cannot be anticipated may arrive at any time, then analytic cognition simply cannot be used. There are too many factors to consider and, even worse, not all the relevant factors are known.

As examples, consider weather forecasting and the act of pulling an under-powered car into heavy traffic. Computer-generated mathematical models have made some progress in the former task, but no human can use them (and in fact this is a remaining area in which the human judge still "adds value" to computer models; Stewart, Roebber, & Bosart, 1997). Too many variables are relevant and they shift too quickly; a human forecaster must out of necessity use intuitive judg-ment or hand the whole task over to a machine. Also, unanticipated variables often arise in weather forecasting, and computer models have no way of using information they are not preprogrammed to interpret.

The calculation of the right moment to pull into traffic could also probably be handed over to a computer, but the human judge does not have the luxury. It is interesting to note that he or she usually does not have the need either. Even though the necessary geometric calculations are much too complex for any human to do in the time allotted, most people usually manage to drive their cars into traffic without colliding with anybody. This is an extremely important fact. It implies that even in domains—such as geometry—in which analytic cognition would seem to be per-fectly appropriate, the typical human judge has an alternative and much more effi-cient mode of reasoning available that yields sufficiently good results.

Moreover, consider the kinds of open-ended situations where analytic cognition would not know where to begin, such as the situation of a decision-making psy-chologist in the process of setting up an optimal algorithmic procedure a for a domain such as medical diagnosis or clinical forecasting. Once she is finished she can be sure of a formula that outperforms intuitive judgment, the literature indi-cates, but where does she begin? Where is the optimal formula that tells her *which* variables to include in her optimal formula? Of course there is none, because the situation is too complex and the system in which it is located is open rather than closed.

Fast

A second important property of intuitive cognition is that it is very fast. Phenom-enologically, it can seem to require no time at all. The person pulling into traffic glances at the oncoming cars and goes, or doesn't. And a person may take one look at somebody else and feel that the person can be trusted, or is dangerous, or does not seem to be very smart. In contexts in which analytic cognition would guarantee a perfect answer every time, intuitive cognition might still be necessary because there is not time to calculate the exactly right answer. In the classic speed–accuracy trade-off, sufficient accuracy combined with great speed can be more useful, sometimes, than exact accuracy combined with great slowness.

Effortless

Intuitive cognition is not just fast, it is phenomenologically easy. It is not something that raises a sweat, literal or metaphorical. You glance at the traffic and go; glance out the window and grab your umbrella; shake hands with someone and be struck that something about the person seems strange. The results of intuitive cognition do not come from hard thinking, they just occur in moments of inspiration, insight, or "gut feeling."

Intuitive cognition not only does not require effort; sometimes it seems like it cannot be prevented. You might not be able to "help thinking" that something is strange about your new roommate, that the neighborhood feels dangerous, or that the weather is about to change. Insights like these often arrive unbidden, unstrived for, and sometimes unwanted.

Implicit and Not Didactically Teachable

When a person who has employed intuitive cognition is asked to explain what he has done, there is typically little or nothing he or she can say. "I can't exactly put it into words," the individual may say, "I just knew." Most people cannot even retrospectively recreate the intuitive geometry that led to their decision to pull into traffic, and veteran weather forecasters sometimes just have to tell you that it looked like rain. Hammond's (1996) book includes some of Mark Twain's fascinating descriptions of the processes by which Mississippi River pilots avoided the hidden and always-changing underwater obstacles along their routes. Even the best of them— and some were very good indeed—could tell you almost nothing about *how* they did it. The best clinical psychologist I ever met once told me how she spotted patients who were likely to be dangerous: "They just give me the creeps."

Expertise that takes this form is not easily transferred. Twain described how novice river pilots begged the veterans for advice, only to be told nothing of the slightest use. My clinical psychologist friend was never able to exactly describe "creepiness" either. Such knowledge is not didactically teachable; no lecture or book can tell you how to detect creepiness or even how to decide the right moment to pull your car into traffic.

So how do we ever learn? The answer is *practice and feedback*. One acts, enjoys, or suffers the consequences, and then acts again. Gradually and eventually, Mark Twain became a capable river pilot. I never learned to usefully diagnose creepiness, but most of us have acquired the necessary skills to guide an automobile through complex traffic situations. Other kinds of procedural knowledge are acquired this way as well. It has been observed that athletic coaches and music teachers are not necessarily excellent players or singers, and some of the most successful never were.

What they do provide is the opportunity for their students to practice, followed by useful feedback. Even our knowledge of emotions has this quality. No logical analysis or amount of words ever captures what a feeling really is, but we all know. We know it from practice, from experience.

Correspondent

Intuitive cognition is evaluated according to *correspondence criteria*. There is no reason, of course, why the results of intuitive cognition should not make logical sense. But the point is that it does not matter whether they do. Intuitive cognition is judged by its results. A weather forecast that predicts rain, followed by rain ensuing, is correct regardless of the way the forecast was made. A deft entry into traffic or a caught ball likewise are examples of successful intuitive cognition, regardless of whether the judge can tell you how the necessary calculations were done (typically he or she cannot) or whether the reported process, if it is described, is internally consistent or makes logical sense.

Robust

As was noted previously, while intuitive cognition might seldom yield answers that are correct to the fourth decimal, it usually gets close. As Brunswik (1956, p. 93) pointed out, "the organic multiplicity of factors entering into the [intuitive judgment] process constitutes an effective safeguard against drastic error." Intuitive judgment uses many different fallible cues at the same time, and so is less dependent on any one (or few) of them. Although it does not zero in on the one or two that might yield the optimal answer, it is also not led astray by a few that might be seriously misleading. In this sense, intuitive cognition is more stable and less prone to catastrophic error and is also the route to seeing the "big picture."

Implications for Improving Accuracy

To some extent personality judgment is surely based on both analytic and intuitive cognition, depending on which attribute is being judged and under what circumstances. As will be discussed later, under most real-life circumstances I suspect that intuitive cognition is more important for personality judgment. But both kinds are surely necessary at least sometimes, and the appropriate tactics for improving analytic and intuitive cognition are very different. Thus, the distinction between analytic and intuitive cognition implies that to improve accuracy, it is necessary to be clear about what kind of judgmental process is being addressed.

Improving Analytic Cognition

As was discussed earlier, analytic cognition is didactically teachable. To the extent this kind of cognition is important for personality judgment, its accuracy could be improved by giving judges lectures or books that describe the cues to personality and how they should best be used. A small but gradually growing body of research is beginning to provide grist for this kind of instruction (e.g., Bond, Berry, & Omar, 1994; Borkenau & Liebler, 1995; Gifford, 1994).

Learning the Right Cues   For example, a judge could be told "if a person speaks in a very loud voice, then the person is probably high on extraversion," because that is indeed what the research literature shows (Scherer, 1978). The judge could also be instructed that people who wear glasses tend to be low on extraversion and openness to experience (Borkenau, 1991) and that "baby faced" men are higher on intimacy and lower on extraversion than those with more mature-appearing facial features (Berry & Landry, 1997). Research also shows that shy, socially anxious people make less eye contact (Asendorpf, 1987; Daly, 1978) and maintain greater interpersonal distance (Pilkonis, 1977). More consequentially, judges could be taught that a boy who physically attacks others and associates with deviant peers is at risk for delinquency, but that the degree to which he irritates his mother at home is not relevant (Bank, Duncan, Patterson, & Reid, 1993). Very recent research indicates that valid cues to personality can even be found in the appearance of an individual's bedroom! People with cluttered rooms full of personal possessions tend to be unconscientious, and those who decorate with a distinctive style and possess a variety of books and magazines tend to be open to experience (Pryor, Chuang, Craik & Gosling, 1998).

This research provides a promising beginning, but didactic instruction on how to judge personality more accurately faces a couple of formidable obstacles. First, many different cues are relevant to personality assessment, often simultaneously, and their interpretation typically depends on the exact situational context (e.g., Borman, 1974; Gifford & Gallagher, 1985). To judge someone's personality, typically you must watch him or her do several things at once, some of which are relevant and some of which are not, and adjust your interpretation of these behaviors according to the context in which they occur. What the judge must be taught, therefore, is a complex multivariate combination of cues interacting with constantly changing circumstances. The loud voice of someone falling off a cliff is not necessarily a sign of extraversion, but the loud voice of someone who drowns out everyone else at a party probably is.

The second obstacle is even more formidable and somewhat embarrassing for the field of psychology. Even if psychologists were to gear up an intensive program for teaching people how to judge personality more accurately, on surveying the research literature they would find they still have surprisingly little of use to teach. Despite the examples of connections between overt behaviors and personality traits that were summarized earlier, such research is in fact very rare (and the summary offered here includes nearly every study I could find). As was discussed in Chapter 2, personality psychologists have seldom attempted to measure the overt behaviors that are associated with personality traits. As was discussed in

Chapter 3, social psychology has been dominated by investigations of error rather than of accuracy.

Avoiding Error   As a result, the principal advice the social psychological literature seems to offer for improving accuracy is to avoid the vast number of errors it has cataloged. Unfortunately, that approach does not work, for two reasons (see Chapter 3). First, in every study that has tried it so far, training people to make fewer errors has made accuracy worse rather than better (Borman, 1975; Funder, 1987). This is probably because errors reveal processes that are an important part of accurate judgment, just as visual illusions reveal processes that aid the accurate perception of size and space (Funder, 1987). Second, an overemphasis on the possibilities of error could serve to undermine judges' confidence. When judges are less confident, their information processing suffers and they tend to become less accurate (Bandura, 1989; Wilson & Schooler, 1991; Wood & Bandura, 1989). Training to improve accuracy should seek to improve judges' confidence, this research suggests, not undermine it in the way a constant harping on possible errors is likely to do.

Toward Didactic Instruction   The kind of research that would have yielded the most useful information would have examined, as directly and in as wide a range of contexts as possible, the behavior of large numbers of subjects who were separately assessed on a variety of personality traits. If research like this had been done by many investigators over many years—if it had been done, for example, by the same number of investigators who researched error over the past two decades—psychology would now possess a large catalog of the relations between personality and behavior. These relations could have been systematized into something we could didactically teach to judges of personality and thereby improve accuracy through the time-honored method of scientific research.

Alas, the situation just described is so far but a pipe dream. A few investigators have examined a few behaviors in a few contexts. But overall these efforts comprise but a small, if important, pioneering,start on what is truly needed.

We can at least hope this situation will change in the future. The obstacles were discussed in Chapter 2. Here, I will just reiterate one important point. Our explicit knowledge of the connections between personality and behavior will only grow to the extent that researchers begin to include direct behavioral observation—not just questionnaires—into their personality assessments. Perhaps even more important, this knowledge will only grow to the extent grant reviewers and funding agencies allow investigators the resources to do this difficult, painstaking work,and journal reviewers and editors will allow their results to be published. This work is valuable even if any one study shows the connection between personality and behavior in just one context. Over time, knowledge will accumulate, and the course syllabus for "how to judge personality accurately" will at last be able to include enough actual content to be useful.

Improving Intuitive Cognition

The research agenda just described offers an important degree of promise for efforts to improve the accuracy of personality judgment. It certainly deserves to be tried. But in the final analysis I suspect that, in most circumstances, the accuracy of personality judgment depends more on the quality of intuitive cognition.

This insight first dawned on me after I gave a talk at a professional meeting that concluded with my expressing the pipe dream described earlier—that someday we would assemble a catalog of connections between personality and behavior that could be didactically taught to judges. Afterward, a psychologist who was in the audience—and unfortunately I do not recall his name—approached me and said something like, "Nice talk, but that idea at the end will never work." Why not, I asked.

He asked me whether I thought people were as complicated as the weather, then explained he had done research on improving the accuracy of weather forecasters.[4] Specifically, as I recall, the problem involved predicting wind shear, violent cold downdrafts that can take aircraft at low altitudes and thrust them onto the ground. It turned out that the valid indicators of wind shear that appear on radar screens were known, but they were complex and interactive. Many different variables were important at once, and their relevance and relative value constantly changed according to other environmental factors. When attempts were made to teach these patterns to forecasters, it proved to be too much. The poor forecaster peering at the radar screen was a little like the person in an old, underpowered car using a slide rule to decide when to enter onrushing traffic. There were too many variables to remember, the calculations were too complex and, perhaps most important, there simply was not enough time.

But the news was not all bad. It turned out there was a way to improve forecasters' accuracy, and those who recall the earlier discussion of intuitive judgment will not be surprised by what it was (though I was, at the time). What worked was practice and feedback. Forecasters were shown radar displays, asked for their judgment, then told whether they were right or wrong. Then they did another. Over many, many trials, accuracy slowly improved even though the forecasters could not say, explicitly, what they were learning to do. They were learning, on an intuitive level, what wind shear looks like.

Let's assume that human personality is almost as complex as the weather. From the lessons of this story and our understanding of the processes of intuitive judgment, how would we go about improving the judgment of it? In this light, the answer is obvious: Use practice and feedback.

This could be done in two ways. One is as part of a formal training program, modeled on the weather researcher's technique rather than more traditional class-

---

[4]Ken Hammond (personal communication, August, 1998) tells me that this individual may have been himself (which I doubt) or Tom Stewart, but that I seem to have misremembered exactly what I was told. Perhaps it is better to regard this little tale as apocryphal.

room instruction. People could be shown videotapes or other displays of the behavior of an individual then asked for their judgments of his or her personality. Then they would be given feedback. This feedback could be a look at the individual's self-description, the way he or she was described by an expert panel, or even his or her future behavior. Then they would go through the whole process again with another stimulus individual.[5] Over time, research might reveal the best criterion to use, but in the early stages the goal would be for judges to attain whatever criterion is employed ever more closely with each trial. The next step for research would be to assess the generalizability of the results of such training: Do the judges subsequently do better in real life?

The development and evaluation of training programs like this deserves to be tried, and will of course require a large amount of both resources and time. Such training using practice and feedback has already been shown to improve empathic accuracy, the ability to guess the thoughts and feelings of a particular target (Marangoni, Garcia, Ickes, & Teng, 1995) and, in particular, the detection of deception (Zuckerman, Koestner, & Alton, 1984; Zuckerman, Koestner, & Colella, 1985). Kenneth Hammond has made a strong case that practice-and-feedback training ought to utilize, wherever possible, what he called "cognitive feedback" (1996, p. 270). This is feedback that identifies not just whether a judgment was right or wrong but which specific cues might have been used correctly and incorrectly. Such training is possible, of course, only in circumstances in which the valid and invalid cues to judgment have been reliably ascertained by previous research. Although the development of training programs like these is an exciting future direction, we might well ask whether, in the meantime, something else might be done as well. The answer is yes.

The second, more informal way to improve the intuitive judgment of personality is for anyone who would judge his or her peers to acquire as much practice and feedback as possible. Get out more, be an extravert (see Chapter 6). The same advice applies to those who would improve their self-knowledge (see Chapter 7). Mix with many different people in a wide range of social settings. Travel. Meet the kind of people you do not ordinarily meet. Most important, *be sure to seek feedback.*

The lack of good feedback is the missing link in much ordinary social experience (Hammond, 1996) and may be the reason many of us are not as good judges of personality as we should be. If we give up on a new acquaintance because we think we will not like him or her over time, we lose the chance to learn whether this prediction was right. In general, to the degree we are guided in our selections of who to interact with by our first impressions, for those individuals who fail to make the cut these impressions will remain forever inviolate, and we will never know how inaccurate (or even accurate) they might have been. Or if we fail to let our

---

[5] The stimulus person perhaps need not even be real. Perhaps excerpts could be shown of well-developed characters in the cinema and trainee's judgments evaluated against clinicians' expert judgments of the same characters.

acquaintances feel free to express themselves, perhaps because we interrupt, are easily offended, or just fail to show interest, we will be cutting ourselves off from potentially useful knowledge about what they, and people like them, are really like. Unless the people we encounter feel free to be themselves, we will never be in a position to learn about what they are really like. By the same token, if we would know ourselves, we should encourage and be open to feedback from others concerning the nature of our own personalities.

It may take all the creativity and social insight at one's command just to seek feedback. We need to stay with people long enough to test our expectations of them, trust them (provisionally) long enough to let them prove themselves or not, and never assume that our judgment of someone is right until and unless we have a chance to test it. This is no easy prescription to follow.

THE JUDGE'S SITUATION

The preceding discussion has an important limitation. All analyses that focus on the utilization stage, including the error paradigm, place the entire onus for accuracy on the judge. That is, if the judge makes an incorrect judgment, the judge must be the source of the problem. There is something lacking in the judge; the judge must be fixed.

The irony in this point of view, as was noted in Chapter 3, is that it amounts to a variant of the so-called "fundamental attribution error" so often ascribed to nonpsychologists. It makes the judge responsible for errors and the sole locus for improving accuracy. But what about the judge's *situation*? If the judge is in an impossible situation, then any failure of accuracy is not the judge's fault, and all the tinkering in the world with his or her cognitive processes will not improve accuracy one iota.

The aspect of the judge's situation that is important for accuracy is the amount and quality of the relevant information that is available to his or her judgment. According to the Realistic Accuracy Model, each stage is *necessary* for accuracy. If the judge does not have relevant information available, accurate judgment is impossible, no matter how optimal his or her perceptual and cognitive processes might otherwise be.

Thus, the general perspective of RAM implies not one, but two general prescriptions for improving the accuracy of personality judgment. The first, associated with the detection and utilization stages, is to improve the judge's relevant capabilities for analytic and intuitive cognition. The second, associated with the relevance and availability stages, is to improve the quantity and quality of the information in the judge's environment. In other words, the judge needs to use the available information better, but also needs for better information to be available.

The traditional subject matter of social psychology concerns the relationship between social information, once provided, and the way it is processed by the lay perceiver, so research in this field will be most helpful for the first approach. The traditional subject matter of personality psychology concerns the connection between personality and behavior, so it is (improved) research in this field that will be most helpful for the second approach. This is further evidence, if more were needed, that the traditional distinctions between social and personality psychology are arbitrary and sometimes insidious. It will take both fields, working together, to fully understand and finally to improve the accuracy of personality judgment.

References

Adams, H. F. (1927). The good judge of personality. *Journal of Abnormal and Social Psychology, 22,* 172–181.

Ahadi, S., & Diener, E. (1989). Multiple determinants and effect size. *Journal of Personality and Social Psychology, 56,* 398–406.

Aiken, L. S., West, S. G., Sechrest, L., & Reno, R. R. (1990). Graduate training in statistics, methodology and measurement in psychology: A survey of PhD programs in North America. *American Psychologist, 45,* 721–734.

Akert, R. M., & Panter, A. T. (1988). Extraversion and the ability to decode nonverbal communication. *Personality and Individual Differences, 9,* 965–972.

Albright, L., & Forziati, C. (1996). Cross-situational consistency and perceptual accuracy in leadership. *Personality and Social Psychology Bulletin, 21,* 1269–1276.

Albright, L., Kenny, D. A., & Malloy, T. E. (1988). Consensus in personality judgments at zero acquaintance. *Journal of Personality and Social Psychology, 55,* 387–395.

Allport, G. W. (1937). *Personality: A psychological interpretation.* New York: Holt, Rinehart & Winston.

Allport, G. W. (1950). Prejudice: A problem in psychological and social causation. *Journal of Social Issues, 4*(6).

Allport, G. W. (1958). What units shall we employ? In G. Lindzey (Ed.), *Assessment of human motives* (pp. 239–260). New York: Rinehart.

Allport, G. W. (1961). *Pattern and growth in personality.* New York: Holt, Rinehart & Winston.

Allport, G. W. (1966). Traits revisited. *American Psychologist, 21,* 1–10.

Allport, G. W., & Odbert, H. S. (1936). Traitnames. A psycho-lexical study. *Psychological Monographs, 47,* 211:171.

Allport, G. W., & Vernon, P. E. (1933). *Studies in expressive movement.* New York: Macmillan.

Alloy, L. B., & Abramson, L. Y. (1979). Judgment of contingency in depressed and nondepressed students: Sadder but wiser? *Journal of Experimental Psychology: General, 108,* 441–485.

Ambady, N., Hallahan, M., & Rosenthal, R. (1995). On judging and being judged accurately in zero-acquaintance situations. *Journal of Personality and Social Psychology, 69,* 518–529.

Ambady, N., & Rosenthal, R. (1992). Thin slices of expressive behavior as predictors of interpersonal consequences: A meta-analysis. *Psychological Bulletin, 111,* 256–274.

Andersen, S. M. (1984). Self-knowledge and social inference: II. The diagnosticity of cognitive/affective and behavioral data. *Journal of Personality and Social Psychology, 46,* 294–307.

Anderson, D. E., Ansfield, M. E., & DePaulo, B. M. (in press). Love's best habit: Deception in the context of relationships. In P. Philippot, R. S. Feldman, & E. J. Coats (Eds.), *The social context of nonverbal behavior.* Cambridge: Cambridge University Press.

Anderson, E. M., Bohon, L. M., & Berrigan, L. P. (1996). Factor structure of the private self-consciousness scale. *Journal of Personality Assessment, 66,* 144–152.

Anderson, N. H. (1990). A cognitive theory of judgment and decision. In N. H. Anderson (Ed.), *Contributions to information integration theory* (pp. 105–142). Hillsdale, NJ: Erlbaum.

Argyle, A. M. (1987). *The psychology of happiness.* London: Methuen.

Aronson, E., Brewer, M., & Carlsmith, J. M. (1985). Experimentation in social psychology. In G. Lindzey & E. Aronson (Eds.), *Handbook of social psychology* (Vol. 1, pp. 441–485).

Aronson, E., & Mettee, D. R. (1968). Dishonest behavior as a function of differential levels of induced self-esteem. *Journal of Personality and Social Psychology, 9,* 121–127.

Asch, S. E. (1946). Forming impressions of personality. *Journal of Abnormal and Social Psychology, 9,* 258–290.

Asendorpf, J. B. (1987). Videotape reconstruction of emotions and cognitions related to shyness. *Journal of Personality and Social Psychology, 53,* 542–549.

Asendorpf, J. B., & van Aken, M. A. G. (1991). Correlates of temporal consistency of personality patterns in childhood. *Journal of Personality, 59,* 689–703.

Azibo, D. A. (1991). An empirical test of the fundamental postulates of an African personality metatheory. *Western Journal of Black Studies, 15,* 183–195.

Bandura, A. (1989). Human agency in social cognitive theory. *American Psychologist, 44,* 1175–1184.

Bandura, A. (1997). *Self-efficacy: The exercise of control.* New York: W. H. Freeman.

Bandura, A., & Wood, R. E. (1989). Effect of perceived controllability and performance standards on self-regulation of complex decision-making. *Journal of Personality and Social Psychology, 56,* 805–814.

Bank, L., Duncan, T., Patterson, G. R., & Reid, J. (1993). Parent and teacher ratings in the assessment and prediction of antisocial and delinquent behaviors. *Journal of Personality, 61,* 693–709.

Bargh, J. A., & Pratto, F. (1986). Individual construct accessibility and perceptual selection. *Journal of Experimental Social Psychology, 22,* 293–311.

Baron, J. (1988). *Thinking and deciding.* Cambridge, England: Cambridge University Press.

Baron, R. M., Albright, L., & Malloy, T. E. (1995). Effects of behavioral and social class information on social judgment. *Personality and Social Psychology Bulletin, 21,* 308–315.

Baumeister, R. E., & Tice, D. M. (1988). Metatraits. *Journal of Personality, 30,* 571–597.

Baumgardner, A. H., & Brownlee, E. A. (1987). Strategic failure in social interaction: Evidence for expectancy disconfirmation process. *Journal of Personality and Social Psychology, 52,* 525–535.

Bem, D. J. (1972). Self-perception theory. In L. Berkowitz (Ed.), *Advances in experimental social psychology* (Vol. 6, pp. 1–62). New York: Academic Press.

Bem, D. J. (1983). Further déjà vu in the search for cross-situational consistency: A response to Mischel and Peake. *Psychological Review, 90,* 390–393.

Bem, D. J., & Allen, A. (1974). On predicting some of the people some of the time: The search for cross-situational consistencies in behavior. *Psychological Review, 81,* 506–520.

Bem, D. J., & Funder, D. C. (1978) Predicting more of the people more of the time: Assessing the personality of situations. *Psychological Review, 85,* 485–501.

Bem, D. J., & McConnell, H. K. (1970). Testing the self-perception explanation of dissonance phenomena: On the salience of premanipulation attitudes. *Journal of Personality and Social Psychology, 14,* 23–31.

Bender, I. E., & Hastorf, A. H. (1950). The perception of persons: Forecasting another person's responses on three personality scales. *Journal of Abnormal and Social Psychology, 45,* 566–561.

Bentler, P. M. (1995). *EQS: Structural equations program manual.* Encino, CA: Multivariate Software.

Berglas, S., & Jones, E. E. (1978). Drug choice as a self-handicapping strategy in response to noncontingent success. *Journal of Personality and Social Psychology, 36,* 942–952.

Berman, J. S., & Kenny, D. A. (1976). Correlational bias in observer ratings. *Journal of Personality and Social Psychology, 34,* 263–273.

Bernardin, H. J., & Pence, E. C. (1980). Effects of rater training: Creating new response sets and decreasing accuracy. *Journal of Applied Psychology, 65,* 60–66.

Bernieri, F., & Gillis, J. S. (1995). Personality correlates of accuracy in a social perception task. *Perceptual and Motor Skills, 81,* 168–170.

Bernieri, F. J., Gillis, J. S., Davis, J. M., & Grahe, J. E. (1996). Dyad rapport and the accuracy of its judgment across situations: A lens model analysis. *Journal of Personality and Social Psychology, 71,* 110–129.

Bernieri, F. J., Zuckerman, M., Koestner, R., & Rosenthal, R. (1994). Measuring person perception accuracy: Another look at self-other agreement. *Personality and Social Psychology Bulletin, 20,* 367–378.

Bernstein, W. M., & Davis, M. H. (1982). Perspective-taking, self-consciousness, and accuracy in person perception. *Basic and Applied Social Psychology, 3,* 1–19.

Berry, D. S. (1990). Taking people at face value: Evidence for the kernel of truth hypothesis. *Social Cognition, 8,* 343–361.

Berry, D. S. (1991). Accuracy in social perception: Contributions of facial and vocal information. *Journal of Personality and Social Psychology, 61,* 298–307.

Berry, D. S., & Brownlow, S. (1989). Were the physiognomists right? Personality correlates of facial babyishness. *Personality and Social Psychology Bulletin, 15,* 266–279.

Berry, D. S., & Finch-Wero, J. L. (1993). Accuracy in face perception: A view from ecological psychology. *Journal of Personality, 61,* 497–520.

Berry, D. S., & Landry, J. C. (1997). Facial maturity and daily social interaction. *Journal of Personality and Social Psychology, 72,* 570–580.

Berry, D. S., & McArthur, L. Z. (1986). Perceiving character in faces: The impact of age-related craniofacial features on social perception. *Psychological Bulletin, 100,* 3–18.

Berry, D. S., & Pennebaker, J. W. (1993). Nonverbal and verbal emotional expression and health. *Psychotherapy & Psychosomatics, 59,* 11–19.

Bhaskar, R. (1978). *A realist theory of science.* Hassocks, Sussex: Harvester Press.

Blackman, M. C., & Funder, D. C. (1998). The effect of information on consensus and accuracy in personality judgment. *Journal of Experimental Social Psychology, 34,* 164–181.

Blanchard, E. B., & Epstein, L. H. (1978). *A biofeedback primer.* Reading, MA: Addison-Wesley.

Block, J. (1965*)*. *The challenge of response sets: Unconfounding meaning, acquiescence, and social desirability in the MMPI.* New York: Appleton-Century Crofts.

Block, J. (1977). Advancing the science of personality: Paradigmatic shift or improving the quality of research? In D. Magnusson & N. S. Endler (Eds.), *Personality at the crossroads: Current issues in interactional psychology* (pp. 37–63). Hillsdale, NJ: Erlbaum.

Block, J. (1978). *The Q-sort method in personality assessment and psychiatric research.* Palo Alto, CA: Consulting Psychologists Press. (Original work published 1961)

Block, J. (1989). Critique of the Act Frequency Approach to personality. *Journal of Personality and Social Psychology, 56,* 234–245.

Block, J. (1993). Studying personality the long way. In D. C. Funder, R. D. Parke, C. Tomlinson-Keasey, & K. Widaman (Eds.), *Studying lives through time: Personality and development* (pp. 9–41). Washington, DC: American Psychological Association.

Block, J., Buss, D. M., Block, J. M., & Gjerde, P. F. (1981). The cognitive style of breadth of categorization: The longitudinal consistency of personality correlates. *Journal of Personality and Social Psychology, 40,* 770–779.

Block, J., von der Lippe, A., & Block, J. H. (1973). Sex-role and socialization patterns: Some personality concomitants and environmental antecedents. *Journal of Consulting and Clinical Psychology, 41,* 321–341.

Block, J., Weiss, D. S., & Thorne, A. (1979). How relevant is a semantic similarity interpretation of personality ratings? *Journal of Personality and Social Psychology, 37,* 1055–1074.

Block, J. H., & Block, J. (1980). The role of ego-control and ego-resiliency in the organization of behavior. In W. A. Collins (Ed.), *Minnesota symposium on child psychology* (Vol. 13). Hillsdale, NJ: Erlbaum.

Bodenhausen, G. V. (1993). Emotion, arousal, and stereotypic judgment: A heuristic model of affect and stereotyping. In D. Mackie & D. Hamilton (Eds.), *Affect, cognition and stereotyping: Interaction processes in intergroup perception.* San Diego: Academic Press.

Bond, C. F., Berry, D. S., & Omar, A. (1994). The kernel of truth in judgments of deceptiveness. *Basic and Applied Social Psychology, 15,* 523–534.

Borkenau, P. (1990). Systematic distortion and systematic overlap in personality ratings. In G. L. Van heck, S. E. Hampson, J. Reykowski, & J. Zakrzewski (Eds.), *Personality psychology in Europe. Vol. 3: Foundations, models and inquiries* (pp. 3–29). Lisse, Netherlands: Swets & Zeitlinger.

Borkenau, P. (1991). Evidence of a correlation between wearing glasses and personality. *Personality and Individual Differences, 12,* 1125–1128.

Borkenau, P., & Liebler, A. (1992a). The cross-modal consistency of personality: Inferring strangers' traits from visual or acoustic information. *Journal of Research in Personality, 26,* 183–204.

Borkenau, P., & Liebler, A. (1992b). Trait inferences: Sources of validity at zero acquaintance. *Journal of Personality and Social Psychology, 62,* 645–657.

Borkenau, P., & Liebler, A. (1993). Convergence of stranger ratings of personality and intelligence with self-ratings, partner ratings, and measured intelligence. *Journal of Personality and social Psychology, 65,* 546–553.

Borkenau, P., & Liebler, A. (1994). Effects of communication among judges on the validity of their judgments. *European Journal of Psychological Assessment, 10,* 10–14.

Borkenau, P., & Liebler, A. (1995). Observable attributes as manifestations and cues of personality and intelligence. *Journal of Personality, 63,* 1–25.

Borkenau, P., & Müller, B. (1992). Inferring act frequencies and traits from behavior observations. *Journal of Personaltiy, 60*, 553–574.

Borkenau, P., & Ostendorf, F. (1987a). Fact and fiction in implicit personality theory. *Journal of Personality, 55*, 415–443.

Borkenau, P., & Ostendorf, F. (1987b). Retrospective estimates of act frequency: How accurately do they reflect reality? *Journal of Personality and Social Psychology, 52*, 626–638.

Borman, W. C. (1974). The rating of individuals in organizations: An alternate approach. *Organizational Behavior and Human Decision Processes, 12*, 105–124.

Borman, W. C. (1975). Effects of instructions to avoid halo error on reliability and validity of performance evaluation ratings. *Journal of Applied Psychology, 60*, 556–560.

Borman, W. C. (1977). Consistency of rating accuracy and rating errors in the judgment of human performance. *Organizational Behavior and Human Performance, 20*, 238–252.

Borman, W. C. (1979a). Format and training effects on rating accuracy and rater errors. *Journal of Applied Psychology, 64*, 410–421.

Borman, W. C. (1979b). Individual difference correlates of accuracy in evaluating others' performance effectiveness. *Applied Psychological Measurement, 3*, 103–115.

Borman, W. C. (1982). Validity of behavioral assessment for predicting military recruiter performance. *Journal of Applied Psychology, 67*, 3–9.

Bower, G. H., & Hilgard, E. R. (1981). *Theories of learning* (5th ed.). Englewood Cliffs, NJ: Prentice-Hall.

Bowers, K. S. (1973). Situationism in psychology: An analysis and critique. *Psychological Review, 80*, 863–872.

Brickman, P., Coates, D., & Janoff-Bulman, R. (1978). Lottery winners and accident victims: Is happiness relative? *Journal of Personality and Social Psychology, 36*, 917–927.

Brodt, S., & Ross, L. (1998). The role of stereotyping in overconfident social prediction. *Social Cognition, 16*, 225–252.

Brody, N. (1996). Intelligence and public policy. *Psychology, Public Policy and the Law, 2*, 473–485.

Bronfenbrenner, U., Harding, J., & Gallwey, M. (1958). The measurement of skill in social perception. In D. McClelland (Ed.), *Talent and society: New perspectives in the identification of talent*. New York: Van Nostrand.

Brown, J. D. (1986). Evaluations of self and others: Self-enhancement biases in social judgment. *Social Cognition, 4*, 353–376.

Brunswik, E. (1956). *Perception and the representative design of experiments*. Berkeley: University of California Press.

Buck, R. (1984). *The communication of emotion*. New York: Guilford.

Buck, R. (1993). The spontaneous communication of interpersonal expectations. In P. D. Blanck (Ed.), *Interpersonal expectations: Theory, research and applications* (pp. 227–241). New York: Cambridge University Press.

Buck, R., Miller, R. E., & Caul, W. F. (1974). Sex, personality, and physiological variables in the communication of affect via facial expression. *Journal of Personality and Social Psychology, 30*, 587–596.

Burton, R. V. (1963). Generality of honesty reconsidered. *Psychological Review, 70*, 481–499.

Buss, D. M., & Craik, K. H. (1983). The act frequency approach to personality. *Psychological Review, 90*, 105–126.

Cairns, R. B., (1979). *The analysis of social interactions: Methods, issues and illustrations.* Hillsdale, NJ: Erlbaum.

Cairns, R. B., & Green, J. A. (1979). How to assess personality and social patterns: Observations or ratings? In R. B. Cairns (Ed.), *The analysis of social interactions: Methods, issues and illustrations* (pp. 209–226). Hillsdale, NJ: Erlbaum.

Camerer, C. (1981). General conditions for the success of bootstrapping models. *Organizational Behavior and Human Performance, 27,* 411–422.

Campbell, J. D., & Fehr, B. (1990). Self-esteem and perceptions of conveyed impressions: Is negative affectivity associated with greater realism? *Journal of Personality and Social Psychology, 58,* 122–133.

Cantor, N., & Kihlstrom, J. F. (1987). *Personality and social intelligence.* Englewood Cliffs, NJ: Prentice-Hall.

Carroll, J. S., Perkowtiz, W. T., Lurigio, A. J., & Weaver, F. M. (1987). Sentencing goals, causal attributions, ideology, and personality. *Journal of Personality and Social Psychology, 52,* 107–118.

Caspi, A. (1998). Personality development across the life course. In N. Eisenberg (Ed.), *Handbook of child psychology* (5th ed., pp. 311–387).

Cattell, R. B., & Cattell, H. E. P. (1995). Personality structure and the new fifth edition of the 16PF. *Educational and Psychological Measurement, 55,* 926–937.

Chapdelaine, A., Kenny, D. A., & LaFontana, K. M. (1994). Matchmaker, matchmaker, can you make me a match? Predicting liking between two unacquainted persons. *Journal of Personality and Social Psychology, 67,* 83–91.

Chaplin, W. F., & Goldberg, L. R. (1984). A failure to replicate the Bem and Allen study of individual differences in cross-situational consistency. *Journal of Personality and Social Psychology, 47,* 1074–1090.

Cheek, J. M. (1982). Aggregation, moderator variables, and the validity of personality tests: A peer-rating study. *Journal of Personality and Social Psychology, 43,* 1254–1269.

Christensen-Szalanski, J. J. J., & Beach, L. R. (1984). The citation bias: Fad and fashion in the judgment and decision literature [Comment]. *American Psychologist, 39,* 75–78.

Clark, A. (1987). From folk psychology to naíve psychology. *Cognitive Psychology, 11,* 139–154.

Clark, J. M., & Paivio, A. (1989). Observational and theoretical terms in psychology: A cognitive perspective on scientific language. *American Psychologist, 44,* 500–512.

Cliff, N. (1983). Some cautions concerning the application of causal modeling methods. *Multivariate Behavioral Research, 18,* 115–126.

Cline, V. B., & Richards, J. M., Jr. (1960). Accuracy of interpersonal perception – A general trait? *Journal of Abnormal and Social Psychology, 60,* 1–7.

Cloyd, L. (1977). Effect of acquaintanceship on accuracy of person perception. *Perceptual and Motor Skills, 44,* 819–826.

Colvin, C. R. (1993a). Childhood antecedents of young-adult judgability. *Journal of Personality, 61,* 611–635.

Colvin, C. R. (1993b). Judgable people: Personality, behavior, and competing explanations. *Journal of Personality and Social Psychology, 64,* 861–873.

Colvin, C. R., & Block, J. (1994). Do positive illusions foster mental health? An examination of the Taylor and Brown Formulation. *Psychological Bulletin, 116,* 3–20.

Colvin, C. R., Block, J., & Funder, D. C. (1995). Overly positive self-evaluations and personality: Negative implications for mental health. *Journal of Personality and Social Psychology, 68,* 1152–1162.

Colvin, C. R., & Funder, D. C. (1991). Predicting personality and behavior: A boundary on the acquaintanceship effect. *Journal of Personality and Social Psychology, 60,* 884–894.

Colvin, C. R., Vogt, D., & Ickes, W. (1997). Why do friends understand each other better than strangers do? In W. Ickes (Ed.), *Empathic accuracy* (pp. 169–193). New York: Guilford.

Conley, J. J. (1984). Relation of temporal stability and cross-situational consistency in personality: Comment on the Mischel-Epstein debate. *Psychological Review, 91,* 491–496.

Cook, M. (1984). *Issues in person perception.* London: Methuen.

Cook, T. D., & Campbell, D. T. (1979). *Quasi-experimentation: Design and analysis issues for field settings.* Chicago: Rand McNally.

Crandall, C. S. (1984). The overcitation of examples of poor performance: Fad, fashion or fun [Comment]? *American Psychologist, 39,* 1499–1500.

Creed, A., & Funder, D. C. (1998). The two faces of private self-consciousness: Self-report, peer-report, and behavioral correlates. *European Journal of Personality, 12,* 411–431.

Cronbach, L. J. (1955). Processes affecting scores on "understanding of others" and "assumed similarity." *Psychological Bulletin, 52,* 177–193.

Cronbach, L. J. (1958). Proposals leading to analytic treatment of social perception scores. In R. Tagiuri & L. Petrullo (Eds.), *Person perception and interpersonal behavior,* pp. 353–379. Stanford, CA: Stanford University Press.

Cronbach, L. J., Gleser, G. C., Nanda, H., & Rajaratnam, N. (1972). *The dependability of behavioral measurements: Theory of generalizability for scores and profiles.* New York: Cambridge University Press.

Cronbach, L. J., & Meehl, P. E. (1955). Construct validity in psychological tests. *Psychological Bulletin, 52,* 281–302.

Crow, W. J., & Hammond, K. R. (1957). The generality of accuracy and response in interpersonal perception. *Journal of Abnormal and Social Psychology, 54,* 384–390.

Csikszentmihalyi, M., & Larson, R. (1992). Validity and reliability of the Experience Sampling Method. In M. V. DeVries (Ed.), *The experience of psychopathology: Investigating mental disorders in their natural settings* (pp. 43–57). Cambridge, England: Cambridge University Press.

Daly, S. (1978). Behavioral correlates of social anxiety. *British Journal of Social and Clinical Psychology, 17,* 117–120.

Darley, J. M., & Butson, C. D. (1973). "From Jerusulem to Jerrono": A study of situational and dispositional variables in helping behavior. *Journal of Personality and Social Psychology, 27,* 100–108.

Darley, J. M., & Latane, B. (1968). Bystander intervention in emergencies: Diffusion of responsibility. *Journal of Personality and Social Psychology, 8,* 377–383.

Davidson, K. W. (1993). Suppression and repression in discrepant self-other ratings: Relations with thought control and cardiovascular reactivity. *Journal of Personality, 61,* 669–691.

DePaulo, B. M. (1992). Nonverbal behavior and self-presentation. *Psychological Bulletin, 11,* 203–243.

DePaulo, B. M., & Friedman, H. S. (1998). Nonverbal communication: In D. T. Gilbert, S. T. Fiske, & G. Lindzey (Eds.), *Handbook of social psychology* (4th ed., Vol. 2., pp. 3–40). New York: Oxford University Press.

Diener, E. (1984). Subjective well-being. *Psychological Bulletin, 95,* 542–575.

Donahue, E. M., Robins, R. W., Roberts, B. W., & John, O. P. (1993). The divided self: Concurrent and longitudinal effects of psychological adjustment and social roles on self-concept differentiation. *Journal of Personality and Social Psychology, 64,* 834–846.

Drasgow, F., & Hulin, C. L. (1990). Item response theory. In M. D. Dunnette & L. M. Hough (Eds.), *Handbook of industrial and organizational psychology, Vol. 1* (2nd ed.), pp. 577–636. Palo Alto, CA: Consulting Psychologists Press.

Dymond, R. F. (1949). A scale for the measurement of empathic ability. *Journal of Consulting Psychology, 13,* 127–133.

Dymond, R. F. (1950). Personality and empathy. *Journal of Consulting Psychology, 14,* 343–350.

Dunning, D., Perie, M., & Story, A. L. (1991). Self-serving prototypes of social categories. *Journal of Personality and Social Psychology, 61,* 957–968.

Dunning, D., & Story, A. L. (1991). Depression, realism, and the overconfidence effect: Are the sadder wiser when predicting future actions and events? *Journal of Personality and Social Psychology, 61,* 521–532.

Duval, S., & Wicklund, R. A. (1972). *A theory of objective self-awareness.* New York: Academic Press.

Ekman, P. (1991). *Telling lies: Clues to deceit in the marketplace, politics, and marriage.* New York: W. W. Norton.

Ekman, P., & O'Sullivan, M. (1991). Factual expression: Methods, means, and moves. In R. S. Feldman & B. Rime (Eds.), *Fundamentals of nonverbal behavior: Studies in emotion and social interaction,* pp. 163–199. New York: Cambridge University Press.

Epstein, S. (1979). The stability of behavior: I. On predicting most of the people much of the time. *Journal of Personality and Social Psychology, 37,* 1097–1126.

Epstein, S. (1980). The stability of behavior: II. Implications for psychological research. *American Psychologist, 35,* 790–806.

Epstein, S. (1983). The stability of confusion: A reply to Mischel and Peake. *Psychological Review, 90,* 179–184.

Epstein, S. (1994). Integration of the cognitive and the psychodynamic unconscious. *American Psychologist, 49,* 709–724.

Epstein, S., & O'Brien, E. J. (1985). The person-situation debate in historical and current perspective. *Psychological Bulletin, 98,* 513–537.

Erdelyi, M. H. (1974). A new look at the new look: Perceptual defense and vigilance. *Psychological Review, 81,* 1–25.

Estes, S. G. (1938). Judging personality from expressive behavior. *Journal of Abnormal and Social Psychology, 33,* 217–236.

Evans, J. St. B. (1984). In defense of the citation bias in the judgment literature [Comment]. *American Psychologist, 39,* 1500–1501.

Eysenck, M. W. (1990). *Happiness: Facts and myths.* East Sussex, England: Erlbaum.

Festinger, L., & Carlsmith, J. M. (1959). Cognitive consequences of forced compliance. *Journal of Abnormal and Social Psychology, 58,* 203–210.

Fine, R. (1986). *Narcissism, the self and society.* New York: Columbia University Press.

Fishbein, M., & Ajzen, I. (1974). Attitudes toward objects as predictors of single and multiple act criteria. *Psychological Review, 81,* 59–74.

Fiske, S. T., & Taylor, S. E. (1991). *Social cognition* (2nd ed.). New York: McGraw-Hill.

Fiske, S. T., & Von Hendy, H. M. (1992). Personality feedback and situational norms can control stereotyping processes. *Journal of Personality and Social Psychology, 62,* 577–596.

Fletcher, G. (1993, October). *Empathic accuracy in married couples.* Paper presented at the meeting of the Society for Experimental Social Psychology, Santa Barbara, CA.

Flink, C., & Park, B. (1991). Increasing consensus in trait judgments through outcome dependency. *Journal of Experimental Social Psychology, 27,* 453–467.

Frank, M. G., & Ekman, P. (1997). The ability to detect deceit generalizes across different types of high-stake lies. *Journal of Personality and Social Psychology, 72,* 1429–1439.

Frank, M. G., & Gilovich, T. (1989). Effect of memory perspective on retrospective causal attributions. *Journal of Personality and Social Psychology, 57,* 399–403.

Freedman, D. (1991). Statistical models and shoe leather. *Sociological Methodology, 21,* 291–313.

Fuhrman, R. W., & Funder, D. C. (1995). Convergence between self and peer in the response-time processing of trait-relevant information. *Journal of Personality and Social Psychology, 69,* 961–974.

Funder, D. C. (1980a). On seeing ourselves as others see us: Self-other agreement and discrepancy in personality ratings. *Journal of Personality, 48,* 473–493.

Funder, D. C. (1980b). The "trait" of ascribing traits: Individual differences in the tendency to trait ascription. *Journal of Research in Personality, 14,* 376–385.

Funder, D. C. (1982). On assessing social psychological theories through the study of individual differences: Template matching and forced compliance. *Journal of Personality and Social Psychology, 43,* 100–110.

Funder, D. C. (1983). Three issues in predicting more of the people: A reply to Mischel and Peake. *Psychological Reivew, 90,* 283–289.

Funder, D. C. (1987). Errors and mistakes: Evaluating the accuracy of social judgment. *Psychological Bulletin, 101,* 75–90.

Funder, D. C. (1989). Accuracy in personality judgment and the dancing bear. In D. Buss & N. Cantor (Eds.), *Personality psychology: Recent trends and emerging directions* (pp.210–223). New York: Springer-Verlag.

Funder, D. C. (1991). Global traits: A neo-Allportian approach to personality. *Psychological Science, 2,* 31–39.

Funder, D. C. (1992). Everything you know is wrong (review of *The Person and the Situation,* by L. Ross and R. E. Nisbett). *Contemporary Psychology, 37,* 319–320.

Funder, D. C. (1993a). Judgments as data for personality and developmental psychology: Error versus accuracy. In D. C. Funder, R. D. Parke, C. Tomlison-Keasey, & K. Widaman (Eds.), *Studying lives through time: Personality and development* (pp. 121–146). Washington, DC: American Psychological Association.

Funder, D. C. (1993b). Judgments of personality and personality itself. In K. H. Craik, R. Hogan, & R. N. Wolfe (Eds.,) *Fifty years of personality psychology* (pp. 207–214). New York: Plenum.

Funder, D. C. (1995a). On the accuracy of personality judgment: A realistic approach. *Psychological Review, 102,* 652–670.

Funder, D. C. (1995b). Stereotypes, baserates, and the fundamental attribution mistake: A content-based approach to judgmental accuracy. In L. Jussim, Y-T. Lee, & C. McCauley (Eds.), *Stereotype accuracy: Toward appreciating group differences* (pp. 141–156). Washington, DC: American Psychological Association.

Funder, D. C. (1997a). *The personality puzzle.* New York: W. W. Norton.

Funder, D. C. (1997b). What do you think of me? *Psychological Inquiry 7,* 275–278.

Funder, D. C. (1998). Why does personality psychology exist? *Psychological Inquiry, 9,* 150–152.

Funder, D. C. (in press). The Realistic Accuracy Model and Brunswik's approach to social judgment. In R. Hammond & T. R. Stewart (Eds.), *The Essential Brunswik: Beginnings, explications, applications.* Oxford: Oxford University Press.

Funder, D. C., & Colvin, C. R. (1988). Friends and strangers: Acquaintanceship, agreement, and the accuracy of personality judgment. *Journal of Personality and Social Psychology, 55,* 149–158.

Funder, D. C., & Colvin, C. R. (1991). Explorations in behavioral consistency: Properties of persons, situations, and behaviors. *Journal of Personality and Social Psychology, 60,* 773–794.

Funder, D. C., & Colvin, C. R. (1997). Congruence of self and others' judgments of perosnality. In R. Hogan, J. Johnston & S. Briggs (Eds.), *Handbook of personality psychology* (p. 617–647). San Diego: Academic Press.

Funder, D. C., & Dobroth, K. M. (1987). Differences between traits: Properties associated with interjudge agreement. *Journal of Personality and Social Psychology, 52,* 409–418.

Funder, D. C., Furr, R. M., & Colvin, C. R. (1998). *The behavioral Q-sort: A tool for the description of social behavior.* Unpublished manuscript, University of California, Riverside

Funder, D. C., & Harris, M. J. (1986). On the several facets of personality assessment: The case of social acuity. *Journal of Personality, 54,* 528–550.

Funder, D. C., Kolar, D. C., & Blackman, M. C. (1995). Agreement among judges of personality: Interpersonal relations, similarity, and acquaintanceship. *Journal of Personality and Social Psychology, 69,* 656–672.

Funder, D. C., & Ozer, D. J. (1983). Behavior as a function of the situation. *Journal of Personality and Social Psychology, 44,* 107–112.

Funder, D. C., Parke, R. D., Tomlinson-Keasey, C., & Widaman, K. (Eds.). (1993). *Studying lives through time: Personality and development.* Washington, DC: American Psychological Association.

Funder, D. C., & Sneed, C. D. (1993). Behavioral manifestations of personality: An ecological approach to judgmental accuracy. *Journal of Personality and Social Psychology, 64,* 479–490.

Funder, D. C., & West, S. G. (1993). Consensus, self-other agreement, and accuracy in personality judgment: An introduction. *Journal of Personality, 61,* 457–476.

Gage, N. L., & Cronbach, L. J. (1955). Conceptual and methodological problems in interpersonal perception. *Psychological Review, 62,* 411–422.

Gangestad, S. W., Simpson, J. A., DiGeronimo, K., & Beik, M. (1992). Differential accuracy across traits: Examination of a functional hypothesis. *Journal of Personality and Social Psychology, 62,* 688–698.

Gergen, K. J. (1985). The social constructionist movement in modern psychology. *American Psychologist, 40,* 266–275.

Gergen, K. J. (1994). *Realities and relationships.* Cambridge, MA: Harvard University Press.

Gergen, K. J., & Semin, G. R. (1990). Everyday understanding in science and daily life. In G. R. Semin & K. J. Gergen (Eds.), *Everyday understanding: Social and scientific implications. Inquires in social construction.* London: Sage.

Gibson, J. J. (1979). *The ecological approach to visual perception.* New York: Harper & Row.

Gifford, R. (1994). A lens-mapping framework for understanding the encoding and decoding of interpersonal dispositions in nonverbal behaviors. *Journal of Personality and Social Psychology, 66,* 398–412.

Gifford, R., & Gallagher, T. M. (1985). Sociability: Personality, social context, and physical setting. *Journal of Personality and Social Psychology, 48,* 1015–1023.

Gifford, R., & Hine, D. W. (1994). The role of verbal behavior in the encoding and decoding of interpersonal dispositions. *Journal of Research in Personality, 28,* 115–132.

Gifford, R., Ng, C-F., & Wilkinson, M. (1985). Nonverbal cues in the employment interview: Links between applicant qualities and interviewer judgments. *Journal of Applied Psychology, 70,* 729–736.

Gilbert, D. T., Pelham, B. W., & Krull, D. S. (1988). On cognitive business: When person perceivers meet persons perceived. *Journal of Personality and Social Psychology, 54,* 733–740.

Goldberg, L. R. (1992). The social psychology of personality. *Psychological Inquiry, 3,* 89–94.

Goldberg, L. R. (1993). The structure of phenotypic personality traits. *American Psychologist, 48,* 26–34.

Golding, S. L. (1975). Flies in the ointment: Methodological problems in the analysis of the percentage of variance due to person and situations. *Psychological Bulletin, 82,* 278–288.

Gottman, J. M., & Porterfield, A. L. (1981). Communicative competence in the nonverbal behavior of married couples. *Journal of Marriage and the Family, 43,* 817–824.

Gough, H. G. (1990). The California Psychological Inventory. In C. E. Watkins, Jr. & V. L. Campbell (Eds.), *Testing in counseling practice. Vocational psychology* (pp. 37–62). Hillsdale, NJ: Erlbaum.

Greenwald, A. G., & Pratkanis, A. R. (1984). The self. In R. S. Wyer & T. K. Srull (Eds.), *Handbook of social cognition* (pp. 129–178). Hillsdale, NJ: Erlbaum.

Grice, H. P. (1975). Logic in conversation. In P. Cole & J. L. Morgan (Eds.), *Syntax and semantics* (Vol. 3, pp. 41–58). San Diego, CA: Academic Press.

Grove, W. M., & Meehl, P. E. (1996). Comparative efficiency of informal (subjective, impressionistic) and formal (mechanical, algorithmic) prediction procedures: The clinical-statistical controversy. *Psychology, Public Policy and the Law, 2,* 293–323.

Haig, B. D. (1992). From nuisance variables to explanatory theories: A reformulation of the third variable problem. *Educational Philosophy and Theory, 24,* 78–97.

Hall, J. A. (1990). *Nonverbal sex differences; Accuracy of communication and expressive style.* Baltimore: Johns Hopkins University Press.

Hammond, K. R. (1996). *Human judgment and social policy.* New York and Oxford: Oxford University Press.

Harackiewicz, J. M., & DePaulo, B. M. (1982). Accuracy of person perception: A component analysis according to Cronbach. *Personality and Social Psychology Bulletin, 8,* 247–256.

Hartshorne, H., & May, M. A. (1928). *Studies in deceit.* New York: Macmillan.

Hastie, R., & Rasinski, K. A. (1988). The concept of accuracy in social judgment. In D. Bar-Tal & A. W. Kruglanski (Eds.), *The social psychology of knowledge* (pp. 193–208). Cambridge, England: Cambridge University Press.

Hastorf, A. H., & Bender, I. E. (1952). A caution respecting the measurement of empathic ability. *Journal of Abnormal and Social Psychology, 47,* 574–576.

Hathaway, S. R., & Meehl, P. E. (1951). *An atlas for the clinical use of the MMPI.* Minneapolis: University of Minnesota Press.

Havenstein, N. M., & Alexander, R. A. (1991). Rating ability in performance judgments: The joint influence of implicit theories and intelligence. *Organizational Behavior and Human Decision Processes, 50,* 300–323.

Hayes, W. L. (1973). *Statistics for the social sciences* (2nd. ed.). New York: Holt, Rinehart and Winston.

Heider, F. (1958). *The psychology of interpersonal relations.* New York: Wiley.

Hirsch, J. (1986). Behavior-genetic analysis. In J. Medioni & G. Vaysse (Ed.), *Readings from the 19th International Ethological Conference: Genetic approaches to behavior* (pp. 129–138). Toulouse, France: Privat Publisher.

Hixon, J. G., & Swann, W. B. (1993). When does introspection bear fruit? Self-reflection, self-insight, and interpersonal choices. *Journal of Personality and Social Psychology, 64,* 35–43.

Hoch, S. J. (1987). Perceived consensus and predictive accuracy: The pros and cons of projection. *Journal of Personality and Social Psychology, 53,* 221–234.

Hofstee, W. K. B. (1994). Who should own the definition of personality? *European Journal of Personality, 8,* 149–162.

Hogan, R. (1982). A socioanalytic theory of motivation. *Nebraska Symposium on Motivation,* 55–89.

Hogan, R. (1998). Reinventing personality. *Journal of Social & Clinical Psychology, 17,* 1–10.

Hogan, R., & Hogan, J. (1991). Personality and status. In D. G. Gilbert & J. J. Connolly (Eds.), *Personality, social skills and psychopathology: An individual differences approach* (pp. 137–154). New York: Plenum.

Hogan, R., & Nicholson, R. A. (1988). The meaning of personality test scores. *American Psychologist, 43,* 621–626.

Hoyle, R. H. (Ed.), (1995). *Structural equation modeling: Concepts, issues and applications.* Thousand Oaks, CA: Sage Publications.

Hull, J. G. (1981). A self-awareness model of the causes and effects of alcohol consumption. *Journal of Abnormal Psychology, 90,* 586–600.

Ickes, W. (1983). A basic paradigm for the study of unstructured dyadic interaction. *New Directions for Methodology of Social and Behavioral Science, 15,* 5–21.

Ickes, W. (1993). Empathic accuracy. *Journal of Personality, 61,* 587–610.

Ickes, W. (Ed.). (1997). *Empathic accuracy.* New York: Guilford.

Ickes, W., Bissonette, V., Garcia, S., & Stinson, L. L. (1990). Implementing and using the dyadic interaction paradigm. *Review of Personality and Social Psychology, 11,* 16–44.

Ickes, W., Stinson, L., Bissonnette, V., & Garcia, S. (1990). Naturalistic social cognition: Empathic accuracy in mixed-sex dyads. *Journal of Personality and Social Psychology, 59,* 730–742.

Jackson, D. N. (1982). Some preconditions for valid person perception. In M. P. Zanna, E. T. Higgins, & C. P. Herman (Eds.), *Consistency in social behavior: The Ontario symposium* (Vol. 2, pp. 251–279). Hillsdale, NJ: Erlbaum.

Jackson, D. N., Neill, J. A., & Bevan, A. R. (1969). Interpersonal judgmental accuracy and bias as a function of degree of acquaintance. *Proceedings of the 77th Annual Convention of the American Psychological Association, 4,* 135–136.

James, W. (1915). *The will to believe and other essays in popular philosophy.* London: Longmans, Green. (Original work published 1897)

John, O. P., & Robins, R. W. (1993). Determinants of interjudge agreement on personality traits: The big five domains, observability, evaluativeness, and the unique perspective of the self. *Journal of Personality, 61,* 521–551.

John, O. P., & Robins, R. W. (1994). Accuracy and bias in self-perception: Individual differences in self-enhancement and narcissism. *Journal of Personality and Social Psychology, 66,* 206–219.

Jones, E. E. (1979). The rocky road from acts to disposition. *American Psychologist, 34,* 107–117.

Jones, E. E. (1985). Major developments in social psychology during the past five decades. In G. Lindzey & E. Aronson (Eds.), *The handbook of social psychology* (3rd ed., pp. 47–107). New York: Random House.

Jones, E. E. (1990). *Interpersonal perception.* New York: W. H. Freeman.

Jones, E. E., & Harris, V. A. (1967). The attribution of attitudes. *Journal of Experimental Social Psychology, 3,* 1–24.

Jones, E. E., & Nisbett, R. E. (1971). *The actor and the observer: Divergent perspectives on the causes of behavior.* Morristown, NJ: General Learning Press.

Joreskog, K. G., & Sorbom, D. (1993). *LISREL 8 user's reference guide.* Chicago: Scientific Software.

Jourard, S. M. (1971). *Self-disclosure: An experimental analysis of the transparent self.* New York: Wiley.

Jussim, L. (1991). Social perception and social reality: A reflection–construction model. *Psychological Review, 98,* 54–73.

Jussim, L. (1993). Accuracy in interpersonal expectations: A reflection-construction analysis of current and classic research. *Journal of Personality, 61,* 637–668.

Jussim, L., Lee, Y-T, & McCauley, C. (Eds.). (1995). *Stereotype Accuracy: Toward appreciating group differences.* Washington, DC: American Psychological Association.

Kahneman, D. T., & Tversky, A. (1973). On the psychology of prediction. *Psychological Review, 80,* 237–251.

Kane, J. S., & Lawler, E. E., III. (1978). Methods of peer assessment. *Psychological Bulletin, 85,* 555–586.

Keating, C. F. (1985). Human dominance signals: The primate in us. In S. L. Ellyson & J. F. Dovidio (Eds.), *Power, dominance, and nonverbal behavior* (pp. 89–108). New York: Springer-Verlag.

Kelley, H. H. (1973). The processes of causal attribution. *American Psychologist, 28,* 107–128.

Kenny, D. A. (1991). A general model of consensus and accuracy in interpersonal perception. *Psychological Review, 92,* 155–163.

Kenny, D. A. (1994). *Interpersonal perception: A social relations analysis.* New York: Guilford Press.

Kenny, D. A. (1997). *Peqson: A general model for understanding interpersonal perception, unpublished manuscript, University of Connecticut.*

Kenny, D. A., & Albright, L. (1987). *Accuracy in interpersonal perception: A social relations analysis. Psychological Bulletin, 102,* 390–402.

Kenny, D. A., Albright, L., Malloy, T. E., & Kashy, D. A. (1994). Consensus in interpersonal perception: Acquaintance and the big five. *Psychological Bulletin, 116,* 245–258.

Kenny, D. A., Bond, C. F., Jr., Mohr, C. D., & Horn, E. M. (1996). Do we know how much people like one another? *Journal of Personality and Social Psychology, 71,* 928–936.

Kenny, D. A., & DePaulo, B. M. (1993). Do people know how others view them? An empirical and theoretical account. *Psychological Bulletin, 114,* 145–161.

Kenny, D. A., Horner, C., Kashy, D. A., & Chu, L. (1992). Consensus at zero aquaintance: Replication, behavioral cues, and stability. *Journal of Personality and Social Psychology, 62,* 88–97.

Kenny, D. A., Kieffer, S. C., Smith, J. A., Ceplenski, P., & Kubo, J. (1996). Circumscribed accuracy among well-acquainted individuals. *Journal of Experimental Social Psychology, 32,* 1–12.

Kenny, D. A., & LaVoie, L. (1984). The social relations model. In L. Berkowitz (Ed.), *Advances in experimental social psychology* (Vol. 18, pp. 141–179). New York: Academic Press.

Kenny, D. A., Mohr, C. D., & Levesque, M. J. (1998). *A social relations partitioning of variance of dyadic behavior.* Unpublished manuscript, University of Connecticut.

Kenrick, D. T., & Funder, D. C. (1988). Profiting from controversy: Lessons from the person-situation debate. *American Psychologist, 43,* 23–34.

Kenrick, D. T., McCreath, H. E., Govern, J., King, R., & Bordin, J. (1990). Person-environment intersections: Everyday settings and common trait dimensions. *Journal of Personality and Social Psychology, 58,* 685–698.

Kenrick, D. T., & Stringfield, D. O. (1980). Personality traits and the eye of the beholder: Crossing some traditional philosophical boundaries in the search for consistency in all of the people. *Psychological Review, 87,* 88–104.

Kirouac, G., & Dore, F. Y. (1985). Accuracy of the judgment of emotions as a function of sex and level of education. *Journal of Nonverbal Behavior, 9,* 3–7.

Klein, S. B., & Loftus, J. (1988). The nature of self-referent encoding: The contributions of elaborative and organizational processes. *Journal of Personality and Social Psychology, 55,* 5–11.

Klein, S. B., Loftus, J., & Burton, H. A. (1989). Two self-reference effects: The importance of distinguishing between self-descriptiveness judgments and autobiographical retrieval in self-referent encoding. *Journal of Personality and Social Psychology, 56,* 853–865.

Kleugel, J. R. (1990). Trends in Whites' explanations of the Black-White gap in socioeconomic status, 1977–1989. *American Sociological Review, 55,* 521–525.

Knapp, M. L., & Hall, J. A. (Eds.). (1992). *Nonverbal communication in human interaction* (3rd ed.). New York: Harcourt, Brace, Jovanovich.

Koestner, R., Bernieri, F., & Zuckerman, M. (1989). Trait-specific versus person-specific moderators of cross-situational consistency. *Journal of Personality, 57,* 1–16.

Koestner, R., Bernieri, F., & Zuckerman, M. (1994). Self-peer agreement as a function of two kinds of trait relevance. *Social Behavior and Personality, 22,* 17–30.

Kolar, D. W. (1995). *Individual differences in the ability to accurately judge the personality characteristics of others.* Unpublished doctoral dissertation, University of California, Riverside.

Kolar, D. W., Funder, D. C., & Colvin, C. R. (1996). Comparing the accuracy of personality judgments by the self and knowledgable others. *Journal of Personality, 64,* 311–337.

Krebs, D. L., & Denton, K. (1997). Social illusions and self-deception: The evolution of biases in person perception. In J. A. Simpson & D. T. Kenrick (Eds.), *Evolutionary Social Psychology* (pp. 21–48). Mahwah, NJ: Erlbaum.

Kruglanski, A. W. (1989). The psychology of being "right": The problem of accuracy in social perception and cognition. *Psychological Bulletin, 106,* 395–409.

Krull, D. S. (1993). Does the grist change the mill? The effect of the perceiver's inferential goal on the process of social inference. *Personality and Social Psychology Bulletin, 19,* 340–348.

Kuhn, T. S. (1962). *The structure of scientific revolutions.* Chicago: University of Chicago Press.

Kuiken, D. (1981). Non-immediate language style and inconsistency between private and expressed evaluations. *Journal of Experimental Social Psychology, 17,* 183–196.

Kunda, Z. (1987). Motivated inference: Self-serving generation and evaluation of causal theories. *Journal of Personality and Social Psychology, 53,* 636–647.

Kunda, Z., & Nisbett, R. E. (1986). The psychometrics of everyday life. *Cognitive Psychology, 18,* 195–224.

Lanning, K. (1988). Individual differences in scalability: An alternative conception of consistency for personality theory and measurement. *Journal of Personality and Social Psychology, 55,* 142–148.

Lerner, M. J. (1980). *The belief in a just world: A fundamental delusion.* New York: Plenum Press.

Lester, D. (1991). Accuracy of recognition of genuine versus simulated suicide notes. *Personality and Individual Differences, 12,* 765–766.

Levesque, M. J., & Kenny, D. A. (1993). Accuracy of behavioral predictions at zero acquaintance: A social relations analysis. *Journal of Personality and Social Psychology, 65,* 1178–1187.

Lewin, A. Y., & Zwany, A. (1976). Peer nominations: A model, literature critique and a paradigm for research. *Personnel Psychology, 29,* 423–447.

Locher, P., Unger, R., Sociedade, P., & Wahl, J. (1993). At first glance: Accessibility of the physical attractiveness stereotype. *Sex Roles, 28,* 729–743.

Lopes, L. L. (1991). The rhetoric of irrationality. *Theory and Psychology, 1,* 65–82.

Lopes, L. L., & Oden, G. C. (1991). The rationality of intelligence. In E. Eells & T. Marusqewski (Eds.), *Probability and rationality: Studies on L. Jonathan Cohen's philosophy of science* (pp. 199–223). Amsterdam: Rodopi.

Lusk, C. M., & Hammond, K. R. (1991). Judgment in a dynamic task: Microburst forecasting. *Journal of Behavioral Decision Making, 4,* 55–73.

Lyubomirsky, S., & Nolen-Hoeksema, S. (1993). Self-perpetuating properties of dysphoric rumination. *Journal of Personality and Social Psychology, 65,* 339–349.

Maddi, S. R. (1996). *Personality theories: A comparative analysis* (6th ed.). Pacific Grove, CA: Brooks/Cole.

Madon, S., Jussim, L., & Eccles, J. (1997). In search of the powerful self-fulfilling prophecy. *Journal of Personality & Social Psychology, 72,* 791–809.

Malloy, T. E., & Albright, L. (1990). Interpersonal perception in a social context. *Journal of Personality and Social Psychology, 58,* 419–428.

Malloy, T. E., Albright, L., Kenny, D. A., Agatstein, F., et al. (1997). Interpersonal perception and metaperception in nonoverlapping social groups. *Journal of Personality and Social Psychology, 72,* 390–398.

Manicas, P. T., & Secord, P. F. (1983). Implications for psychology of the new philosophy of science. *American Psychologist, 38,* 399–413.

Marangoni, C., Garcia, S., Ickes, W., & Teng, G. (1995). Empathic accuracy in a clinically relevant setting. *Journal of Personality and Social Psychology, 68,* 854–869.

Markus, H. (1977). Self-schematia and procssing information about the self. *Journal of Personality and Social Psychology, 35,* 63–78.

Markus, H. (1983). Self-knowledge: An expanded view. *Journal of Personality, 51,* 543–565.

Markus, H., & Kitayama, S. (1991). Culture and the self: Implications for cognition, emotion, and motivation. *Psychological Review, 98,* 224–253.

Markus, H., Smith, J., & Moreland, R. L. (1985). Role of the self-concept in the perception of others. *Journal of Personality and Social Psychology, 49,* 1494–1512.

Maslow, A. H. (1987). *Motivation and personality* (3rd ed.). New York: Harper & Row.

McArthur, L. Z., & Baron, R. M. (1983). Toward an ecological theory of social perception. *Psychological Review, 90,* 215–238.

McClelland, D. C. (1972). Opinions reflect opinions: So what else is new? *Journal of Consulting and Clinical Psychology, 38,* 325–326.

McClelland, D. C. (1984). Is personality consistent? In D. McClelland (Ed.), *Motives, personality and society* (pp. 185–211). New York: Praeger.

McCrae, R. R. (1982). Consensual validation of personality traits: Evidence from self-reports and ratings. *Journal of Personality and Social Psychology, 43,* 293–303.

McCrae, R. R., & Costa, P. T. (1995). Trait explanations in personality psychology. *European Journal of Personality, 9,* 231–252.

McGowen, J., & Gormly, J. (1976). Validation of personality traits: A multicriteria approach. *Journal of Personality and Social Psychology, 34,* 791–795.

McKay, J. R., O'Farrell, T. J., Maisto, S. A., Connors, G. J., & Funder, D. C. (1989). Biases in relapse attributions made by alcoholics and their wives. *Addictive Behaviors, 14,* 513–522.

Mead, G. H. (1934). *Mind, self, and society.* Chicago: University of Chicago Press.

Meehl, P. E. (1954). *Clinical vs. statistical prediction: A theoretical analysis and a review of the evidence.* Minneapolis: University of Minnesota Press.

Meehl, P. (1970). Nuisance variables and the ex post facto design. *Minnesota Studies in the Philosophy of Science, 4,* 373–402.

Messick, S. (1989). Validity. In R. L. Linn (Ed.), *Educational measurement* (3rd ed., pp. 13–104). New York: Macmillan.

Milgram, S. (1975). *Obedience to authority.* New York: Harper/Colophon.

Miller, D. T., & Ross, M. (1975). Self-serving biases in the attribution of causality: Fact or fiction? *Psychological Bulletin, 82,* 213–225.

Miller, G. A. (1969). Psychology as a means of promoting human welfare. *American Psychologist, 24,* 1063–1075.

Mischel, W. (1968). *Personality and assessment.* New York: Wiley.

Mischel, W. (1973). Toward a cognitive social learning reconceptualization of personality. *Psychological Review, 80,* 252–283.

Mischel, W., & Peake, P. K. (1982). Beyond déjà vu in the search for cross-situational consistency. *Psychological Review, 89,* 730–755.

Monson, T. C., & Snyder, M. (1977). Actors, observers, and the attribution process: Toward a reconceptualization. *Journal of Experimental Social Psychology, 13,* 89–111.

Moore, B. S., Sherrod, D. R., Liu, T. J., & Underwood, B. (1979). The dispositional shift in attribution over time. *Journal of Experimental Social Psychology, 15,* 553–569.

Moskowitz, D. S. (1982). Coherence and cross-situational generality in personality: A new analysis of old problems. *Journal of Personality and Social Psychology, 43,* 754–768.

Moskowitz, D. S., & Schwarz, J. C. (1982). Validity comparison of behavior counts and ratings by knowledgeable informants. *Journal of Personality and Social Psychology, 42,* 518–528.

Neimeyer, R. A., Neimeyer, G. L., & Landfield, A. W. (1983). Conceptual differentiation, integration and empathic prediction. *Journal of Personality, 51,* 185–191.

Neisser, U. (1976). *Cognition and reality: Principles and implications of cognitive psychology.* San Francisco: W. H. Freeman.

Neisser, U. (1980). On "social knowing." *Personality and Social Psychology Bulletin, 6,* 601–605.

Neuberg, S. L. (1989). The goal of forming accurate impressions during social interactions: Attenuating the impact of negative expectancies. *Journal of Personality and Social Psychology, 56,* 374–386.

Neuberg, S. L., & Fiske, S. T. (1987). Motivational influences on impression formation: Outcome dependency, accuracy-driven attention, and individuating processes. *Journal of Personality and Social Psychology, 53,* 374–386.

Neuberg, S. L., & Newson, J. R. (1993). Personal need for structure: Individual differences in the desire for simpler structure. *Journal of Personality and Social Psychology, 65,* 113–131.

Nisbett, R. E. (1980). The trait construct in lay and professional psychology. In L. Festinger (Ed.), *Retrospections on social psychology* (pp. 109–130). New York: Oxford University Press.

Nisbett, R. E., Caputo, C., Legant, P., & Marecek, J. (1973). Behavior as seen by the actor and as seen by the observer. *Journal of Personality and Social Psychology, 27,* 154–165.

Nisbett, R. E., & Ross, L. (1980). *Human inference: Strategies and shortcomings of social judgment.* Englewood Cliffs, NJ: Prentice-Hall.

Noller, P. (1981). Gender and marital adjustment level differences in decoding messages from spouses and strangers. *Journal of Personality and Social Psychology, 41,* 272–278.

Norman, W. T., & Goldberg, L. R. (1966). Raters, ratees, and randomness in personality structure. *Journal of Personality and Social Psychology, 4,* 681–691.

Nowicki, S., Jr., & Mitchell, J. (1998). Accuracy in identifying affect in child and adult faces and voices and social competence in preschool children. *Genetic, Social and General Psychology Monographs, 124,* 39–59.

Ozer, D. J. (1985). Correlation and the coefficient of determination. *Psychological Bulletin, 97,* 307–315.

Ozer, D. J., & Reise, S. P. (1994). Personality assessment. *Annual Review of Psychology, 45,* 357–388.

Park, B., & Judd, C. M. (1989). Agreement on initial impressions: Differences due to perceivers, trait dimensions, and target behaviors. *Journal of Personality and Social Psychology, 56,* 493–505.

Park, B., & Judd, C. M. (1989). Agreement in initial impressions: Differences dues to perceivers, trait dimensions, and target behaviors. *Journal of Personality and Social Psychology, 56,* 493–505.

Park, B., Kraus, S., & Ryan, C. S. (1997). Longitudinal changes in consensus as a function of acquaintance and agreement in liking. *Journal of Personality and Social Psychology, 72,* 604–616.

Parkinson, B. (1985). Emotional effects of false autonomic feedback. *Psychological Bulletin, 98,* 471–494.

Passini, F. T., & Norman, W. T. (1966). A universal conception of personality structures? *Journal of Personality and Social Psychology, 4,* 44–49.

Patterson, M. L. (1994a). Interaction behavior and person perception: An integrative approach. *Small Group Research, 25,* 172–188.

Patterson, M. L. (1994b). Strategic functions of nonverbal exchange. In J. A. Daly & J. M. Wiemann (Eds.), *Strategic interpersonal communication* (pp. 273–293). Hillsdale, NJ: Erlbaum.

Patterson, M. L. (1995). A parallel process model of nonverbal communication. *Journal of Nonverbal Behavior, 19,* 3–29.

Patterson, M. L., Churchill, M. E., Farag, F., & Borden, E. (1991–1992). Impression management, cognitive demand, and interpersonal sensitivity. *Current Psychology: Research and Reviews, 10,* 263–271.

Paulhus, D. L., & Bruce, M. N. (1992). The effect of acquaintanceship on the validity of personality impressions: A longitudinal study. *Journal of Personality and Social Psychology, 63,* 816–824.

Paunonen, S. V. (1989). Consensus in personality judgments: Moderating effects of target-rater acquaintanceship and behavior observability. *Journal of Personality and Social Psychology, 56,* 823–833.

Paunonen, S. V., & Jackson, D. N. (1987). Accuracy of interviewers and students in identifying the personality characteristics of personnel managers and computer programmers. *Journal of Vocational Behavior, 31,* 26–36.

Pennebaker, J. W. (1997). *Opening up: The healing power of expressing emotions* (rev. ed.). New York: The Guilford Press.

Perry, J. (Ed.) (1975). *Personal identity.* Berkeley: University of California Press.

Psychology. San Francisco: W. H. Freeman.

Peterson, C. (1980). Memory and the "dispositional shift." *Social Psychology Quarterly, 43,* 372–380.

Pilkonis, P. (1977). The behavioral consequences of shyness. *Journal of Personality, 45,* 596–611.

Pryor, M. R., Chuang, A. C., Craik, K. H., & Gosling, S. D. (1998, August). *Reliability and validity of personality impressions based on bedrooms.* Paper presented at the 108th Annual Meeting of the American Psychological Association, San Francisco.

Quattrone, G. A. (1982). Overattribution and unit formation: When behavior engulfs the person. *Journal of Personality and Social Psychology, 42,* 593–607.

Raskin, R., Novacek, J., & Hogan, R. (1991). Narcissistic self-esteem management. *Journal of Personality and Social Psychology, 60,* 911–918.

Reise, S. P., & Waller, N. G. (1993). Traitedness and the assessment of response pattern scalability. *Journal of Personality and Social Psychology, 65,* 143–151.

Reisman, J. M. (1990). Intimacy in same-sex friendships. *Sex Roles, 23,* 65–82.

Resnick, H. E., Fries, B. E., & Verbrugge, L. M. (1997). Windows to their world: The effect of sensory impairments on social engagement and activity time in nursing home residents. *Journals of Gerontology: Series B: Psychological Sciences and Social Sciences, 52B,* S135–S144.

Robins, R. W., & John, O. P. (1997). Effects of visual perspective and narcissism on self-perception: Is seeing believing? *Psychological Science, 8,* 37–42.

Rorer, L. G. (1965). The great response-style myth. *Psychological Bulletin, 63,* 129–156.

Rosenthal, R. (1994). Interpersonal expectancy effects: A 30-year perspective. *Current Directions in Psychological Science, 3,* 176–179.

Rosenthal, R., Hall, J. A., DiMatteo, M. R., Rogers, P. L., & Archer, D. (1979). *Sensitivity to nonverbal communication: The PONS test.* Baltimore: Johns Hopkins University Press.

Rosenthal, R., & Rosnow, R. L. (1984). *Essentials of behavioral research: Methods and data analysis.* New York: McGraw-Hill.

Rosenthal, R., & Rubin, D. B. (1982). A simple, general purpose display of magnitude of experimental effect. *Journal of Educational Psychology, 74,* 166–169.

Ross, L. (1977). The intuitive psychologist and his shortcomings. In L. Berkowitz (Ed.), *Advances in experimental social psychology* (Vol. 10, pp. 174–214). New York: Academic Press.

Ross, L., & Nisbett, R. E. (1991). *The person and the situation: Perspectives of social psychology.* New York: McGraw-Hill.

Ross, L., Greene, D., & House, P. (1977). The false consensus phenomenon: An attribution bias in self-perception and social perception processes. *Journal of Experimental Social Psychology, 13,* 279–301.

Rothbart, M., & Park, B. (1986). On the confirmability and disconfirmability of trait concepts. *Journal of Personality and Social Psychology, 50,* 131–142.

Ryle, G. (1967). *The concept of mind.* New York: Barnes & Noble. (Originally published 1947).

Sartre, J. P. (1965). *The philosophy of Jean-Peal Sartre* (R. D. Cumming, Ed.). New York: Random House.

Scheier, M. F., Buss, A. H., & Buss, D. M. (1976). Self-consciousness, self-report of aggressiveness, and aggression. *Journal of Research in Personality, 44,* 637–644.

Scherer, K. R. (1978). Personality inference from voice quality: The loud voice of extraversion. *European Journal of Social Psychology, 8,* 467–487.

Schneider, D. J., Hastorf, A. H., & Ellsworth, P. C. (1979). *Person perception* (2nd ed.). Reading, MA: Addison-Wesley.

Sedikides, C. (1993). Assessment, enhancement, and verification determinants of the self-evaluation process. *Journal of Personality and Social Psychology, 65,* 317–338.

Sedikides, C., & Skowronski, J. J. (1993). The self in impression formation: Trait centrality and social perception. *Journal of Experimental Social Psychology, 29,* 347–357.

Shaklee, H. (1991). An inviting invitation [Review of *An invitation to cognitive science: Vol. 3. Thinking*]. *Contemporary Psychology, 36,* 940–941.

Sherrod, D. R. (1989). The influence of gender on same-sex friendships. In C. Hendrick (Ed.), *Close relationships: Review of personality and social psychology* (Vol. 10). Newbury Park, CA: Sage.

Shrauger, J. S., & Schoeneman, T. J. (1979). Symbolic interactionist view of self-concept: Through the looking glass darkly. *Psychological Bulletin, 86,* 549–573.

Shweder, R. A. (1975). How relevant is an individual differences theory of personality? *Journal of Personality, 43,* 455–484.

Shweder, R. A., & Broune, E. J. (1982). Does the concept of person vary cross-culturally? In A. J. Marsella & G. M. White (Eds.), *Cultural conceptions of mental health and therapy* (pp. 97–137). London: Reidel.

Shweder, R. A., & D'Andrade, R. G. (1979). Accurate reflection or systematic distortion: A reply to Block, Weiss and Thorne. *Journal of Personality and Social Psychology, 37,* 1075–1084.

Sillars, A. L., & Scott, M. D. (1983). Interpersonal perception between intimates: An integrative review. *Human Communication Research, 10,* 153–176.

Simpson, J., Ickes, W., & Blackstone, J. (1995). When the head protects the heart: Empathic accuracy in dating relationships. *Journal of Personality and Social Psychology, 69,* 629–641.

Skarzynska, K. (1982). Person perception accuracy and perceptual perspective. *Polish Psychological Bulletin, 13,* 143–152.

Skinner, B. F. (1931). The concept of the reflex in the description of behavior. *Journal of General Psychology, 5,* 427–458.

Skinner, B. F. (1966). *The behavior of organisms: An experimental analysis.* New York: Appleton-Century-Crofts. (Originally published 1938)

Skitka, L. J. (in press). Ideological and attributional boundaries on public compassion: Reactions to individuals and communities affected by a natural disaster. *Personality and Social Psychology Bulletin.*

Skitka, L. J., & Tetlock, P. E. (1993). Providing public assistance: Cognitive and motivational processes underlying liberal and conservative policy preferences. *Journal of Personality and Social Psychology, 65,* 1205–1223.

Snodgrass, S. E. (1985). Women's intuition: The effect of subordinate role on interpersonal sensitivity. *Journal of Personality and Social Psychology, 49,* 146–155.

Snodgrass, S. E. (1992). Further effects of role versus gender on interpersonal sensitivity. *Journal of Personality and Social Psychology, 62,* 154–158.

Snodgrass, S. E., Hecht, M. A., & Ploutz-Snyder, R. (1998). Interpersonal sensitivity: Expressivity or perceptivity? *Journal of Personality and Social Psychology, 74,* 238–249.

Snyder, C. R., Smith, T. W., Augelli, R. W., & Ingram, R. E. (1985). On the self-serving function of social anxiety: Shyness as a self-handicapping strategy. *Journal of Personality and Social Psychology, 48,* 970–980.

Snyder, M. (1987). *Public appearances, private realities: The psychology of self-monitoring.* New York: W. H. Freeman.

Snyder, M., & Ickes, W. (1985). Personality and social behavior. In G. Lindzey & E. Aronson (Eds.), *Handbook of social psychology* (3rd ed., Vol. 2, pp. 883–948). Reading, MA: Addison-Wesley.

Snyder, M., Tanke, E. D., & Berscheid, E. (1977). Social perception and interpersonal behavior: On the self-fulfilling nature of social stereotypes. *Journal of Personality and Social Psychology, 35,* 656–666.

Spain, J. (1994). *Personality and daily life experience: Evaluating the accuracy of personality judgments.* Unpublished doctoral dissertation, University of California, Riverside.

Srull, T. K., & Wyer, R. S. (1989). Person memory and judgment. *Psychological Review, 96,* 58–83.

Stanovich, K. E. (1991). Cognitive science meets beginning reading. *Psychological Science, 2,* 70–81.

Stein, L. M., & Bienenfeld, D. (1992). Hearing impairment and its impact on elderly patients with cognitive, behavioral or psychiatric disorders: A literature review. *Journal of Geriatric Psychiatry, 25,* 145–156.

Stewart, T. R., Roebber, P. J., & Bosart, L. F. (1997). The importance of the task in analyzing expert judgment. *Organizational Behavior and Human Decision Processes, 69,* 205–219.

Stich, S. P. (1996). *Deconstructing the mind.* New York and Oxford: Oxford University Press.

Stiff, J. B., Kim, H. T., & Ramesch, C. N. (1992). Truth biases and aroused suspicion in relational deception. *Communication Research, 19,* 326–345.

Stinson, L., & Ickes, W. (1992). Empathic accuracy in the interactions of male friends vs. male strangers. *Journal of Personality and Social Psychology, 62,* 787–797.

Storms, M. D. (1973). Videotape and the attribution process: Reversing actors' and observers' points of view. *Journal of Personality and Social Psychology, 27,* 165–175.

Strickland, L. H. (1958). Surveillance and trust. *Journal of Personality, 26,* 200–215.

Strongman, K. (1998). *Postmodernism and psychology.* Colloquium delivered at the Department of Psychology, University of Canterbury, Christchurch, New Zealand, March 25.

Swann, W. B., Jr. (1984). Quest for accuracy in person perception: A matter of pragmatics. *Psychological Review, 91,* 457–477.

Swann, W. B., Jr. (1997). The trouble with change: Self-verification and allegiance to the self. *Psychological Science, 8,* 177–180.

Swann, W. B., & Ely, R. J. (1984). A battle of wills: Self-verification versus behavioral confirmation. *Journal of Personality and Social Psychology, 46,* 1287–1302.

Swann, W. B., & Gill, M. J. (1997). Confidence and accuracy in person perception: Do we know what we think we know about our relationship partners? *Journal of Personality and Social Psychology, 73,* 747–757.

Swann, W. B., Stein-Seroussi, A., & McNulty, S. E. (1992). Outcasts in a white-lie society: The enigmatic worlds of people with negative self-conceptions. *Journal of Personality and Social Psychology, 62,* 618–624.

Swann, W. B., Stephenson, B., & Pittman, T. S. (1981). Curiosity and control: On the determinants of the search for social knowledge. *Journal of Personality and Social Psychology, 40,* 635–642.

Taft, R. (1955). The ability to judge people. *Psychological Bulletin, 52,* 1–23.

Taft, R. (1966). Accuracy of empathic judgments of acquaintances and strangers. *Journal of Personality and Social Psychology, 3,* 600–604.

Tagiuri, R., & Petrullo, L. (Eds.) (1958). *Person perception and interpersonal behavior.* Palo Alto, CA: Stanford University Press.

Taylor, S. E., & Brown, J. D. (1988). Illusion and well-being: A social psychological perspective on mental health. *Psychological Bulletin, 103,* 193–210.

Tellegen, A. (1988). The analysis of consistency in personality assessment. *Journal of Personality, 56,* 621–663.

Tetlock, P. E., & Levi, A. (1982). Attribution bias: On the inconclusiveness of the cognition-motivation debate. *Journal of Experimental Social Psychology, 18,* 68–88.

Thomas, G. (1998). *Accuracy in person perception.* Unpublished doctoral dissertation, University of Canterbury (Christchurch, New Zealand).

Thorne, A. (1989). Conditional patterns, transference, and the coherence of personality across time. In D. Buss & N. Cantor (Eds.), *Personality: Recent trends and emerging directions.* New York: Springer-Verlag.

Thurstone, L. L. (1935). *The vectors of mind.* Chicago: University of Chicago Press.

Triandis, H. C. (1994). *Culture and social behavior.* New York: McGraw-Hill.

Trickett, P. K., & Putnam, F. W. (1993). Impact of child sexual abuse on females: Toward a developmental, psychobiological integration. *Psychological Science, 4,* 81–87.

Trope, Y. (1986). Identification and inferential processes in depositional attribution. *Psychological Review, 93,* 239–257.

Valins, S. (1966). Cognitive effects of false heart-rate feedback. *Journal of Personality and Social Psychology, 4,* 400–408.

Vernon, P. E. (1933). Some characteristics of the good judge of personality. *Journal of Social Psychology, 4,* 42–58.

Vogt, D. S., & Colvin, C. R. (1998). *The good judge of personality: Gender differences, personality correlates, and Cronbachian "artifacts."* Unpublished manuscript, Northeastern University.

Vonnegut, K. (1966). *Mother night.* New York: Delacorte.

Waller, N. G., & Reise, S. P. (1989). Computerized adaptive personality assessment: An illustration with the absorption scale. *Journal of Personality and Social Psychology, 57,* 1051–1058.

Watson, D. (1989). Strangers' ratings of the five robust personality factors: Evidence of a surprising convergence with self-report. *Journal of Personality and Social Psychology, 57,* 120–128.

Watson, D., & Clark, L. A. (1991). Self versus peer ratings of specific emotional traits: Evidence of convergent and discriminant validity. *Journal of Personality and Social Psychology, 60,* 927–940.

Wegner, D. M. (1994). Ironic processes of mental control. *Psychological Review, 101,* 34–52.

Westbrook, M. (1974). Judgment of emotion: Attention vs. accuracy. *British Journal of Social and Clinical Psychology, 13,* 383–389.

Westen, D. (1998). Unconscious thought, feeling, and motivation: The end of a century-long debate. In R. F. Bornstein & J. M. Masling (Eds.), *Empirical perspectives on the psychoanalytic unconscious* (pp. 1–43). Washington, DC: American Psychological Association.

Wiggins, J. S. (1973). *Personality and prediction: Principles of personality assessment.* Reading, MA: Addison-Wesley.

Williams, L. J. (1995). Covariance structure modeling in organization research: Problems with the method versus applications of the method. *Journal of Organizational Behavior, 16,* 225–233.

Wilson, E. O. (1998). Back from chaos. *Atlantic Monthly, 281,* 41–62 (esp. p. 59).

Wilson, T. D., & Schooler, J. W. (1991). Thinking too much: Introspection can reduce the quality of preferences and decisions. *Journal of Personality and Social Psychology, 60,* 181–192.

Woll, S. B., & McFall, M. E. (1979). The effects of false feedback on attributional arousal and rated attractiveness in female subjects. *Journal of Personality, 47,* 214–229.

Wood, R. E., & Bandura, A. (1989). Impact of conceptions of ability on self-regulatory mechanisms and complex decision-making. *Journal of Personality and Social Psychology, 56,* 407–415.

Wyer, R. S., & Srull, T. K. (1986). Human cognition in its social context. *Psychological Review, 93,* 322–359.

Zajonc, R. B. (1976). Preface: Emergence of individual differences in social context. In L. H. Strickland, F. E. Aboud, & K. J. Gergen (Eds.), *Social psychology in transition* (pp., 155–156). New York: Plenum.

Zebrowitz, L. A., & Collins, M. A. (1997). Accurate social perception at zero acquaintance: The affordances of a Gibsonian approach. *Personality and Social Psychology Review, 1,* 204–233.

Zuckerman, M., Bernieri, F., Koestner, R., & Rosenthal, R. (1989). To predict some of the people some of the time: In search of moderators. *Journal of Personality and Social Psychology, 57,* 279–293.

Zuckerman, M., Koestner, R., & Alton, A. O. (1984). Learning to detect deception. *Journal of Personality and Social Psychology, 46,* 519–528.

Zuckerman, M., Koestner, R., & Colella, M. J. (1985). Learning to detect deception from three communication channels. *Journal of Nonverbal Behavior, 9,* 188–194./REF

Index